CHILD OF THE FOREST

JACK L. GROSSMAN
and JAMES BUCHANAN

Based on the Life Story
of Charlene Perlmutter Schiff

SPARK Publications
Charlotte, North Carolina

Child of the Forest
By Jack Grossman and James Buchanan

Designed, produced, and published by SPARK Publications, SPARKpublications.com
Charlotte, NC

Cover Design by Jack Grossman and SPARK Publications.

This story is based on the true life story of Charlene Perlmutter Schiff and recreates events, locations, and conversations to the best of her recollection. Individual's names may have been changed in instances where Charlene could not recall actual names of people she met in passing. Any similarity between the fictitious names with actual names or characters is purely coincidental.

Printed in the United States of America.
Hardcover, October 2018, ISBN: 978-1-943070-48-0
Paperback, October 2018, ISBN: 978-1-943070-49-7
E-book, October 2018, ISBN: 978-1-943070-50-3
Library of Congress Control Number: 2018956806

Dedication

To all of the precious, innocent souls who perished in or survived the Holocaust. NEVER AGAIN.

To the many people, including my wife, Kristie, and our daughters, who believed in me and supported me throughout this journey.

To my grandparents, parents, and the many relatives and friends, living and deceased, whom I love deeply.

And to my dear friend Charlene, the most amazing person I ever met. Your kind soul and gentle spirit will forever live in me.

Table of Contents

Foreword

On Memorial Day of 2006, I visited the United States Holocaust Memorial Museum for the third time in four years. It was a day I will never forget. The field trip I helped chaperone arrived at the break of dawn in Washington, D.C., by bus from Charlotte, North Carolina. Just like my previous trips, we started the day with a prayer service at the Vietnam War Memorial as silhouettes in the background laid memorials at the base of the wall while others transcribed names from the wall onto paper. It was a perfect prelude to what I was about to experience.

I was accompanied by my youngest daughter, a bus load of other twelve-year-old children, and a few other chaperones. After the short and reverent prayer service, we were off to the Holocaust Memorial, and I prepared mentally for the familiar, somber experience. I went expecting to feel the same level of deep sadness that I felt on my previous trips, but I did not expect to be so profoundly moved. My view of life was forever altered when I heard a story about a young girl and her experiences during the Nazi invasion of her small town in Eastern Poland during the early 1940s. The more I listened to her story, the more I questioned whether I heard it correctly. I kept asking myself, "Did I really just hear that?"

Charlene was known as Shulamit Perlmutter but lovingly called Musia (pronounced Moosha) by everyone who knew her. Her story was so moving it literally embedded into my subconscious. I could not run from its presence. In fact, for the remainder of the day and the next day traveling home, I couldn't get it out of my head. I kept repeating to myself, "Did I hear her story correctly? Did this really happen?"

Upon arriving home, I greeted my family and, without hesitation, went immediately to the computer. I searched the Internet hoping to find a book or movie about this young girl and her experiences during one of humanity's darkest times. I kept thinking how she must have felt and if I would be as brave. I so badly wanted to share this story with my family, but I also wanted to confirm that I heard it correctly; I wanted answers to my burning questions. I searched and searched the Internet but to no avail. I thought, "How can this be? I had just heard the most compelling story of my entire life, and it has not been documented in a book or film for others to experience?" It was right then and there that I looked up to my wife from my chair and said, "I am going to make sure Charlene's story is told to the world ... whatever it takes."

And yes, I heard her story correctly. And yes, it really did happen, but it was even more incredible than I first thought and more compelling than I could ever imagine.

Jack Grossman
September 2018
North Carolina

"Hope is a fiction. It's a dream that tomorrow will be different, or some miracle will happen to save you. It's not sufficient; it's not enough to keep you alive in the ghetto, the camps. When a person is drowning, and they reach for air, it's not hope that propels that fight. The drive to live is what pushes us toward life, but it's stronger in some and can make the difference between life and death. Why stronger in some? It's always love. Love is what allows us to keep our humanity and know that someone needs us to survive."

– Estelle Laughlin, Holocaust survivor
and personal friend of Shulamit "Musia" Perlmutter

Liquidation

Our last morning in the ghetto, Mama was gentle as she woke me.

"Musia, darling, time for us to go."

She brushed a wisp of hair from my eyes. Her trembling fingers lingered against my skin.

"Come, you need to open your eyes, *neshomeleh*."

I breached the surface but let myself drift back into the warmth of somnolent waters.

"My neshomeleh, you must wake up. We have to go." The softness in her voice belied the strain on Mama's nerves. "Please, Musia."

I opened my eyes, and in one, deep breath the acidic odor of human rot burned my nostrils, eyes, and throat. Mama's face hung above me like a dimmed, emaciated moon, her eyes smudged by exhaustion.

"Musia, do you remember how to get to the Voitenkos'?" she whispered.

"Yes, Mama."

"They live in Skobelka."

"I know, Mama."

"When we cross the river, we walk across the field until we

reach the road to Skobelka."

"I know, I know, Mama; you've told me so many times—"

"Musia, please, whisper." Her eyes wandered toward Mrs. Joselewicz, sitting on a bed of wood laths torn from a wall and supported by scavenged bricks. At forty, Mrs. Joselewicz' sallow, jaundiced face and withdrawn eyes made her look like an old woman.

Mama continued. "You must not forget—"

"I remember their farm from before—"

"—because if you lose me, you will have to find the Voitenkos' on your own." Mama's eyes welled.

"I know, Mama. I'm twelve, not a little girl."

She took a deep breath and seemed to regain some strength. "Promise me you will go to the Voitenkos'."

I sat up and looked into Mama's eyes. "I promise."

"We have to go now." She steadied herself with one arm and stood. Her dress swayed as if draped on a wooden clothes hanger.

An aching nausea roused itself in me. I held my arms against my belly to soothe the pain and hunger, but they were little comfort.

"Put your clothes on like I told you," Mama said as she wrapped a sweater around her body. "Do you remember?"

"Yes, Mama."

"And wear your winter shoes."

"It's August, Mama. They'll be too hot."

Mama looked to Mrs. Joselewicz, who was taking an interest in our conversation. Mrs. Cukier looked up as well. She lay on her own bed of lath and brick, cradling her wheezing five-year-old daughter Ania to her withered bosom. Ania's body was bony and pitted, head shaved and flecked by abscesses that wept rancid yellow pus where lice had burrowed into her skin. Florid blooms of reddened skin covered the rest of her body. Her eyes were glassy and impassive, mouth fixed in a gaping, oblong O. She was more cadaver than child.

"We're never coming here again, and it will be cold soon," Mama whispered.

"I'm worried about Tchiya, Mama."

Mama's fingers ran through her coarse, gray-streaked hair and tied it into a loose knot.

Before the ghetto, her hair was thick and sinuous, black as india ink, and she wore it braided into a tight chignon. In the evenings, she brushed her hair, so it flowed back from a slight widow's peak and fell along the natural curve of her celloesque body to her waist. A smile passed over her lips; she was aware of how Papa glanced up from his book every so often to admire her.

"I am too," she said. "Now, please get dressed."

"Will we see Tchiya?"

A thin, dust-flecked beam of moonlight diffused into the room. It shone like a little star through a knothole in a board.

"No, neshomeleh. Tchiya will have to remain hidden with the Yelenyuks until its safe for us to get her." Mama's ashen face and pustule scars were accentuated by a halo of moonlight.

I pulled a sock over my foot—there was a hole near the heel—then put on the other one and wiggled my big toe as it poked through. I rubbed the aching stub that was my ring finger and remembered the SS officer who stabbed it off in a fit of rage.

"Does it hurt?" Mama asked.

I nodded, and she reached out to me, and I gave her my hand to rub. "You need to wear all your socks," she said then let my hand go. "Be quick please."

I had only three threadbare pairs, but together they covered my feet. I pushed my foot into one of my ankle-high winter shoes. The black leather was well past scuffed, the low heel worn down to bare wood. I looked up at Mama. "Do you think she's alive?"

"Tchiya's a bit older, perhaps a bit wiser than you." She smiled. "I think, too, that your sister has a healthy sense of fear."

"Healthy?" I pulled the frayed shoelaces tight, careful not to break them.

"She's a careful girl." She wet her lips and whispered, "It's been three days since she left, so I'm sure she's made it to the Yelenyuks. We would know if she hadn't, right?"

"Yes, Mama."

Mama's eyes wandered down to her hands. "The people you love can't completely disappear."

"Papa did." My lower jaw jutted out.

Mama looked into my eyes, "Get dressed, neshomeleh."

"I don't want you to ever lie to me again, Mama."

Mama looked at Mrs. Joselewicz and Mrs. Cukier, who pretended not to listen. "Musia Perlmutter, please be quiet."

"Papa disappeared, poof." I popped open the fingers of both hands.

"I know, neshomeleh."

"Please promise me you won't lie to me again."

"I promise."

"I love you."

"I love you too, neshomeleh. Now, please, put your clothes on."

Satisfied, I pulled my two best dresses over my body and tied the arms of a brown sweater around my waist. No matter what Mama said, the sweater was too thick to wear in August. Mama handed me one of her long-sleeved blouses to wear over the dresses. I frowned but put it on. I had argued with her enough.

I lifted my coat from the corner of my bed and felt the weight of a few gold coins—the jewelry was already used— Mama had sewn into the seams.

"Those things are for a rainy day, nothing else." Her stern eyes, deep in their sockets, focused on me. "Wherever we go, whatever we do, you take that coat."

"Yes, Mama."

On the front and back of the coat was a ghost of the Star of David. The Germans forced us to sew these on all our clothes when they came to Horochów, but mama removed them during the night.

I kept a small penknife in the breast pocket of my coat and the heavy, brass key to our family's home in Horochów. It had a pendant heart etched in the bow and notched teeth at the end of a cylindrical shank. When the Germans forced us to leave our home, I slid it off its hook without Mama or Tchiya seeing as I passed through the front door.

I checked both pockets to be sure my things were still in them and buttoned them closed. Then I folded the coat so that the pockets wouldn't spill and held it in my arms. The air was so warm and the coat so much bigger than me, it might have made me trip or made noise as it dragged on the ground.

Mama pulled together two bundles made of two worn scarves—one for her and one for me—wrapped with food she'd managed to scavenge, a few potatoes and a small block of dense, hard bread. She picked up both and cradled them in one arm.

"Let's go," she said.

My stomach ached, and my body shook. Suddenly, I was afraid to leave the ghetto. "Mama?"

Mama ran her fingers through my hair and caressed the nape of my neck. "Each day there are more Germans, more Ukrainian guards, more dogs wandering through the ghetto. Outside the walls, they are busy preparing for something horrible."

"Maybe if we hide, they won't find us."

Mama gave a brief, worried look toward Mrs. Cukier and Mrs. Joselewicz then whispered into my ear. "There is nowhere to hide that they won't find us."

I pressed my coat tighter to my aching belly. "If they catch us, they'll kill us."

"Then we'd better not let them catch us." Mama grasped my hand in hers. "Remember, to get to the Voitenkos' we cross the river then go across the field until we reach the road that goes to Skobelka."

"I know, Mama, I know."

Aged floorboards creaked as we stepped toward the door. Mrs. Cukier and Mrs. Joselewicz watched us pass through a ray of silver moonlight. No one spoke. Mama's hand tightened around mine as she opened the door. I looked into Mrs. Cukier's bitter eyes. She pulled Ania's panting body closer to her chest. We had our plan for what was to come; she had hers.

The brass latch clicked as Mama closed the door behind us. Plaster dust coated the hallway floor and walls. A wide shaft of moonlight shone through a lone window at the end of the hall, creating an iridescent quadrangle on the floor and up one-third of the wall. Anything white glowed with a violet hue, including our dirty, white blouses.

"Put your coat on," Mama said as she pushed her arms through the sleeves of her own.

The wool felt heavy, and the hem dragged in the dust. "Mama, if we run, I'll trip."

"We won't run."

Mama crouched, so she wouldn't cast a silhouette in the window. She reached back with one hand and fluttered it as a signal for me to do the same. We made the first few steps, then stood. The stairs were dark, and bits of plaster and paint chips, swept aside by passing feet, lay piled along the edges.

On the second-floor landing, Mama stopped and pressed her hand to my chest. Lit by an elongated, uneven shaft of light was the emaciated body of a young girl. Her legs splayed in dust and paint chips, her back tilted against a wall, her hands rested on either side of her hips, palms open. The soft darkness gave her blouse and pitted face an ethereal appearance. The girl's face tilted toward us; her vacant eyes staring at Mama.

I pushed Mama's hand from my chest, "It's Nava."

"Shush, neshomeleh."

Behind a door across from Nava's body, the floor creaked. "Nava?" a woman's voice called.

Mama motioned for me to follow, and with quick, stooped steps, we turned and made our way down the stairway to the door that led out to the street. Nine parallelograms of light passed through nine panes of glass in the door and stretched out across the floor and up the sides of the entryway. Mama eased up to the door and peered out.

"Oh, Nava, no, my love. Oh, my love," sobbed the woman in the stairway above us.

Mama looked up, "Quick, we have to go." Then she paused, "Remember, you must get to the Voitenkos'."

My lower jaw jutted, "I know, Mama. I know."

Mama looked into my eyes, "Do you know why I call you 'neshomeleh'?"

Above us, the woman mourned, "Nava, Nava ...," and wept in convulsions.

I turned from Mama's eyes. "I'm your 'little soul.'"

Another woman pleaded, "Haya, please, you'll be heard!"

Haya continued to mourn.

"Think of the rest of us," a third woman hissed.

Mama reached out and held my hand. She felt the little, fleshy stump of my finger, and her eyes saddened. "Yes, Musia, you are my little soul."

Outside the door, a dog barked, and hobnail boots rushed towards us, clacking on the cobblestones.

Mama's eyes widened. "Come." She pulled me a few steps down the hallway and pressed my body into a shallow doorway. "Don't move. Quiet." She grabbed my bundle and tossed both it and hers across the hall, under the stairwell. Then she flattened her body into a doorway across from me.

The door crashed open, and a German shepherd ran in, followed by four soldiers.

A woman's voice called out, "Look what you've done."

I looked at the soldiers without moving my head. They stood at the foot of the stairs, listening for the source of the voices. All four of them wore gray-green woolen uniforms with SS insignia on their collars, not the all-black uniforms of the Ukrainian militia. The soldier holding the shepherd's leash gripped a small pistol in his free hand. The other three carried blunt, ugly machine guns. They were SS too.

The dog bared its teeth at me.

"Nava, oh Nava," groaned Haya.

"*Die treppe hinauf!*" said the soldier, giving the leash a sharp tug. *Upstairs.*

"Damn you," a woman barked. "Damn you." A door slammed.

The dog strained against its leash and pulled the soldier up each step in powerful leaps. Hobnails clicked as the other men followed.

Haya groaned, "No, no, no ..."

Then a single pistol shot.

"*Brechen die tür auf,*" shouted a soldier. The door cracked open with a single kick, the dog barked, men yelled, "*Herauskommen drecksau,*" and their guns fired in short, grotesque bursts.

Mama jerked my hand. "Come."

She reached under the steps to pick up our bundles, then pulled me through the door and down the stoop. Above us came the metallic spitting of guns and the shepherd's husky bark. Down the street, a short distance beyond the edge of our building, the river flowed quietly and powerfully.

• • •

From the window above came the sound of a few sporadic shots thudding into soft flesh. Otherwise, the street was silent. In the darkness, behind scavenged boards, within false walls, tucked deep into basement corners with rats and spiders, more than four thousand people—most of them women and young girls—hid and prayed, all of them feverish with the impulse to survive.

Pale brick walls hemmed the ghetto in on three sides. A wide, deep, and often turbulent river served as the fourth barrier. The buildings in the ghetto hugged cramped, claustrophobic streets. Alleys leading to small, shared courtyards separated the buildings. In each courtyard was a small outbuilding with a bucket to serve as the toilet for a hundred or more people. A solid, rock wall connected the buildings that ran parallel to the river. The only opening to the river was at the end of our cobblestone street, which was usually a sewer because residents dumped buckets of urine and feces into the gutter, so the rain would wash the waste into the river.

Mama pulled me from the stoop to the edge of our building. A broad strip of dirt and scrubby grass passed between us and a wide thicket of tall, reedy bulrushes and arrowroot that ran along the riverbank and faded out into deeper water.

In the moonlight, the far side of the river tantalized. It bent gently so that spring rains and meltwater eroded the bank into a steep, root- and rock-strewn wall of soft dirt. Not far beyond the river's edge was a wide, dirt path, lined by linden trees with broad crowns and skinny, limbless trunks. There, in the daytime, farmers guided their carts, pulled by horses and overloaded with hay or wheat past the ghetto. From the other bank, they would stare into our tight, semiurban abattoir. We would stare back at people almost untouched by war, their overloaded carts a cruel reminder that we starved as they fed the German army.

For some in the ghetto, living became an unbearable burden. Loss piled upon loss to the point where no one was left to live for. These people came to the river. Heads bowed, hands clasped at their bellies, eyes desolate, they walked with grim, funereal precision down our street. They paused where the cobblestones faded into dirt that was etched by fanning sluices of rainwater.

They knew eyes were upon them. One last, full breath, and they stepped onto the dirt. A shot, maybe two; their bodies crumpled to the ground.

The corpses would lie for days until Ukrainian guards allowed a small detail of Jews to step onto the dirt to collect them. The workers would swat away clusters of flies; maggots spilled from the bodies as shaking hands rolled them onto blankets and dropped them into a cart. The smell of rotting flesh, a metallic-blood tang, spread across the ghetto. It made my saliva sour, and it lingered for days.

. . .

Now Mama let go of my hand and turned to me. "Remember, across the river, cross the field to the road to Skobelka."

Above us, I heard the dog barking and soldiers banging against walls and floors, looking for more Jews to kill. My stomach tightened and quivered. "Mama, you're frightening me. Are you coming? Are you coming with me across the river?"

"Yes, neshomeleh, of course I am." She pulled me close to her. "I live for you, my dear girl."

"I know how to get to the Voitenkos'. I told you, I know."

The soldiers grew louder as their zeal to kill burned into rage.

Mama kneeled and pulled me down with her in the shadow of a building. She rested her other hand on a drainpipe that ran down the wall.

Deep in our building, a door splintered.

"*Raus Juden*," yelled a soldier, "*hände hoch*!" A pistol popped, followed by bursts of machine guns.

Mama's legs tensed; her hand felt its way down my shoulder and grabbed my coat sleeve.

"Mama, no."

"Neshomeleh, we have to."

"They'll shoot us."

"They're in the house shooting."

Mama poked her head around the corner, then looked up

at the moon. Phosphorescent moonlight lit the river. Sporadic bursts of gunfire sounded deeper within the building.

A fat, dark cloud passed in front of the moon, and Mama squeezed the clump of coat in her hand and pulled me around the corner. Bent low, our shoulders bumped over each stone as we slid along the wall towards the opening. I waited for the inevitable shot.

My chest tightened. The dirt, Mama's back, the wall, the river, everything felt dreamlike. I closed my eyes, and the memory of a doll in a shop window—a doll I'd prayed, pleaded, and cried for—came to me. As I scraped along that wall, body stiff, braced for a bullet to tear through me, the doll's blushing ceramic cheeks, dark, coarse hair, its pretty dress, the odor of its newness, comforted my trembling heart.

A tug on my coat and a breath of marshy air plucked me from the memory and away from the wall. We raced across the open ground, and then my shoes sank into cool, liquid mud. It seeped through broken seams and over the cuff, soaking my socks and feet. The bulrushes closed around us; Mama slowed each step to a cautious breath. We arched our bodies to pass through without jostling or leaving a wake in the reeds.

Spraying bullets thudded behind the wall.

The water rose above my knees. With each step, mud sucked at our shoes. Water pulled at the skirts of our dresses and splashed in soft, unnerving surges as we pushed our legs forward.

How do they not hear us? I thought. A pressure built in my chest and rushed up through my eyes and forehead. I felt sick and hollow. The reeds, mud, water, Mama's bowed body—everything closed around me and looked distorted and unreal.

"Mama?"

She turned. "What?"

"I don't feel good."

Her lips clamped together hard enough to turn white.

"Neshomeleh, you're all right."

I closed my eyes and imagined the acrylic scent of the doll, the starched itch of its dress, and its blank, false eyes. It stared up at me, cradled in my arms.

A breeze rolled through the bulrushes, and an insect hissed over my head. Mama ducked. I covered my scrunched eyes with my hands and tried to drift further into memory, but another hissing bee shattered bulrush stalks as it passed.

Mama grabbed my coat and pulled me down into the thigh-high water. We knelt in the mud, our faces just a few inches above the water's surface, and looked back. Nobody stood on the riverbank shooting at us, but the deep thrum of diesel engines and lights bounced through the ghetto. Not far away we heard men yell, "*Raus Juden*." Others shouted, in accented Polish, "Rats, your time is up."

I looked up at the buildings and saw a darkened schema of boarded-up windows, like lifeless eyes staring out over the river. Each one, I thought, hid a man with a gun waiting to shoot Mama and me.

A few bullets hissed over our heads, and the number of voices yelling for the ghetto's residents to come out from hiding grew. Screams of women, children, an occasional male voice, pleading, "No ... no ...," were followed by successive pistol or rifle shots. For most, their hearts burst or lungs filled with blood, and life left them quickly. Others groaned until a final bullet sent them from the world.

I looked up and down the river, beyond the thicket of bulrushes and past the edges of the ghetto. Every apartment, every building, held hungry people happy to receive a bounty from the Germans for a Jew.

More diesel engines and lights wound through the ghetto; brakes squealed, then voices shouted, "*Schnell, schnell ... herauskommen jüdisch huren.*"

Mama and I hid deep in the bulrushes, but like the flicker of a movie reel we saw light and movement through the stalks and grass-like leaves. A boy, a woman, a girl—some person ran into the reeds and splashed through the water, followed by bullets. The body fell forward.

Doors splintered, and orders barked, "*Hände hoch!*" People were walking from their cramped apartments to the main square of the Horochów ghetto, heads low, resigned.

Beyond the ghetto walls and on the other side of the river, our former neighbors—most of them once our friends, colleagues, teachers, butchers, grocers, bakers, the people of Horochów—remained silent, impassive.

"We've got to try to cross while it's dark," Mama said, wiping water from her face.

I clenched my eyes.

"Musia, no!" Mama whispered. "We can't wish this away or hope for someone to save us."

"Yes, Mama." I lowered my face and felt the water on my lips. The stub of my missing finger ached.

Behind Mama, the light of a fire grew, and her eyes softened. "To save ourselves we have to put wishes away. We must live for each other. Do you understand?"

The light of two more fires rose behind Mama. The rapid spitting of large machine guns replaced the more laborious killing of pistols and rifles. Men yelled in German, Ukrainian, and Polish. Women and children screamed, pleaded, and died in one, painful, lingering wail.

Mama caressed my cheek with the palm of her hand. "Do you understand that hope is not enough?"

"Yes, Mama," I lied.

We stayed low, faces just above the water, and Mama did her best to guide me through the bulrushes without disturbing them.

The open river was still impossibly far away when a spray of bullets tore through the bulrushes. Mama stopped, and we looked back toward the bank. Lying low, the stalks of bulrushes were thin and leafless, which created a porous curtain. The flickering firelight gave the scene on the riverbank a surreal quality, like a movie spool moving too slowly through a lens.

We saw outlines, then images, then shadows, as light waxed and waned. Three dark bodies lay splayed in the dirt. One of them, a woman, I think, lifted her head and a bullet struck it.

More people ran from the street into the weeds and leafy stalks.

Four men, Ukrainian militia, stepped from the shadows of the street into the firelight. One of them looked back up the street and raised his arm. A bright beam of light shone out from up the street and ranged over the bulrushes and then into the river. Its source was a mystery to me, but its concentrated beam made the green of the bulrushes and the darkness of the river vivid.

One of the soldiers raised his rifle and shot into the river. I turned to look, but the reeds were too thick. The man levered the bolt of his gun to chamber another round. His friends watched him aim and squeeze the trigger. I turned but saw nothing, then heard a splash out past the bulrushes.

"Chort!" the man yelled as he loaded another round. I saw the dark outline of his body raise the rifle and slowly take aim. In the river, I heard a person splashing. The rifle fired. A thud echoed off the water, and one of the soldiers patted the shooter on the back.

"Khoroshyy postril Valentyn!" one of the men shouted. The beam of light drew down from the river into the bulrushes.

"Come out, Jews, and we'll send you to a work camp. You get to live!"

Mama squeezed my hand. "Stay still," she whispered.

Through the stalks, I saw six shadows in the light emerge from the bulrushes, their hands hung loose by their sides. The anonymous beam of light swept over them, then held steady as they walked. I think most were women; two, maybe three, were children my age. One woman held the hand of a smaller figure. I believe the shadow was her daughter.

They walked toward the soldiers, heading into the source of the light, their heads bowed. The four watched as they passed, guns cradled in their arms. One woman turned to the soldier nearest her and yelled, "*Pierdolec!*" Then spat in the face of the black-uniformed man. He wiped the spit from his face as another soldier quickly raised his gun and shot her in the chest and she collapsed.

The remaining prisoners stopped. The beam of light cut around them, casting long shadows into the bulrushes and river. Their clothes were wet and hung off their fragile bodies like moss swaying from tree branches in the light of a full moon.

The soldiers raised their rifles and shot them. One woman dropped immediately. Two others, a mother holding her girl's hand, shuddered then fell. The soldiers worked the bolts on their rifles and shot the remaining two.

Three of the soldiers walked past the bodies—one of them wiping his face—into the light and disappeared up the street.

The fourth gave a last look into the lit bulrushes. He took his cap off with one hand and wiped sweat from his forehead with the cuff of his uniform. He leaned down, hands on his knees, and spat into the dirt like an exhausted farmer.

"Mama, this is like work for them."

"Yes, neshomeleh." The water in front of her lips rippled as she spoke.

Behind us, the first pink aura of sunlight radiated from the horizon and colored the river.

"We can't go now," I said.

"No." Mama looked to the bodies along the bank. "We can't."

■ ■ ■

For hours, we sat in water up to our necks. No more people tried to run to the river, and we didn't see any soldiers, Ukrainian or SS. We heard the steady pounding of small and large machine guns. The dying screamed. A woman separated from her child or a child from her mother wailed, then was silent. Men roared in voices that were cold and metallic, furious and delirious, primal and inhuman, "*Raus Juden*," "*Schnell Juden*," or the command to shoot, "*Schießen.*

I closed my eyes and drew out memories of the doll: its scent; the feel of coarse fabric; its eyelids lolling back into its head to expose animated, round, blue eyes; its pouting smile.

"Neshomeleh?"

"Yes, Mama." I opened my eyes and looked into hers. Filthy water soaked through my coat and clothes. My body itched, and the froggy odor of the water made my tummy queasy.

"You have to be strong, my love." She cradled my cheek in her hand. "Please don't give up."

The sun was high above us now and hot. "I want to take my coat off."

Mama looked back to the bank. Smoke rose from more fires. Entire buildings burned, and I imagined the people hiding in them burning to death or running into the street to be shot.

Mama looked at me, then the water. Her eyes brightened a little. "Our coats are the same color as the water."

"I'm hot, wet, and itchy."

"Try to bear through it please?" She looked to the other side of the river. "Remember—"

My jaw stiffened, "I know how to get to the Voitenkos', Mama."

"Not that," Mama said, a little too loud. "Neshomeleh, remember '*Umhoo.*' Greet a Jew—"

"Yes, Mama—"

"—with this word, and they will know you."

"I remember my Yiddish, Mama." My eyes drooped. "I'm tired."

"I am too." Mama looked at the partially submerged corpse of a tree exposed when the water receded. She held the sleeve of my coat and pulled me toward it. She was slow and deliberate and made only a wrinkle in the water. "Lay your head here," she said, placing her hand on a bit of exposed trunk. "I'll hold you to be sure you don't float away."

I curled up to the sodden log and rested my head on it. Mama swept her arms around me. A sharp, broken branch poked my chest, so I wiggled away from it into Mama's chest. Despite the misery so close to us, hunting for us, I felt secure. I let my eyes close and drifted into sleep.

• • •

My eyes opened to evening light and Mama prodding me. One of her hands covered my mouth. A mix of froggy water and smoke filled my nostrils. "Shhhh," she whispered into my ear. I looked up to her eyes, but her focus was on the riverbank near the end of the cobblestone street. A machine gun fired, and I shifted my weight. Two SS men stood near the bulrushes amid stiffened, contorted bodies.

The sun was low behind the ghetto so that the buildings cast long shadows that darkened the two men. Their movements seemed weary, and as they shot into the bodies, their arms shuddered with the jolt of each burst.

They stopped and reloaded their guns. One of the SS men pulled out a pack of cigarettes and offered one to his friend then pulled one out for himself. He lit his friend's and then his cigarette, then he squatted, his behind resting on a woman's body as he smoked. The other urinated into the water. The orange, lit end of the cigarette dangled from his lips. He tilted his head to avoid the smoke.

We held our eyes just above the water. Mama's knotted hair floated in an arc behind her head.

The ghetto was still on fire. Lapping flames glowed in the encroaching darkness. Guns still fired; the dying still wept.

The SS men flicked their cigarettes into the water, snapped a lever on the sides of their guns to cock them, and strolled back to the work of killing.

...

Although the late-August air was warm, my body shivered. "Mama, I'm so cold and hungry."

She reached into one of our bundles and pulled out a soggy clump of bread that almost melted between her fingers. "Here."

The sight of it made me queasy. I shook my head.

"Eat it, Musia."

"It's disgusting."

Her eyes narrowed, lips pressed together. "Eat."

I opened my mouth and she shoved the bread in and wiped it off her fingers on the side of my cheek. I swallowed, but my stomach and throat clenched, forcing the bread into the back of my throat. I swallowed again, and this time it stayed down.

Mama pulled me close to her body and wrapped her arms around me. I felt so sick, so very tired. Her hands pressed against my belly, and I felt them almost touch my spine. "You can feel the bumps along my back, can't you?"

"No, neshomeleh, your body feels strong, ready."

"Ready for what?"

She nestled her cheek to mine. "For what you will need to do."

"I'm scared, Mama. What if—"

"Musia, remember what your father told you when you have bad thoughts?"

"They are like birds; let them fly away."

"Yes, let them fly away, my love."

Firelight lapped and flicked across the water. Machine guns screeched. It was taking the soldiers a long time to kill the thousands of people in our ghetto. "They don't want to leave, Mama."

She held me tighter.

"No, no, no, no ...," A woman chanted. Mama and I turned to see the outline of her body standing at the riverbank in front of us. A dress hung from her wasted body, and she held a bundle to her chest. Firelight pulsed behind her casting a living, jagged shadow.

She moved in short, painful steps toward Mama and me.

A moment later, two black-uniformed Ukrainians— thin, boyish builds—jogged around the corner, past the cobblestones onto the dirt riverbank. One cradled his rifle in the crook of an arm and pulled a fresh clip of bullets from a pouch on his leather belt. The other struggled with the bolt on his rifle. He trotted in awkward steps, eyes rising to follow the woman, then back down to his fumbling hands.

Mama edged her body in front of me, and we dipped lower in the water.

Light bent around her face as her head turned toward the young soldiers. "It's Mrs. Cukier," I whispered. The bundle she carried was Ania's body. With each painful step, Ania's head flopped like a rag doll.

The bolt handle slid forward. The soldier raised his gun, aimed, and fired. Mrs. Cukier stumbled and dropped to her knees. The soldier slowed, worked the bolt again, and walked closer to Mrs. Cukier and Ania. He raised the rifle to his shoulder and fired. The bullet snapped Mrs. Cukier's spine. Her torso bent almost in half, her body remained kneeling as if in some perverse prayer. Ania fell from her arms and lay beneath her.

Flames in the ghetto lapped skyward, casting light over the riverbank tableau of bent bodies and youthful killers. Firelight reached into the bulrushes and river.

The first soldier pushed a new clip into his rifle and snapped the bolt handle forward. The other soldier's eyes searched across the water, then into the bulrushes. They stopped where Mama and I hid.

Mama's weight shifted. The soldier's eyes fixed, as if he were staring into Mama's eyes. He half raised his rifle.

"*Pryyikhaty*," said the other soldier.

The second soldier waved him off with one hand, eyes tranquil, menacing.

"*Hier kommen, jetzt!*" yelled an SS soldier from the cobblestones.

The Ukrainian frowned. He lowered his rifle, and the two Ukrainians disappeared up the street with the German.

"We'll wait a little longer, then cross," Mama said.

"Yes." I shook with relief.

"Neshomeleh, when we get across, go to the Voitenkos', across the field to the road to Skobelka, then north—"

I pulled away from Mama. "Stop repeating it!" Doesn't she believe I know my way? Why am I always so helpless?

"Shush, Musia."

I turned and leveled my eyes at hers. "I know how to get there. We used to buy butter, milk, cheese from them. I know him. I know his name. I know his family. Trudka and I were in the same grade in school. I. Know. Where. They. Live."

"Yes, Musia. I'm sorry." Mama looked back to the cobblestones. "Please, quiet, neshomeleh." She reached for me and held me close.

My muscles were tired and weak. I pulled my knees close to my chest and rattled in Mama's arms. I was so cold. Mama draped her coat around us both. "Try to sleep, my love. Rest, and we'll cross the river together in a little bit."

I closed my eyes and let my mind drift in soft currents, which dissolved into an image of Papa. He was such an elegant man, always in a black wool suit with a vest. Pince-nez glasses rested on the bridge of his nose; a wisp of black mustache crossed above his lips; black, wavy hair was held in place with pomade. His eyes were serious and kind, his demeanor gentle and reassuring. Each morning he wrapped his long arms around me, then put his coat on, plucked an umbrella—rain or shine—from the stand by the front door, and left to catch the train to his life's work as a philosophy professor at the University of Lwów.

In the dream, he held a wooden box cage filled with small, red-faced birds spreading their yellow wings, shaking with the desire to fly. I reached with a finger to touch one through two wooden bars, but Papa pulled a peg from a clasp and lifted the wooden top. In a heartbeat, the birds darted into the air and circled Papa and me.

"What are they?" I asked.

He looked down at me and smiled, lips parted. "*Tzadikim, neshomeleh.*"

I reached out to catch one of the circling birds, but my hands were too slow. "Help me, Papa."

"Help you what?"

"Help me catch one."

The cage was no longer in his hands, and he shooed the birds away.

My cheeks warmed, and my chest tightened. "Mama and I need one, and they're gone now, Papa!"

"They're needed elsewhere, neshomeleh."

"No, Papa!"

"Yes, Musia." He looked at me. Any trace of a smile left his lips and eyes. "You must find your own way."

I searched the sky. The *Tzadikim* were gone. I reached for Papa, to hold on to him, but he'd gone too, leaving me in a small forest clearing.

I woke with a deep breath. The smell of smoke and water, the metallic odor of burning blood returned. I looked for Mama. There was only the moon shining down. I tried to sit up, but my coat hung on the broken end of a branch on the drowned tree. I twisted and pulled the coat to free it and looked into the bulrushes, but I couldn't see Mama.

Too scared to yell, I called for her in a hushed voice. "Mama, where are you, Mama?" There was no answer. Mrs. Cukier's bent, broken body with Ania's trapped within it was still there, but not Mama. I looked to where the other bodies lay but didn't see one in a wool coat. The fires had died down, so there was little light other than the moon. The far bank of the river was dark, quiet.

"Maaammmmaaaa," I called. Except for periodic bursts of machine guns or the occasional lone shot, there was only silence.

I took my wet coat off and wrapped it over my shoulder. Mama's bundle was gone, so I picked up my own. "Oh, Mama, which way did you go?"

Across the river, I thought. *She must have gone across the river.*

"I'm so sorry, Mama." Tears fell down my cheeks. "I didn't mean to disappoint you." I crawled toward the edge of the bulrushes, mumbling, "I didn't mean to get so angry, Mama. Mama, do you hear me?"

Past the thicket of bulrushes, the water deepened. I hunched into it, my feet pushing off the soft riverbed. I splashed it on my face to wash salty tears from my eyes. Soon, the water was so deep I had to stand to keep my face above the surface. Then it was over my head. I paddled with my arms and feet, unable to swim in my shoes and with the heavy coat draped over my shoulder and bundle in one hand.

"Mama?" I felt like I was drowning. If I let my breath out, I sank deeper into the water. I thought to let go of the coat, but Mama's voice didn't let me. *Wherever we go, whatever we do, you take that coat.* The current pushed me farther from the burning ghetto. My lungs burned, my body hollow, my muscles drained of strength.

I let a breath out, prepared to drift to the bottom. My legs flailed, useless. Water seeped over my eyes, and I felt the coat, its sodden weight and hidden valuables, pulling me down.

I gave one last kick, but rather than flying through water, my foot hit solid riverbed. I pushed off and my head broke through the river's surface. I drew in a quick breath and bobbed with the current for a moment.

I took bouncing steps, bobbing up and then down until the river became shallower. When the water was waist high, I looked to the ghetto. Smoke and the dim light of small fires rose into the sky.

I stayed low in the water to avoid the searching eyes of soldiers. When I reached the steep riverbank, I tossed the wet bundle up then scrambled up the bank and through tall grass at its top. With the bundle in hand, I crawled to a linden tree near the dirt path, pulled the coat from my shoulders, and sat with my back against its trunk.

Trees lined the other side of the road. Through them, I looked across a broad field of amber wheat. Breezes passed over grain stalks and caught their brown brushes in rippling, moonlit waves.

"Mama, where are you?"

Mama's voice whispered through the wheat with the wind. *Across the field, neshomeleh.*

"Yes, Mama."

The Voitenkos' Farm

My sodden hands looked pale white and wrinkled in the moonlight.

A warm breath passed through the immense wheat field and across my cheek. I looked from my hands back toward the ghetto. Thousands of fading embers glowed softly, and the river was a trickling murmur.

I sat under a linden tree, my legs stretched in front of me, the hard contours of its bark pressing against my damp back. The tree's heart-shaped leaves rustled over my head, and a honey-sweet aroma drifted down from the tree. I felt for the sweater I'd wrapped around my waist as Mama and I dressed, but it was gone, taken by the river. *How long ago did we sneak into the bulrushes?* I wondered. *Was it two days? Three?*

Vast swathes of bristled tassels, slouching from their burden of grain-filled husks, rippled like linen shaken out across a moonlit, golden bed. The field was alive with movement and a steady thrum of chirping crickets. Small frogs peeped from the riverbank.

The field ran flat for a long way until it climbed up a gentle slope and disappeared over a broad, rounded hill. To my left ran the edge of a deep hardwood forest, and to my right more fields, bounded by wagon tracks, rose and fell into the horizon. From visiting farmers with Mama, I knew that shake- and thatch-roofed cottages and barns huddled in darkened vales.

The first hint of morning grew over the far horizon. I had little experience in the habits of farmers; my world before the ghetto was school, private tutors, kids, and the intellectual friends of my parents, but I knew the people who belonged to these fields woke up with first light.

I looked back to the smoldering ghetto. The skirt of bulrushes was too thick for me to see the bodies on the far bank, but I knew they were there, lying in a heap. My eyes wandered over the reeds and then into the river. "Mama," I called, but my voice was lost in the murmur of water, the din of crickets and frogs, and the breeze sweeping over the field. I searched for any sign of movement, for the dark bent figure of Mama searching for me, but nothing.

"Mama, I'm so sorry. Please, please come to me." I raised my hands to my face, but the raw odor of slough water disgusted me, and saliva from an unknown well filled the back of my throat. "Mama, please, I'll be good, like Tchiya." I looked into the immensity of the field spreading out before me and thought, *How could I let this happen?*

"Mama, where are you?" I sat up onto my knees and closed my eyes. Listening with all my might, I heard a faint whisper. *The field, neshomeleh, into the field.* I squinted into the sun's first yellow light and far away, in the deepest part of the field, saw the rounded back of a rock bulging above the rolling sea of amber. A slender, elongated shadow stretched from the rock's leeward side, and within it, snug against the rock, a hollow formed a small, protected place.

Mama, are you afraid to call to me? In my heart, I knew Mama wouldn't leave me. I pulled my coat—with its valuables and my small penknife—to my side and placed the bundle Mama had put together for me in a sleeve of the coat. My body felt like water, but I was able to crawl over the two wheel ruts of the dirt track, past the second row of linden trees, and across a skirt of grass and wild flowers into the field.

Within the forest of wheat stalks I lay on the ground and rested a moment. I closed my eyes again and listened for people looking for Jews but heard only the gentle energy of a living field: crickets chirping, ants crawling to-and-fro, and the rustle of something small darting, then stopping, then darting again. As the air warmed and the light matured into a muted sheen of goldenrod, thin clouds of insects floated from the field, which brought swallows from their nooks diving at the flying bugs. Every so often a blue-green dragonfly hummed overhead on its zigzagging path.

My stomach ached, and my body shook from hunger. I reached into my small bundle and pulled out a damp, withered potato. Water and rot puckered the skin and softened the flesh. I bit into it, and my mouth welcomed its juice, but its soured flavor stung my throat, and I gagged on its mealy pulp. I remembered the river-soaked bread but couldn't bear putting it into my mouth.

Not hearing any human sounds, I pushed myself up on my knees and then stood on wobbly legs. The stalks were almost as tall as me. I looked to see if any people were on the wagon path near the river but saw only the burnt ruins of the ghetto. Smoke rose from a handful of far-off chimneys, but there were no humans, no guns firing, or no grinding of trucks or machinery. The lack of human sounds gave the scene an eerie quality.

The tall wheat made it hard to see the rock, but I felt Mama there, waiting. *I must get to her quick as I can.*

As I crawled through the dirt, crickets bounced off my face and hands. Small stones and bits of chaff and straw stuck to my hands and knees and my wet clothes. My body itched, and the back of my neck felt tight and sore, but I kept crawling, dragging my coat behind me.

I'm coming, Mama, I'm coming, I repeated in my mind. If I didn't reach her soon, she'd leave. She didn't know I was here. I'd have to go to the Voitenkos' alone.

At the thought, my stomach cramped, and I vomited up a small mouthful of potato but forced it back down.

I broke a wheat stem off at the root and chewed on it to ease the taste of vomit from my dry mouth, but then a shiver ran through me. I turned to see a thin trail of bent and broken stalks, straight as a pencil, leading from the edge of the field to me.

Stupid, useless me.

I closed my eyes and softly but urgently called out, "Are you there, Mama?" Nothing. A cricket smacked into my ear, and I slapped at it. Tears bubbled from my eyes. "Please be there, Mama. Please, I can't be alone any longer." I tried to crawl without leaving any broken stems, but I had to get to Mama. *She's waiting. I know it. I must hurry.* I wiped tears from my face and kept crawling.

Finally, I reached the rock. I squinted but did not see Mama. I edged closer and in a loud whisper said, "Mama, are you there? Please be there." But there was no response.

I crawled around the rock and looked for any sign of her, but nothing.

I rested my back against the rock. *I've let you down again.*

■ ■ ■

I woke to sun in my face. My mouth was dry, and my lips were coarse and sore. My body was hollow, and my mind raced with thoughts of Mama and my loneliness. I rubbed the stump of my ring finger, which ached. Filthy water and scraping it on the ground as I crawled inflamed the folded skin at the stub. Dirty blood seeped from small cuts and scratches on my hands.

"Mama, are you here?" I whispered as loud as I dared but heard only the wind through the wheat—still no human voices, no sounds of people. I leafed through my bundle and ate another soft, shriveled potato then broke a wheat stalk and chewed it to take the rancid flavor from my mouth.

I refused to believe Mama wasn't waiting for me or looking for me. I knew she wasn't among the bodies near the river, and in my heart, I could feel her; I could feel her heart, her kind soul. She wasn't a cinder burning up toward the sky.

I had to find her, and I had to ask her, my perfect mother, to forgive me for being such a bad daughter, for being angry and getting lost.

I licked my lips to soothe them but didn't have enough moisture on my tongue. I worried about soldiers finding me, and I worried about getting lost, even though I'd told Mama I knew the way. A memory of Papa pushed its way into my mind. In it, I raced into Papa's library, and in a burst of girlish urgency shouted, "Zofia found a hurt baby rabbit in the garden!"

A handful of his elder friends, people as dignified and rigid as Papa's beautiful books, looked at me, then to Papa. "Musia," he said, tilting his head so that his eyes peered above his wire-frame, pince-nez glasses, "you're being rude and a pest. Please leave." The eyes of the men followed me as I walked away, a tear falling to my blouse.

I found Mama in the kitchen, and she looked down on me as she wiped her hands with a towel. "Musia, what were you thinking?" Her voice was tense and tired. She noticed the teardrop running down my cheek. "My darling, Papa is nervous because those are important men, and he wants to be one of them."

"I'm a pest."

"No, Musia, you're my neshomeleh." She tucked the towel into her apron. "Now, let's see if we can't help your friend Zofia with the little baby."

■ ■ ■

How will I live without you, Mama?

I shaded my eyes with one hand and looked up through the stalks and bearded tassels into the sky. Two sparrows, white-chests, black-wings, and brown-throats, skimmed over the field, and in an instant, their bodies spiraled upward, nearly collided, then fell away from each other.

They weren't as pretty as the *Tzadikim* in the dream, but I did remember Papa's words, *You must find your own way.*

The hot sun shone down. I unbuttoned Mama's blouse and peeled it off, still damp with river water and sweat. I balled it up and brought it to my nose. The faintest scent of Mama lingered—not the lavender oil she wore for Papa but her body, her truest essence. I laid the shirt out next to me as best I could among the wheat stems to dry, hoping it wouldn't lose this last tangible piece of Mama until I found her.

I know the Voitenkos; they are good people, I thought. *Mama must be very worried waiting for me.* But I couldn't go to the Voitenkos' until nightfall; it was too dangerous to walk in the open during daylight.

"Sorry to make you wait, Mama," I whispered. The sparrows let loose a sharp series of melodic trills as their bodies whorled like kites through the air. I knew the *Tzadikim* had left, gone elsewhere to help the world, but if there are sparrows and swallows, I could let bad thoughts fly away with them.

■ ■ ■

The sun dipped, and shadows grew longer as afternoon light matured into evening. The blue horizon grew crimson, and the field took on the deep hue of a golden-haired child. Small frogs peeped, and crickets joined the choir of night hymns. In the distance, smoke rose from a chimney, but I saw no lights. The world of humans was in hiding, trying to regain its soul after so much death.

I pushed my body up against the rock and looked back to the still-smoldering ghetto. The lights of Horochów remained dimmed or concealed behind black air-raid curtains. Darkness had not yet descended; instead, the glow of fading summer sunlight backlit the dark buildings. I remembered Mama calling for me in this light as she stood at the edge of our garden. My friend Zofia's mother called her in this light too. Zofia waved goodnight and hurried to her mother's voice.

I resisted and often hid among our small orchard of pear and apple trees where the grass grew a little taller. Near the house were flower beds with rose bushes, azaleas, bright-red corn poppies, violet asters, pink lilies, yellow freesia, and indigo-blue irises. Running around the house was a low, white fence and stone steps leading up to the front door. Tall, aged chestnut trees lined our street. It was a world of beauty and security, within which I used to immerse my mind and body until the last burgundy glow of sun faded into night. Only when I heard frustration shade her voice would I give myself over to Mama and the indoors.

Now I slid around the rock and pretended my ears were radio receivers, able to detect any sound of danger. With the setting sun at my back, I hitched the coat with the bundle in the sleeve up over a shoulder and started walking through the wheat stalks toward the darkening horizon. I tied Mama's blouse around my waist and raised it to breathe in her scent. I was sure Mama was worried because I'd not arrived at the Voitenkos' farm, and I hoped she wasn't too mad.

My stomach ached with hunger, so I ate another soft potato and swallowed some bread, which had dried into a pulp-like paste, more like sawdust than flour.

My mind churned on thoughts of German soldiers and Ukrainian militia, their ugly gray-green uniforms and guns, the smiles on their faces as they killed Jews. I imagined a rifle pointed at my face or a noose around my neck. My chest tightened, and my stomach knotted into a painful cramp. To sweep these worries away I thought of Mama and my sister Tchiya. I imagined Tchiya, her belly fed, lying in some farmer's root cellar sleeping, safe, knowing Mama would come to her. Then I felt worse for putting them both at risk if soldiers found me, and so my mind churned again on thoughts of soldiers and their guns and death. *Look at the trouble I cause. I wish I hadn't fallen asleep in the river. If only I could go back.* Round and round went my mind, unable to turn itself off. Each memory of Mama or Tchiya brought me to guilt or despair or fear and eventually to soldiers and death. For a moment I thought of Papa, but that brought memories of the day the Germans took him. I thought of playing in the garden and woods near our home with Zofia, her blue eyes wide with fun and mischief and her blond braids bouncing as she ran, but it bled into a memory of her emaciated, lifeless face lying in the center of the ghetto.

Worry led to fear, led to anxiety, led to panic. My lips trembled, and I wept as I pushed through the wheat toward the edge of the field and the road to Skobelka. I wiped my eyes with a dirty hand that still smelled of rot and river water. *Mama, I need you!*

I stopped walking. The last embers of day burned behind me, and I raised my hands up to the waxing moon and stretched my fingers out toward it. The air, drenched in silver moonlight on one horizon and the sun's dying fire on the other, tickled the little blond hairs on my bare arms, and my anxious, child's brain paused. I mumbled a song Mama sang, a song lost to me for too long.

Goodnight, goodnight,
Goodnight, my small one,
Goodnight gray eyes half closed,
For all good children,
Watched by a good angel.

I repeated the lyrics until they flowed as a single sentence, broken only by my breathing. The anguish eased, and I lowered my arms. I pulled Mama's blouse to my face and breathed her in. *She's alive and waiting for me. The Voitenkos are good people, and she is with them.*

I walked as quickly as I could. Even though I could see to the next field, it took forever to get to it, and once I did, another lay beyond it.

Finally, in darkness broken by a waning full moon, I came to a weathered and rutted gravel road. I walked down it, taking the chance of someone seeing me. I was exhausted, and Mama's song could carry me only so far.

On either side of the road spread large, broad fields of clover, recently cut and raked into meandering windrows to cure in the sun. I recognized these fields from trips with Mama to the Voitenkos'. I knew I was nearing their farm when the road climbed a gentle slope and then dipped into a small valley between two hills that looked like slowly rising bread. The thought that I was near Mama lightened my mind, heart, and body. I thought of her smile when she saw me, safe, that soldiers hadn't found me, that I had made it to her on my own.

The tree-shaded house and barn formed an *L* with a space at the angle, but no light shone in the house, and no smoke drifted from the chimney. The roofs of the barn and house sagged, and sun and rain had warped many of the shake shingles. Moss grew in clumps where the shingles were most contorted on both roofs, and knots and gaps between the boards mottled the plank walls.

Silver moonlight illuminated the dirt yard between the barn and house. Scattered about were long, wooden feed bins for chickens and two water troughs on either side of the barn door. Somewhere in the dark beyond the barn was a coop with restless chickens roosting for the night. Everything had a thick layer of dirt on it, chicken feathers lay scattered on the ground, and a sour odor of manure wafted heavily in the air.

I knocked on the Voitenkos' door. I listened with my eyes closed but heard no voices or footsteps. I'd hoped they'd be awake, waiting. I knocked harder.

From inside, a dog barked. Its claws scratched on the floor as it ran to the door, never letting up on its warning. I heard his claws on the other side of the door and, above me, the murmur of voices, a man and woman. The dog growled and barked until a man's voice scolded it in Ukrainian. When the dog wouldn't stop growling the man yelled, *"Zatknys!"* and slapped it hard enough for me to hear.

"Who is it?" he asked from behind the door.

"Mr. Voitenko, it's me, Musia Perlmutter, and I am here to hide with my mother. May I come in and see her?"

A bolt gave way, and the door opened slowly. Mr. Voitenko stuck his head past the edge of the door and looked out beyond me into the night. I looked at his face: a bulbous sunburned nose; greasy, matted hair; and fearful eyes. He opened the door wider, and I could see he was wearing a dirty tunic hastily tucked into homemade wool pants; suspenders bulged around his stomach. Behind him, a gaunt German shepherd lay on the floor, his head resting on his front paws, his brows knitted.

Mrs. Voitenko, a tall, angular woman with graying hair and scared eyes, stood behind him, a wool blanket wrapped around her threadbare nightgown. She touched the back of her husband's shoulder, but he shrugged her off. In a thin, quavering whisper, she said, "How is she alive?"

He turned to her. "I don't know."

"I would like to see my mother please," I said.

Again, Mrs. Voitenko touched her husband's shoulder. "How could she not know?"

Mr. Voitenko turned his face toward his wife and then to me. "She isn't here."

With his words my body felt like it would fall into itself. I pulled at the end of my hair with one hand and felt the pain disperse through the nerves of my body. I had done so much.

How could it be true that Mama was not there waiting?

"But we are to meet here. You are to hide us."

Mrs. Voitenko leaned her head in to her husband's ear. "They'll kill our entire family if they find her."

"I know," he said to her.

She pulled the blanket tighter around her body.

I knew better than to believe Mama would break her word. She would never leave me. "Please may I see my mother?"

Mrs. Voitenko craned her neck out like a turtle. "She isn't here, Musia. I'm sorry, but you shouldn't be here either. It's too dangerous."

"Please, *moye kokhannya*," said Mr. Voitenko to his wife. He closed his eyes and rubbed his forehead for a moment, then said to me, "Go to the barn."

"Is my mother there?"

"They'll shoot us, the kids, all of us," Mrs. Voitenko breathed into her husband's ear.

"Go to the barn and wait for me."

■ ■ ■

The barn door was open a little, and I walked into the darkness. A layer of straw matted the packed-dirt floor, and I could hear barn swallows give a peremptory nervous warning from their nooks. Moonlight filtered in through dirt-glazed windows, and my eyes grew used to the light. A low, wood-plank hayloft ran the length of the barn with an opening at one end with a ladder. At that end, two draft horses idled in their stalls. A cat scurried across the floor. Milking stalls lined either side of the barn. Buckets and manure shovels, hay rakes, and scythes—all manner of farm tools hung from pegs hammered into the posts and beams.

It smelled of manure and sour milk.

The door scraped behind me as Mr. Voitenko opened it and walked in carrying a lantern emitting a halo of light around him.

"Where's my mother?"

"She's not here, Musia, and I don't know where she is."

I let my coat fall to the floor. "What do you mean? She's supposed to be here; I'm meeting her here."

"I know, but she isn't here."

If I leave, I thought, *I'll miss Mama when she does come.* "She'll come. Maybe she's checking on Tchiya."

"I don't know, Musia, but you can't wait here."

My chest tightened. I breathed in. "You agreed to hide us."

"Yes, but I changed my mind. It's too dangerous."

My head felt faint, and for a moment, my sight blurred as I realized that I was alone, and it was my fault. If I hadn't fallen asleep, I would still be with Mama, wherever she was.

"Where am I to go? What am I to do?"

"I don't know. There's nothing I can do for you."

My eyes wandered down from his face to the braided watch fob that hung from the pocket of his pants. "What time is it?"

He reached into his pocket and pulled a gold watch out and popped open the cover. "One a.m."

"That's my father's watch."

Mr. Voitenko looked down at his hand, then to me. "No, it isn't."

"Yes, it is. I recognize the chain and the cover. My grandfather gave it to my father."

He snapped the cover shut and put the watch in his pocket. "Don't be a brat. I'll give you some food, but you have to leave when the sun comes up."

"But I have to wait for my mother. I promised her that I would wait for her here."

Mr. Voitenko shrugged his shoulders. "No. It's too dangerous to hide a Jew."

Tears spilled from my eyes as thoughts overwhelmed me— I'd let Mama down; I couldn't survive on my own. "Please, just a couple of days? I know she'll be here for me."

"If you don't leave by morning, I'll report you to the authorities."

As he said this, Mrs. Voitenko came into the barn carrying a bowl of cold broth with a potato in it. Mr. Voitenko gave her a stern look then turned and left. The barn was dark except for drafts of filtered moonlight through the windows.

Mrs. Voitenko led me through the dark barn to the ladder and handed me the bowl and a spoon. "Eat this and hide in the hay. I'll be out to get you before sunrise."

She watched me climb the ladder on shaking legs, with my coat slung over a shoulder and the soup balanced in one hand. I heard her leave the barn, and I curled my body into the hay and ate the soup and potato, my first meal in days.

My belly felt tight and ill, but I didn't get sick. I pulled my coat around me and felt for the penknife and valuables sewn into it for a rainy day, then wondered if this was a rainy day. *Mama, please come, please come, please come,* I prayed to her and for her as my eyes closed and I drifted off to sleep.

The Haystack

Mrs. Voitenko's strong, sharp fingers poked my side as she woke me. The barn was dark except for the lantern Mrs. Voitenko had hung on a hook below the loft. Its flickering light came up from below, casting shadows that exaggerated the jagged features of her face.

"My husband means what he says, Musia. If you want to live, you have to leave." A scarf with a few things wrapped in it rested in her lap. Her lips pressed together. "I remember you and your mother coming here," she said. "I always thought you were good Jews."

She handed the bundle to me and eased her way to the ladder. "My husband will call the authorities, and they'll kill you. You have to leave." Then she climbed down the ladder. The halo of light wobbled with each step she took across the barn and into the yard.

I sat up on the coat, crossed my legs, and opened the scarf. Inside were three eggs, three mostly green apples, a handful of potatoes, a few carrots, and a large chunk of fresh bread. This was more food than I'd seen in almost two years.

A voice in the barnyard drew me to a wide crack in the wall. Although the sun hadn't yet broken over the horizon, I could make out Mr. Voitenko standing with his fists clenched at his sides. "What did you give her?"

Mrs. Voitenko crossed her arms and turned her head. "Food."

"The Nazis, everyone, *everyone* is hunting for Jews, and you gave her food from our house?"

"Yes."

"Do you know what they did to the Babenkos?"

Her body stiffened. "Yes."

"They shot his children and wife in front of him and then hung him from his barn and left their bodies to rot."

She turned her face to his. "I don't want her here, but *God* is watching."

Mr. Voitenko glared at his wife for a moment, then walked toward the barn muttering, "God is watching, like hell."

The door slid open hard, and I crawled back to my coat and packed the two bundles into its sleeves. I brought Mama's blouse to my nose and inhaled her deeply, then tied the blouse to my waist.

"I don't care if your father was Simcha Perlmutter. Get the hell out, or I will turn you in!"

I folded the coat, so the worn outline of the Star of David would not be too visible, threw it over my shoulder and climbed down the ladder. Mr. Voitenko stood in the doorway, the dirt barnyard behind him. His dirty tunic was tucked into his wool pants, held up by suspenders and a belt. A knife jutted from his waistband. His arms were at his sides, his legs wide, and his face tired and dark.

I wanted to beg him to let me stay just a little longer, to say how I knew Mama would be along soon, and we would leave together. I wanted to tell him to give back my father's watch. I wanted to tell him he was an ugly and dishonest man.

Tears burned around my eyes, but I wouldn't let Mr. Voitenko see my fear. As I passed him, I stopped and turned my eyes to the fob of Papa's watch, hanging from his pocket.

"I'll be back for my father's watch."

"You'll be dead."

He followed me into the barnyard. His dog barked from inside the house, and at the kitchen window, I saw the staring faces of his three children: two boys and Trudka, my classmate before the Germans came. I gave them no more than a glance.

Two large oak trees stood on either side of the entryway to the farm. The rising sun lit their leafy tops and glowed across a broad field of hay laid out in windrows.

God, if you exist, bring Mama to me now, I whispered, but only the waxing butternut light answered.

...

I walked down the rutted lane toward the road to Skobelka, hoping I would see Mama's tall, lean figure—starvation and labor eroded the richness of her body—in the distance. The land around me was immense. I knew she was somewhere out there, searching for me. But finding each other seemed impossible. We had no point of reference, no home, no fulcrum. Mama had said to go to the Voitenkos so many times: "We will be safe with them; you will find me there." But as my worn shoes crunched on the gravel, I knew there was no safe place for me. There were only soldiers, all of whom wanted to kill us.

Oh, Mama, where are you? I need you so much. Tears streamed down my cheeks and mixed with thickened saliva as fear seized me. I breathed in short, quick huffs, and my head felt heavy and faint. I stopped in the road, closed my eyes, wrapped my arms around my belly, and listened to a breeze sweetened by curing hay as it passed over the windrows. At first, there was silence, just the air moving across my face, but within it, a thin tendril touched me, and I believed that Mama was alive.

I started walking again. I came to the Skobelka road and

turned toward the small village. I sang as I walked, deadened to any regard for who might hear or see:

Sleep, sleep, beautiful child,
Sleep, sleep, free from worry
and pain

The lyrics carried me forward and eased my panic. Interspersed among vast fields of wheat were fields with cut hay laying out in rows to cure in the sun or piled into massive haystacks. There were also smaller fields of potatoes and beets, their green leaves and stems in thick, neat rows. Behind every house were gardens of varying sizes. I knew, too, that massive forests mottled this land like giant ink blots on a map, and each forest led to even more fields of wheat, barley, rye, potatoes, beets, and hay, folding into more forests, and more fields, and on and on into the broad and wild steppe.

I walked in the middle of the road, singing.

Night, night, the trees rustle,
Night, night, a star is singing,
Go to sleep, blow out the candle

My worn shoes crunched on gravel past the granary at the edge of Skobelka and past the blacksmith and his dark home. I sang as I walked past a small, gold-domed Orthodox church, its ancient graveyard spread out behind it like a marble apron. I walked and sang past the first few low-slung, shake-shingled homes into the center of the village and through the main square marked by a wide well surrounded by more homes.

Dogs barked as I passed, but I walked in the early morning light and sang as if I were a ghost wandering through the realm of the living. I made my way to the end of Skobelka and walked until the sun was firmly above the horizon and ever more fields surrounded me. Dazed and hopeless, I pushed my way through a wall of briars into a field of ripe wheat, walked into the middle of it, and sat.

I spent the next two days sitting in the middle of that field, sleeping and slowly picking from Mrs. Voitenko's bundle. Swallows, larks, and colonies of finches sang and flew overhead. Crickets chirped, and ants were meticulous in their work. The sun beat down, and on the second evening as a thunderstorm passed over, I lay with my mouth open, allowing the heavy drops to fall into it as lightning flickered and thunder cracked.

I thought of releasing my soul from my body as storm clouds billowed overhead, but death would not claim me. *What have I done to deserve this life?* Massive, blinking thunderheads rose far into the sky, and angled rain moved across the field. "I know you're looking for me, Mama!" I yelled into the wet, reverberating air. "I'll come to you."

■ ■ ■

No plan or guidance determined my direction. I obeyed the impulse to walk toward where the sun and moon rose.

I walked and walked through wheat—so much wheat I wondered if the world outside of Horochów was nothing but a single, gigantic wheat field. Every so often I crossed a dirt lane or a hedgerow or passed through a thicket of trees and brush. Sometimes, far away, engines murmured, and once I laid on the ground deep in wheat for quite some time, thinking a man laughed beyond a hedgerow.

Late in the evening, I walked into a forest of pines—tall, lean, and limbless woodland ship masts with opaque canopies rising like church spires high above the small, half-starved girl I'd become. The forest floor was matted by a thick bed of reddish-brown needles and marbled by green patches of ferns or shin-high grass. The air was hot and damp, my eyes were sore, and my arms swung listlessly by my sides, but I couldn't sleep—there were no bushes or underbrush to hide me.

So I kept walking.

Thin, elongated diamonds of silver moonlight filtered through the treetops, but it was so dark that my shoulders scraped against the rough bark of nearly every trunk. Slow and careful, I worked my way through the forest until the first light of day filtered through its distant edge. I was thinking about sleeping beneath a tree when the murmur of a man's voice reached me. I dropped to my knees and crawled forward, my ears pricked. Like a scent floating on a breeze my ears caught the deep tone of his voice again, then the soft timbre of a woman's. *Did I just dream that?*

Beneath both was the slightest acoustic aroma of a small child: "*Muter.*"

Was that Yiddish or German?

The trees gave way to a broad field of cut hay piled into stacks as big as houses. Sitting in a tight circle at the forest's edge were six people, talking quietly—three men and two women. One of the women cradled a little boy. I inched toward them and recognized, from their gaunt bodies and haunted eyes, that they must be Jews.

Mama's voice whispered in my ear, *Greet a Jew with the word 'Umhoo,' and they will know you.*

I pressed my body flat to the ground behind a fat trunk, ready to run away. "Umhoo!"

Immediately, they lay on the ground. The woman covered the child's mouth with her hand and pressed the boy's body into hers. One of the men, with a scraggly beard and bright, wide eyes, peered into the forest.

"Umhoo!" I called again.

They were silent.

"Umhoo!"

One of the men raised his head and replied, "Umhoo, who is it?"

The longing for human contact was stronger than my caution. I stood, so they could see me, and walked toward them. Relieved, the man waved and said, "Come, come."

They sat up and looked deeper into the forest to be sure I was alone. The young woman settled her child and motioned for me to sit next to her. A peasant kerchief was tied around her forehead and behind her ears. Her dress was old and faded, and she wore flimsy sandals. Her son must have been about two and sucked listlessly on his mother's finger.

Next to her sat two young men who made for an odd pair. Unlike those of us from a ghetto, they were well dressed and wore almost new, knee-high boots. However, their suits hung off their bodies as if they were boys wearing their father's clothes. Lying in the grass next to them was a leather briefcase bulging at the seams.

To the left of the young men sat a woman in her mid-thirties. Her eyes moved nervously from me to the forest, then behind us into the field of haystacks. Her hair was disheveled, and she wore a summer dress and light shoes.

By her side was the last of the group, a middle-aged man with red hair whose worn suit looked a size too big. He tugged at his ragged, red beard as his eyes darted from the forest to the woman and back again.

I pulled a carrot from my bundle and handed it to the young mother. She promptly stuck it in her child's mouth. The boy's eyes were dull as he chewed drowsily on the carrot.

"My name is Musia Perlmutter," I said as I tied the bundle tight, "I'm looking for my mother, Fruma Perlmutter. Have you seen her?"

The man and woman's eyes met for a moment. "No, Musia," he said pulling at his beard. "We haven't seen a Fruma Perlmutter. You're the first Jew we've seen for more than a few days."

The young woman's eyes strayed from her child to me. "I don't recognize you, Musia. Were you in the ghetto in Luck?"

"No, Horochów; that's where I lived before the Germans."

"Yes, yes, I had a friend in Horochów, but I suppose no longer?"

Each tug on his beard pulled the corners of the red-haired man's mouth down so that his expression was stern rather than frightened. He reminded me of the tutor Papa hired to teach Tchiya and me math, science, German, and Latin. My eyes met his worried gaze. "Except for my mother, I don't know of any other survivors."

His eyes drifted toward the older woman, and he shook his head. She rested her chin on her hands and turned her vacant stare into the forest. "Welcome. It's good to have another friend," he said. "My name is Jakub Hurwicz, and this is my wife, Tauba."

"I am so glad to meet you," I said, relieved at being greeted as a human and not an object of scorn, available to be killed on a whim. I wasn't safe, but I was safer, and with people like me—those who had the misfortune to be a Jew in a land overrun by Nazis. They were not family, and thoughts of finding Mama did not leave me, but I was no longer alone. And since these people were alive, there must be others; we only had to find them. *Mama may be with them,* I thought.

One of the young men leaned toward me, "I'm Leo Mandelbaum, and this is my brother, Jozef." His brother smiled.

"I am Dora Kalecki, and this is my son Buzio," said the young woman.

Jakub, Tauba, and Dora told me they had escaped with a much larger group from the ghetto in Luck, just north and east of Horochów. I hadn't known a ghetto was there or that other ghettos existed. The world had closed around Mama, Tchiya, and me the day we walked into the ghetto. Jakub said they were separated from the others as they left the city and knew many of their friends were killed as they fled. Like me, the four of them had made it into a large field and then a forest.

"That's where we found each other," Leo interrupted. "My brother and I were hidden in Luck by a tailor friend, but when the Germans liquidated the ghetto, he said it was too dangerous for his family. He gave us these clothes and sent us out into the night."

I told them about the night Mama and I had left our small ghetto apartment and how we hid in the river. Guilt and shame kept me from saying I believed Mama left me in the river because I fell asleep and she could not wake me. Instead, I lied and told them when we swam across, the current swept me farther down than Mama, and I'd gotten lost.

We sat and told our stories for quite some time, oblivious to the world around us. It was such a simple pleasure to be among people, to breathe air unpolluted by the rot of death and decay, to feel a breeze, and to trust for the first time in a very long time that hope was real, not an illusion—that I would find Mama and join Tchiya. Life could be right again.

And then came the screech of a boy. "Jews!" And another. "Jews! There are Jews!" Between two haystacks, a group of boys no older than twelve or thirteen pointed at us. "Jews!" they yelled and ran away across the field and over a small hedgerow.

We knew they would be back with adults, perhaps soldiers. Overcome with fear, we started to run into the forest, but there was nowhere to hide. "In the haystacks!" Jakub yelled. "Hide in the haystacks!"

The urge to run into the forest and never stop beat in my heart, but my legs would not carry me. I turned back to the field and saw the others run toward the haystacks. "You in this one," Jakub said to Leo and Jozef as he pushed Dora, carrying Buzio against her chest, into another. He and Tauba ran to a third. Not knowing any better, I ran to the haystack with Dora and Buzio.

I squirmed into the center of the haystack, dragging my coat in with me. Dora exhaled in huffs from the effort of pushing both her and Buzio deep into the hay. The pile shook from her effort. Buzio wept and moaned, "Muter, muter, muter ..." Finally, the hay calmed, and Dora whispered, "Quiet little one, quiet." She began to sing softly:

> *Sleep, beautiful child,*
> *free from worry and pain*
> *sleep, free from worry and pain*

Dust choked my nose and throat, making it difficult to breathe. The hay scratched at my body so much I thought I would lose my mind. I wished I'd run into the woods and wanted to back out of the hay, but voices came toward us. Not children, but men, and they laughed at the mess we'd made.

"Come out, *blyat* Jews!" One of them yelled.

"Come out, pigs!" another shouted.

More men started screaming for us to come out. Their boots cracked on dried hay stubs as they dug into the stack with their hands, casting about for an arm or a leg. The hay pressed down on my body, and the dust and straw tortured every nerve in my skin. The men yelled louder and groped into the hay with more force.

A hand came close to my foot, but I moved just enough for it to miss. Another hand plunged into the hay and then another and another. The tines of a pitchfork pierced through the hay and Dora yelped in pain. More pitchforks and hands pushed into the hay, probing for the source of the cry.

I didn't know who these men were, but they had to be farmers. There were no gunshots, and their yells, groping hands, and pitchforks were the unfocused violence of a mob rather than soldiers. I gagged on dust in my nose and mouth and fought the incessant scratch of a cough rising in my throat. The fierceness of the searching tines and fingers scared me. That these were the same kind of people Mama and I bought food from made me wonder if every single person in the world was mad, incensed into mass delusion and believing we Jews should be hunted, tortured, and butchered.

Come out, pigs! was their common cry. The hatred within these words, their tone and physicality, were distinct from the quiet observance of the fall slaughter of their food animals. This was cruelty, plain and simple, as though we Jews were savage, feral animals to be put down; its source an utter mystery to me.

A woman screamed, and Buzio cried as he and his mother were pulled from the haystack. Dora's voice diminished into a pitiful sob and plea. "No, please, no, no, no ..." Then came a scream, and another, as Buzio's emaciated cry, "Muter, muter, muter ...," waned into silence.

Tremors rippled through my body, and my heart beat in quick, heavy pulses. A humiliating, wet warmth spread from between my legs, and I covered my ears, wanting to shut out the scream of another dying human. Hands and pitchfork tines churned the hay, and every molecule in my body wanted to run, to escape the dust, the heat, the scratching hay—to run back into the woods, or some huge field of shoulder-high wheat, to sanctuary, where a steel tine would not burst through my head or a strange hand pull me into the intimate act of my murder.

"Here, here," came the husky call of a man's voice, and then a grunt as he strained to pull another human being, another Jew from the hay. "There's another, another," shouted a man. More grunts and screams, as Jakub and Tauba and Leo and Jozef were pulled from the hay and killed by thrusts of a pitchfork.

And then laughter.

Oh Mama, how am I ever going to survive for you?

● ● ●

The men talked, "Good riddance to this trash," one said, and their boots fell heavily on dried and brittle stubs left from the hay as they walked near me. Tobacco smoke seeped into the stack and a rough voice spoke of the money they would get from the Germans for the bodies. It was such a small amount. Papa carried more in his wallet, but they seemed happy for it, with no qualms about the work to earn it.

What is my body worth?

I pressed my hands harder against my ears and focused on each breath: one, then another and another. I inhaled the dense, sickly sweet air deep into my lungs and let it out in a slow, steady sigh. The men laughed and talked and smoked only a few feet away.

Grit oozed down the back of my throat like bitter syrup and congealed tears clotted the corners of my tightly closed eyes. An image of Jakub tugging at his beard came to me, and then how his eyes looked each time he glanced at Tauba. It was fear, worry, concern, wondering, but love too. I remembered that I'd seen a man's eyes communicate like that before.

On June 21, 1941, Hitler broke his agreement with Stalin and attacked Russia. This included the eastern slice of Poland the Russians occupied after the start of the war in 1939 as part of their pact with Hitler. On June 23, the Russians pulled out of Horochów. A few bombs dropped close enough for us to hear the explosions as we hid in our home, and then the Germans occupied our small city. Some stayed, but most passed through in an immense column of tanks, trucks, horse-drawn supply wagons, and an endless river of German soldiers; all of them chasing the Russian army to the east.

For days we lived with a resonant rumble of trucks and tanks and other large machines, and in our house, there was no power, no phone; we were too scared to walk out the door, too scared even to peer from behind our closed drapes into the street. There was only confusion and fear and the terrifying mechanical moan of the Nazi army as it passed. It was a nightmare, but of course, it wasn't the real nightmare.

We were ordered to give the Nazis our gold, silver, jewelry, carpets, radios, anything with any material value whatsoever. Then, on June 29, Papa heard a shout and looked out a front window into the street.

"They're coming," he said as he passed Mama. He walked out the living room, through the kitchen. The front door burst open, and three Ukrainian militia soldiers in black uniforms carrying machine guns ran into the house. A tall, lean, German officer with a dimpled chin and a pistol in one hand followed them in. He stepped up to Mama.

"We are looking for Simcha Perlmutter. Is he here?"

I felt my body withdraw into itself as the officer yelled at Mama. I wanted to run into the kitchen, out the door, and into the garden and grab Papa's hand and show him all my hiding spots, the places he and Mama could never find me, but I was too scared. I stepped back away from Mama and the German and wished for someone to come save us, to tell these people to stop.

"I don't know," she said.

Then a yell from the kitchen door in Ukrainian, "We have him."

The officer glared at Mama; his fingers tightened around the grip of his pistol, and his pointer finger tapped the side of the trigger, but he turned and walked toward the kitchen. Mama and I rushed to the living room door, and Tchiya watched from the stairs as the soldiers hauled Papa past us. Two of them held either arm; the third walked behind him with his gun pointed at Papa's back.

"May I say goodbye—to my family?" he asked.

The officer waved for the soldiers to take Papa into the street. He looked at me, then to Mama. In his eyes were fear, worry, concern, confusion, and love. Out in the street stood fifteen or twenty Jewish men, their eyes expressing that same mix of fear and love as they stared in the directions of their homes, their children and wives.

A mix of black-clad Ukrainian and olive-green uniformed German soldiers surrounded them, their guns held loosely in their hands, their eyes apathetic. I saw Zofia's father, an accountant, as well as Gerda and Julian's father, a professor of chemistry at the University of Lwów. I noticed the white hair of Mr. Tuwim's, who lived four houses down, and little Mr. Slonimski stood with his hands clasped behind his back. I recognized the face of every man there.

And I recognized the faces of five Ukrainian men—civilians not soldiers—talking with the officer as they looked at a list of names. These Ukrainian men were our neighbors, members of our community, and its leaders, as were the scared Jewish men. The officer pointed to a name, then to my father. All five men, without looking at Papa or his family, nodded, *Yes, that's him.*

Tears welled and rolled down my cheeks as Papa walked down our beautiful, tree-lined street toward three large trucks with gated sides. Tchiya touched her hand to my shoulder, and I noticed she was crying too. Mama's eyes looked dark as she gathered us into her arms, but not a tear fell from them nor a word from her mouth. Her body shook with our sobs, but she was steady, loving, and silent.

Two days later, a truck with grated sides pulled up in front of our house. The same German officer climbed out of the passenger side, and three soldiers followed him up our front steps. He knocked on the door and waited for Mama to answer.

"*Guten morgen*, Frau Perlmutter. We are here for Mr. Perlmutter's antiquarian books."

"They're my husband's books," Mama said.

"Not anymore. If you could lead us to his library, we will begin our work."

Tchiya and I watched from the stairway in the front hall. Mama held the door open just a little bit, but we could see the smile on the officer's face. Nothing Mama could say or do would stop him. He pushed past her, with three soldiers following him, and began opening doors until he found the library.

This was Papa's sanctuary. His espresso-finished, maple writing desk stood in the middle of the room, still piled with books and papers left from his work. Next to the desk was a large globe mounted in a specially made oak stand with a numbered, brass meridian ring arching above the globe. Another brass ring marked with months, weeks, days, and hours was mounted on the stand, circling the globe's equator. Its oceans were blue-green, the currents marked by yellow lines, and the countries were muted shades of yellow, orange, green, and tan. Standing on the other side of the desk was a table with a wooden, thirty-drawer card catalogue made of cherry filled with cards for each of the books filling the shelves lining all four walls from floor to ceiling.

Papa collected these books all his life. He traveled long distances to buy them, and people from far away brought him rare editions because they knew he paid well. And there were rules. Before anyone touched a book, they had to wash their hands as they would before prayers, and Papa was the only one allowed to remove a book from a shelf. The library could be cleaned only in his presence. He somehow regulated the temperature in the room, so it was cool and dry in summer and warm in winter. Some shelves were glassed in and heavy curtains covered the library's large windows, so the sun would not fade or damage his beloved books.

His students and colleagues often came to our house for Saturday supper and then shut themselves off in his library to talk, read, and debate. Every now and again, a student failed to show up for these meetings, and then weeks later, a letter would arrive from Jerusalem or Tel-Aviv and be read in the library the following Saturday.

It was an infrequent treat to be allowed in the library. The few times he let me in, we both wore white gloves, and only he could turn a page or close the book. I had no idea why his books were so important to him. Papa tried to explain it several times, but his love for these books was beyond my comprehension.

The officer and soldiers worked through the day, carefully placing the books in crates and hauling them out to the truck. They were polite, and the officer yelled at one of his men when he accidentally bumped into a tea table inherited from Mama's father. When he and his men took a break, he was careful to remove his hat when approaching Mama in the kitchen to ask for a cold drink. She brought them water, all we had, and went back to ignoring their theft of her beloved husband's life's work.

Tchiya and I played cards in the kitchen with Mama. I wanted to run out into the garden, but she insisted we both stay close to her.

"They wouldn't steal me," I said.

"No, of course not," Mama said.

Tchiya's eyes opened wide. "I'd like to practice on the piano."

"No, Tchiya. Let them finish, and when they leave, Musia can go out, and you can play some music for us."

We were quiet; the only sound was the creak of footsteps down the hallway and the soldiers muttering in German.

"I want to go outside," I said again.

"No, Musia."

I hissed back, "Mama, I don't want to sit here while they take Papa's books."

"They will leave, and we will be together and well," she said shuffling the cards. "Patience, neshomeleh."

Frustration welled in my heart, and I banged the heel of one of my shoes against a rung of the chair. "I want Papa."

"I've told you," Mama said, "when Papa comes home we'll have a party with cake, and we'll invite the other men and their families too. It will be a big party, and we'll have it soon. I promise."

After the last crate was packed, the officer entered our kitchen and stood just inside the doorway with a piece of paper in one hand. His bearing was stiff and formal. "Frau Perlmutter," he said holding the paper toward Mama, "this is a receipt for the books. You will be compensated at the end of the war. We are not thieves."

Mama stared at him unsure what to do or make of this offer.

He waved the paper crisply at her. "Madam, please."

Mama stood and took the receipt from his hand. He smiled, stepped forward and kissed both of her cheeks. "*Danke,* Frau Perlmutter."

I mistook his deference and politeness as a sign of Mama's absolute goodness. There is a power within her, I thought, a bit of the divine that must be respected and nurtured.

The next day, the Germans forced all the Jews of Horochów to watch as they burned our synagogue, *shtiebels*, prayer books, and anything else that represented our Jewish identity. On July fourth, Mama, Tchiya, and any Jew older than fourteen were ordered into slave labor.

In late September, the Germans ordered all Jews to move into the ghetto.

...

I don't remember if I slept or was lost in my memories, but when I opened my eyes, there was no light, just the hot, dusty black of the haystack. I pulled my hands from my ears and listened. I heard only the chirping of crickets burrowed around me in the hay. I waited and opened my ears wide, but the men's voices were gone.

I wiggled my shoulders and hips and legs to loosen the hay around me and squirmed backward until first my legs and then my body and finally all of me was free and in the cool night air. I rolled onto my side and spat a gooey wad of saliva from my mouth. I picked what I could from my nose, but my fingers were covered in dust, so I only succeeded in pushing more of the mess into my nose to run down the back of my throat. I rolled onto my back and felt cool air filter into my lungs. A thick mosaic of stars shone above me in the half-moon light, and the Milky Way cut a powdery trail of stars across the sky.

My eyes followed a comet streak down over the horizon, and there, lying a few feet away in the cut grass, a pale foot lolled to one side. I leaned forward and saw the body of Dora. Buzio lay with his face buried in his mother's naked chest, the carrot still grasped in his tiny, milk-white hand. I walked toward them. As I came close, I saw the naked bodies of Jakub, Tauba, Leo, and Jozef arranged in a row. Pitchfork holes mutilated their faces, and their chests were all but ripped open. Dark, dried blood stained their pearl-white flesh.

I'd seen bodies, perhaps hundreds, sprawled out on the ground in all sorts of horrific poses. I'd watched men, women, and children hung and shot for no reason other than that they were Jewish. But all these deaths had happened in the ghetto, a place of ugliness and squalor, a place where rats picked over bodies until starvation led us to kill them for food. It was a place where a truck passed through every few days yanking people—children, women with their babies, old people, anyone not working—off the street and took them to their deaths. I'd watched from my little window as my gray-haired pediatrician Dr. Grossfeld was beaten with sticks then dragged to the back of a truck with grated sides. I'd seen women and children cry out, knowing what was to come: *Dachau* or a bullet to the head, then being dropped into a ditch. I'd watched the trucks slowly pull away and listened to women and children screaming to darkened windows, *Tell my daughter ... Tell my son ... Tell my mother ...*

But I'd never felt like this. Standing over the bodies, I looked up into the deep, starry night and then across the dark field.

These were just men, farmers who did this, Mama. This field, this night, this is not the ghetto; these weren't soldiers.

I know, neshomeleh.

I hugged my arms across my chest.

There is no place for me; there are no people for me—only you, Mama, and Tchiya, beautiful Tchiya.

I'm waiting for you, my love.

I pulled my coat over my shoulder and made my way as quietly as I could into the woods listening for Mama's voice on the breeze.

The Young
SS Officer

The moon cast a quiet light deep into the forest. I didn't know—nor did I care—what direction I took as long as it took my parched mind and body from the bloody row of human kindling lying by the haystack.

Water. Please, Mama, lead me to water.

My toe caught on a root, and I fell onto the pine-matted forest floor, tasting copper as warm blood trickled onto my tongue. Tears wanted to come, but the well had gone dry. Trees groaned as gusts of air caught their upper canopies like sails and bowed them. I wanted to fly up through their needled crowns, to be above the world, a swallow pitching and diving, free from fear and the gnawing ache of loneliness, thirst, and hunger.

There are no miracles here, neshomeleh, only love, and that is what we live for.

But Papa said God is abundant in compassion and God fills the world.

Yes, I know, but his compassion is our love, and that is what we live for.

Yes, Mama.

I dug out an apple and potato from Mrs. Voitenko's bundle, nearly the last of my food, and bit into the potato. Its bitter juice eased my thirst.

The apple was sour, but it gave just enough for me to struggle to my feet and stand on shaking legs.

This is too hard.

My muscles were uncooperative, and I fought against rushes of lightheadedness, but I managed one step and then another, pausing every so often to rest against a tree rather than give in to the temptation to lie exposed on the ground. For how long I walked like this, I don't know. Tall mast-like pines gave way to a mix of broadleaf trees and spruce, balsam, juniper, and larch. I stumbled through spider webs and sharp branches scratched at my face and arms.

Then I heard a murmur that grew into the tender ripple of a small brook. My buckling legs carried me toward the sound to find a tumbling stream. At each of its elbows, webs of twigs and rocks formed narrow riffles that spilled into rock-strewn and sand-bedded pools. Birch, larch, ash, and alder tipped from the low, sloping bank to overhang the brook, the tree's roots sometimes exposed where the water pooled to form a leaf-trapping lattice.

My knees sank into cool, sandy earth at the brook's edge as I plunged my face into the cold water. I gulped in large swallows that chilled me to the center of my belly, then splashed water over my head until it trickled down my neck and back in ticklish rivulets. I laid Mama's blouse and my dresses, socks, and soiled underpants beside the brook and sat naked in a pool with my back to the gurgling chute at its head. The water cooled my stinging thighs, chafed from my ill-fitting, urine-soaked underpants, and I lay back into its trembling current.

Thank you, Mama. I love you.

Afterward, I perched naked on a rock in the warm night air and washed my clothes—except for Mama's blouse and the coat—then walked to a tall, thick pine and hung the clothes on its branches to dry. The bottom branches sloped toward the ground and hid me as I spread the coat out and rested my head against the tree's fat trunk, pulling Mama's blouse over me. With one hand, I poked where the penknife should be and felt its reassuring outline, then did the same for the few coins and Mama's last ring sewn into its hem. My entire body ached, my thoughts unquiet. The screams, ash-white naked bodies, and congealed blood pushed sleep beyond my grasp until all were diffused by the faint burbling of the brook and familiar night sounds of the forest.

...

Glowing, early-morning light sifted through my drowsy eyes. I saw a small clearing dappled by a patchwork of lavender and pollen-yellow wildflowers. The scent of loamy soil and leaves beneath me kindled a vivid memory of white jasmine and violet lilac, their perfume rising in our backyard on the humid air of a late-afternoon storm. I drifted between Mama's delicate blouse and golden morning light and the slap of our screen door behind me as I ran into Mama's kitchen with its pale daffodil and moss-green trimmed cupboards and cabinets, her hum as she leafed through a magazine and the nutty aroma of bread baking in the oven. Home, our home—it was all so real, so beautiful, but I had no tangible proof of it, no photo or any other object I could pull from my bundle to remind me of life before the cruelty began.

I lay under that tree and wondered who my family was. I could visualize their faces, but I strained to remember what it felt like to be with them, in our home, living our lives in all the small ways that make up the moments of a day. Who we were was fading from my memory.

I curled into Mama's blouse and breathed in her body, but the scent was faint. As I fell back into the warm cocoon of sleep, I knew I had to find her soon, before the last trace of her was gone and nothing was left of me.

...

Truck engines stirred me from sleep. I turned to look through the trees toward the noise, but it was impossible to see its source. The gurgling of the brook muddied their words, though I could tell it was not just a few people but a large group. Floating above the din of women and children were a few deep, commanding, male voices. From their inflection I knew they were German.

Nausea crept through me. *Is this a place where they kill Jews?*

I strained my ears, hoping to hear the faint rhythm, a word or phrase of Yiddish or some other identifiably Jewish articulation. I listened for fear and sorrow, for the unmistakable resonance of people like me facing imminent death, but something else was beneath the surface of their collected voices, a cadence I hadn't heard in a long time: happiness. It made me afraid to the point of panic. I wanted to run, to dash through the woods, a deer leaping away from a hunter, but the voices were too near.

I sat up and wrapped Mama's blouse around my body then pulled my clothes from the branches and stuffed them into the sleeves of my coat. No room was left in the sleeves for my tattered shoes, so I covered them with needles, dirt and twigs.

Are there soldiers spreading out, looking for me?

I scrambled up the first branches of the tree, pulling my coat behind me. Pine bark and broken twigs scraped my skin. I was terrified that the shaking branches or the noise of my climb would give me away. My heart beat in big, heavy pumps; sweat stung every scrape and cut.

The air was thick and humid, the kind of day Papa called a weather breeder. "Be careful, Musia," he would have said. "A thunderstorm is on its way by afternoon."

I stopped about two-thirds up the tree, perched on a thin branch with my arms stretched around the rough trunk. The voices now seemed to be coming from the trees and underbrush a little way beyond the brook; its steady babble made it difficult to hear more than a murmur and occasional high-pitched laughter.

They weren't Jews, they were having a picnic. Children hollered to each other as they splashed in the brook. I longed to be in the water, to feel its cool touch on my hot, stinging skin, but I held onto the tree and imagined my body turning into a mottled-brown moth, camouflaged from killers. Errant bits of German and Ukrainian blew into my ears with the laughter of men and women, and I knew death would come with a child's shout from the brook: *Look, a Jew!*

I held the tree tighter and hoped no one would come to pee or catch a furtive kiss beneath my perch. Humid air carried the aroma of sausage cooking on an open fire. That death was so close frightened me, but that something as fundamentally human as a shared meal was also close soothed a deep, vital need. Hunger and thirst are painful, but to a girl like me, the loss of human connection was the most difficult deprivation.

I closed my eyes to let the melody of conversation and laughter feed my lonely heart. As I pressed my nearly naked, burning body against the bark, I knew I could not live without the sound of another human's voice.

I shifted my naked bum on the thin branch.

I love you, Mama and Papa.

● ● ●

I sat in that tree for hours, not moving, peeing and emptying my upset bowels beneath me.

But Papa was right.

A wind from the east blew up, and the tree swayed and creaked with it. Black clouds spun toward us, their bright, white thunderheads rising thousands of feet into the sky; lightning and thunder flashed and barked. The voices hurried and then faded into the woods. The groan of bending trees and blowing leaves and pine boughs overwhelmed all other sounds except for that of a heavy truck firing up and its gears moving the people away.

The tree pitched, branches swirling with each crashing wave of air. Rain smacked the back of my head in hard, mean drops. I turned my face up into the downpour and opened my mouth, thankful for the storm's brief rescue.

"Yes, Papa," I laughed, "today was a good weather breeder."

All hurts and wounds, physical and emotional, died away with the reassuring pressure of Mama's fingers caressing the soft hairs on the back of my neck.

Finally, the rain eased and so too the wind. Cool air followed. In the stillness of the storm's wake, I climbed down into a damp forest of mists. The coat and I were soaked, but the clothes stuffed in the sleeves, as well as the bundles, remained dry. I took Mama's blouse off and held it to my nose. Precious little of her was left in the wet cloth.

Oh, Mama, I'm losing you.

I pressed the blouse into my face and drew in deep, but she was fading from me.

There are no miracles, only love.

The brook burbled, and I pulled the blouse away and breathed in the scent of fresh, rain-beaten earth.

God is abundant in compassion, and God fills the world—

The blouse was soft in my hands.

—but God's kindness is not here.

My head tilted forward, and I again imagined her hand grazing the nape of my neck.

I feel your love, Mama.

A drop of water fell from above and tingled down my spine.

If I feel your love, then you are alive—

My eyes lifted.

—and your love cannot die if I live—

Mist, animated with the patter of spattering drops, hovered above the forest floor.

—because love lives even when hope does not.

I wiped the rain from my eyes and pulled on my underpants, then shimmied into one of the dresses. A particularly large drop splashed into the pool in the brook, and I thought of rinsing Mama's blouse, but instead draped it over my shoulders.

I'm not ready to lose this piece of you just yet.

The holes in my socks were larger now, and it took some figuring to find a combination that covered the entirety of both feet. The shoes were no better.

Webs, some laden with rain, broke on my face and chest as I walked. I brushed them off and wiped at my arms, fearing a spider's bite.

Clear twilight drifted into evening, which gave way to a clear, cool night. I walked under a waning moon, my chapped thighs burning. I crossed a small stream and washed myself with cool water, then continued through the night.

The first tendrils of sunrise rose to the east when I found another large pine with long needles and wide, green branches to hide beneath. My fingers dug into the pine-scented earth and dead needles, and I realized how soft it was. I started to burrow into it with my hands, and soon I'd created a small hole about the size of my curled, sleeping body. With my penknife I cut away small tangles of roots to dig a bit deeper. I lay the coat along the bottom, laid on it and then pulled dead twigs, needles, dirt, and anything else near me over my body. My head rested in my hands, feet and knees curled up into my belly. I closed my eyes and soon slipped into a middle realm between sleep and fear.

Goodnight, Mama. I'm safe in my little grave.

. . .

When I woke, the air was cool and the sky a mix of late morning blue and platinum clouds passing overhead. The sun had dipped a little deeper into the horizon than even the day before, and the first faint whiff of fall was in the air. I thought it must be early September, a time of transition that in the past meant cooler weather, the start of school, harvest, coloring leaves, the beginning of Papa's fall term at the university, the slow demise of the garden, a certain childhood loss of freedom, and then, eventually, winter.

My belly ached, and I realized I hadn't eaten for quite some time. *How long?* I couldn't remember. Only two shriveled potatoes and a carrot were left in Mrs. Voitenko's bundle. I ate them all, but they did little to extinguish my hunger.

I wrapped Mrs. Voitenko's scarf around my head so that my shoulder-length black hair emerged out the back, held away from my eyes. Then I draped the second dress over my body to ward off the chill and started to walk. Now and then, I found berries or greens that looked edible, but these small bits of ground food weren't enough to do more than alter the flavor in my mouth. My stomach was hollow, and the lightness in my head fluttered and palpitated as if consciousness were a faulty clock skipping ticks every so often.

At midday, I came to a broad glade of spindly birches, many of them hunched like old men and women. Sunlight reflected off the ivory bark and lit grasses and ferns as well as patches of small, white flowers that covered the ground.

I weaved among the birches, letting my shoulders bounce from tree to tree. Wisps of grass tickled my ankles, and buzzing flies whizzed around my head and legs. One bit me, and I reached down to slap it but missed. My eyes followed its jagged path, and I reached for it, but it flew away into the grass where it landed on a hand so snowy white it could have been a malformed birch sapling.

Fear buckled my legs, and I hit the ground so hard my breath rushed out of me. I covered my head with my hands, expecting the sound of some human to rise, but heard only the call-and-reply of birdsong and quarreling squirrels. I peeked through my fingers at the hand. It was tilted at the wrist, its fingers stiffened in a delicate pose.

I stood, and as my eyes focused on the radiant patch of grass, I saw the outline of a bent knee, a hint of black hair, and milk-white legs and feet. I listened for danger but heard only the soft voice of the forest. I took slow, tentative steps toward the sunlit glade. As I drew close, the human bits and pieces resolved into the bodies of five women heaped together, bloody bullet holes in their chests and stomachs. Flies hovered and picked at the wounds, walked across unflinching faces, and rubbed their forelegs greedily as they feasted on crusted blood. The women looked no older than Mama, and their clothes were rent to expose their breasts and other parts.

Oh no, Mama.

I ran to them and pulled up each of the women's heads and brushed the flies away praying none of them was Mama. All the bodies were stiff so that I struggled to turn their heads to see them. Clotted blood covered the mouths and ran down the chins of a few of the women, and each face held its own expression of fear or agony, except that of one woman whose lips and eyes evoked a state of demure absence.

Thank God. You're not here, Mama.

No, neshomeleh.

Where are their children?

I sat in the grass.

I need shoes.

Whoever killed them took their shoes.

I need food.

They had only their tattered and bloody dresses and blouses.

My eyes wandered over their bodies looking for anything of use.

Socks, I need socks.

I crawled to the feet of the woman nearest me and removed her wool socks. The other women's feet were bare, but then I noticed a silver band on the ring finger of one woman.

For a rainy day.

Her skin was cold and smooth to touch as I lifted her hand and pulled on the ring, but it didn't slide off. Her body shifted when I tugged harder, and a gasp of air bubbled from her mouth. Her hand dropped from my fingers into the grass.

She's alive?

Her dead, unblinking eyes, imperviousness to the insects crawling in and around her mouth, proved otherwise. I draped what remained of her blouse over her chest and saw the worn shadow from a Star of David. Like Mama and me, she'd torn it from her shirt.

We don't steal, neshomeleh.

The other women had also removed their stars.

I've disappointed you again, Mama.

...

The night Mama sewed the stars onto our clothes she was sitting in the parlor of our home. In her eyes was a somber weariness, and her body slouched from exhaustion after weeks of forced labor. "We will do what we have to, so we can live," she said, "but we will never harm or take from another Jew or person in need, ever."

She finished with my coat and shook it out, careful not to let her silver thimble fall from the middle finger of her left hand. The coat jangled softly from the few gold coins and the last of her jewelry sewn into the hems and seams. She turned to look at me. "Wherever we go, whatever we do, you take this coat."

"I know, Mama."

Tchiya looked up from her book and gave me a sidelong glance.

"You too, Tchiya."

"Yes, Mama."

Love and pain filled Mama's eyes as she recognized the same exhaustion etched in Tchiya's voice and discontented features. Their eyes met in a moment of shared empathy, and it provoked a jealousy within me.

"There was another *łapanka* today," I said using the word to describe the routine roundups of Jews to be killed by the Germans. Some people were taken to pits and shot, others to what the Germans called "work camps," but we knew better.

"How did you hear about it?" Mama asked.

"They came down our street."

Tchiya looked at Mama, then me. "Did they come into the house?"

"No, I was out in the garden playing with Zofia."

Mama's face paled and tightened. "I told you not to go outside when we aren't home."

"I'm sorry, Mama, but it's so boring waiting day after day."

Her voice rose as she spoke. "You must promise me you will stay inside every day. What if they'd found you?"

"Mama, I know how to avoid the Germans."

"What did you do?" Tchiya asked.

"We ran into the cemetery"—a magnificent Christian cemetery slumbered near our house—"and hid in the small chapel."

Tchiya, her eyes wide, placed the book she'd been reading in her lap. "What if Mr. Kijek had seen you?"

"He didn't."

Mama tapped her thimble on the table in an angry, steady beat. "You must promise never to do that again. I love you too much to have to worry more than I already do." She gave one final rap on the table. "Now, to bed, both of you."

Early the next morning, a truck with loudspeakers blaring drove down our street, announcing in Polish and Ukrainian, "All Jews report to the market in one hour. Bring only what you can carry. All Jews report to the market in one hour. Bring only what you can carry."

We raced around the house packing whatever we thought we'd need—clothes, blankets, a pot and spoon for cooking—and passed through our front door into clean, cool, autumn air.

Mr. Kijek watched us from his stoop but said nothing. We met up with Zofia, her mother, and little sister and walked together. By the time we left the early fall brilliance of the chestnut trees lining our street, seven or eight more families, all without their men, joined us. As we neared the market, we saw thousands of people wearing gold stars, carrying suitcases or large bundles filled with the last of their belongings. Most were from Horochów, but some were Jews rounded up by the Germans from nearby towns and villages. All of us were quiet as we walked with the same expressions of fear, worry, concern, wondering, and love that Papa and the other men wore when the Germans took them.

The Germans herded us in a long column from the market to the ghetto they'd built along the river. Mama, Tchiya, and I shared a single room with three other families. There were Mrs. Joselewicz and her two daughters, fourteen-year-old Rosa and fifteen-year-old Belen. Both girls were tall and broad shouldered, and one would have thought they were twins if not for Rosa's wide, owlish eyes. Then Mrs. Cukier and Ania. And then Mrs. Zelinski—a curly-haired woman who looked worried even when she smiled—and her son, Janusz, and daughter, Hannah, ages fifteen and seventeen. With Mama, Tchiya, and me, twelve of us in all inhabited the small hovel. For a toilet we used a single bucket in a shed in the courtyard. More than one hundred people shared one kitchen with a single tap that gave only a dribble of cold water. As days turned to weeks and winter came, we slept with the window open rather than choke on the smell of human rot in our room.

The forced labor continued, except people were walked in groups to their jobs by armed guards, and the work was harder and went from dawn to well after dark. Ania and I didn't work because we were too young, but Hannah didn't either. Before the war, Hannah was a pretty girl. Slender and small breasted, she looked like a ballerina, even if she couldn't force her body to move like one. With the start of the war and then the Russians followed by the Germans and the loss of her father, worry corroded her soft, dancer-like features making them sharp and bitter. She was also born with a clubfoot, which held trivial effect in how anyone perceived her beauty before, but now she was pitiful and ugly.

Mrs. Zelinski was terrified that if the guards or Germans found out Hannah had a clubfoot, she would be taken and killed for being deformed and deemed useless. When they walked into the ghetto, Mrs. Zelinski made Hannah wear a regular shoe rather than her special platform one and walked on one side of her while Janusz walked on the other to hide Hannah's limp.

When a man wearing a suit with a white armband from the *Judenrat*—a committee of Jews assigned by the Germans to manage issues in the ghetto—asked why Hannah couldn't work, Mrs. Zelinski told him she was too young. The man, tall and lean with round, tortoiseshell glasses, eyed Hannah and frowned but placed a check next to her name and moved on. From then on, Hannah watched Ania, so Mrs. Cukier could work and collect a ration.

The Ukrainian guards beat the workers often, and each night I did my best to tend to Mama and Tchiya. For their labor, our daily ration was two slices of bread, a tablespoon of lard, sometimes a piece of fatty meat, a little bit of sugar, and soft, rotted vegetables. Two months later, the Germans eliminated the lard and any meat and reduced the ration to once per week, sometimes not at all.

My view was small, but I knew the Germans had separated us from humankind for a reason.

■ ■ ■

Two weeks after we arrived in the ghetto, early October, an infinite pewter cloud concealed the sky, and a hissing loudspeaker broke the early morning quiet. "Today, we need children for light work. A selection for workers will take place in the square in half an hour."

I grabbed Mama's sleeve. "I can go; I can do this."

"No, Musia. It's too dangerous."

Sometimes, the selection was a *łapanka,* and the people were never heard from again.

"It'll mean more food. I can do this."

Tchiya wiped her red, runny nose. "Musia, listen to Mama. Don't make trouble."

I stomped my foot. "It's not fair! The two of you can leave here and work, and I contribute nothing!"

Mama looked at Tchiya and then the worried eyes of the other mothers in the room.

"It's dangerous, Musia." But Mama's will was weakening.

"I can do this. I promise nothing will happen."

"I don't know."

I had won. "Tchiya is getting sick. The extra food will help her get better."

The guards selected eight of us and marched us to a former hospital, now used by the Germans as an administrative office and dining hall. I scrubbed office floors, peeled lots of potatoes, and polished about thirty pairs of men's boots. The work was inside and warm, and the thought of food made it almost pleasant.

At the end of the day, we were in a large room adjoining a huge kitchen where cooks and their helpers rushed to prepare that night's dinner. Two Ukrainian guards waited for us outside while a broad-shouldered cook with a black shadow of beard picked through a waste can of discarded bread, vegetables, and meat scraps for our pay. I looked at my hands and noticed they were black from shoe polish and dirt.

"May I have some soap?" I asked.

"Soap?" I turned to see a young, blond SS officer standing a few feet away. Two German soldiers stood behind him with their hands resting on their hips. His eyes frightened me, and his voice was sharp, angry. "She wants soap?"

The cook turned and shrugged. "I guess she thinks her hands are dirty from a little work."

The officer smiled at my fear. He reached out and grabbed my arm. "Come."

He pushed me into a small room crowded with several gurneys and ordered me to climb up and lie face down on one. I did.

Other than the sound of my breathing, the room was quiet. Then the point of a wooden cane pushed up my dress and hovered close to my bottom. I felt the air move, then he huffed as he cracked the cane against the back of my thighs. Pain lit through me like fire. Another huff, and the cane came down like a knife slicing through my skin. One blow and then another hit the back of my thighs and bottom. I bit my lip to keep from screaming until blood filled my mouth. Every nerve in my body burned.

Oh, Mama, I'm dying.

With each slap of the cane my chest tightened, and my thoughts slipped into a chaotic spasm of panic, shame, and terror—

Mama, Tchiya!

—that this fair-haired boy incensed with an unknowable rage—

Save me!

—was killing me in as brutal a way as his mind could conjure.

Blood and saliva ran from my lip onto the gurney, their warmth smeared on my chin with the involuntary rattling of my head from the pain and force of each strike. The room dissolved, and my vision narrowed into a solitary pinhole of light as my mind collapsed into a cold, dead place.

Light, breath, and pain surged into me as the other children helped me up and then off the gurney. My underpants were shredded; blood ran down my legs and was splattered across the back of my dress. Two girls wrapped my arms over their shoulders and helped me walk back to the ghetto while the others followed, and black-uniformed guards urged us on with their rifles.

"You didn't scream, Musia, you didn't scream," a girl said softly. "How did you do it?"

Blood and saliva oozed from my mouth like warm syrup. "I hate them."

"Musia," said another girl, "the cook put some extra food in the bag for you."

Tears welled in my eyes, and the familiar flush of guilt warmed my neck and face. *I promised Mama I would be safe.*

Two girls helped me up the stairs and then into the room where Mama and Tchiya were near desperation, worried I was taken in a *łapanka*.

"Oh, my dear child," Mama said rising from her bed.

Mrs. Joselewicz stood and cleared my bed. Belen and Rosa stared at me, concern in their eyes and their mouths opened slightly. Hannah rolled over on her bed and held her stomach with her hands.

Janusz sat up in his bed and scratched at his head, which was shaved to rid him of lice. He scratched so much that small pustules dotted his pale scalp. He'd also been punched by a guard who laughed at the blood that poured from his nose and its crooked, broken angle. The pain caused Janusz' top and bottom eyelids to darken; the effect of it deepened the melancholy in his slender lips and face.

"An SS officer beat her for asking for soap," one of the girls said.

Mama took my arm and guided me to bed and lay me face down.

"Animals," hissed Mrs. Cukier as she rocked Ania in her lap.

"They're animals and murderers," added Mrs. Zelinski.

"She was very brave, Mrs. Perlmutter," said the other girl.

"She always is," Mama said.

"She's too stubborn to be afraid," Tchiya added.

"Tchiya, please get water," Mama said. Janusz watched Tchiya walk to the door. He put his *newsboy* style cap on and followed her out.

"The cook gave her a little extra food," said one of the girls, setting a bag near my bed. Then the two left.

Mama's hands trembled as she lifted my dress.

"Animals," repeated Mrs. Cukier.

"My little neshomeleh," Mama said as she tore one of her blouses into strips.

"I'm sorry, Mama."

Her voice was tender, bathed in compassion. "Whatever for, my love?"

"I promised nothing would happen."

"You're home, and I love you, neshomeleh, that's all that matters."

"I only asked for soap. I didn't know—"

"There's nothing to know, Musia. They hurt us because they can."

"Please forgive me."

"There's nothing to forgive." Then, looking around, she asked, "Where in the world is Tchiya?"

"Here, Mama," Tchiya said coming through the door carrying a basin filled with water, Janusz's broad frame right behind her. Mama glanced at the two of them then looked at me as she dipped a strip of the torn shirt into the water. "I'm sorry, neshomeleh."

I'm sorry too.

■ ■ ■

In the birch grove, I looked into the eyes of the dead woman whose ring I wanted to take. Sadness tightened my chest, and I brushed her cheek with the back of my hand. The sun lit her skin.

They haven't been dead very long.

My eyes searched through the birches.

The people who did this are close.

There was only the music of small animals and birds in the leaves.

I must leave.

I picked up my coat and walked from the birch grove into the denser forest. After an hour, I stopped and climbed as high as I could into a tall tree. The forest stretched out for kilometers in every direction, but to the north a few buildings poked above the far horizon. I climbed down, knowing I had to walk toward those buildings and whoever lived in them.

I don't know where you are—

I picked up Mama's blouse and held it to my nose, breathing in the faintest whisper of her. I felt the material in my hands and against my face and recognized that the residue of her humanity and love saturated its fibers for no other reason than it was hers. A vision of Mama as a *Tzadikim*, a divine person meant to be on this earth, filled my senses and imagination.

—but you are alive.

Hunger

The bellow of a hound in a distant yard sent an electric pulse of fear skittering up my spine. The hound bellowed once more, but without a reply the dog seemed to settle into a wary quiet.

Stupid dogs.

Smoke rose from the chimney of a small, stone, and shim-shingled house. A lamp flickered in the window, but the only sound from inside was the muted flow of conversation in Ukrainian between a man and woman. I crept closer until I was beneath the window. The shutters were left ajar despite the coldness of the night. Their words, each clear and distinct to my starved ears, eased my lonely heart like the warmth of a hearth. My head dipped, and I remembered lying in bed as conversations in Polish, Yiddish, and Ukrainian sifted up through the open louvers of a heating grate.

It was a rare night that Mama and Papa didn't host some group of Horochów friends. The mayor and city council, a collection of Poles, Ukrainians, and Jews, often discussed and debated municipal business well past my bedtime, their animated voices and mingling accents and vocabularies drifting up to my curious ears. The balding Catholic priest sat with Papa after dinner, as did the gray-haired Orthodox priest and often our rabbi, whose pot of a belly protruded from his coat. In the kitchen, Mama and a coterie of like-minded women founded a summer camp for all the children of our mixed community. Our parlor was the scene of piano and violin recitals, and Papa opened his library to poetry readings where Poles, Ukrainians, Jews, everyone felt at home.

Like water seeping into sand, languages soaked into me. I spoke Yiddish, Ukrainian, and Polish in school and with friends. Latin, French, and German tutors came to our home because Papa said these were the languages of art, literature, commerce, and the *Haskalah,* European Judaism's parallel to the Enlightenment. I resisted the tutors and repeatedly questioned the need to learn these languages. Papa, with infinite patience, would look at me, his eyes serious, and say, "You are more than a lovely girl in a nice and untroubled home. You will someday have an important intellectual life, and these are the languages of Voltaire, Diderot, Rouseau, Mendelssohn, and Fürst, the authors of the *Haskalah*."

Yet there are no words in any of the languages I know to accurately describe true hunger. It is pain, need, obsession, futility, frustration, want, and decay experienced as the slow and relentless wasting away of one's mind and body.

Hunger's grasp made me reckless to the point of sneaking toward this home, one of a collection of dreary stone and clapboard houses, barns, dirt yards, and large gardens reduced to stubble with the descent of autumn. These people were no more than subsistence farmers, and the conversation between the man and woman was nothing but the idle chatter of two people consigned to a small life. An image of the dead women I'd left in the woods two days before came to my mind. By now bloat would have contorted their bodies and faces, their flesh gnawed at by animals and swarmed over by flies, but here a man and woman sat in the warmth of their home talking in a way that made clear the war and its violence was a distant thought.

The ground was cold and damp against my knees, and I ached for the warmth of my home.

The things we'll eat when we are together again, Mama.

Yes, neshomeleh, it will be wonderful.

A sliver of silver moon cast a dim light into the yard. Roosting chickens clucked and cooed as they slept in a coop across from the house. Beyond the house stood an aged and weather-beaten barn that leaned into an absent wind. Sporadic lowing of cows rose and fell from a pen attached to the back end of the barn, but there was neither sight nor sound of a watchful dog.

I crept from beneath the window, then darted across the open yard and fell back to my knees in the shadow of the barn. It was difficult to see more than a few feet ahead, so I crept, my coat dragging behind me, searching for an opening. Soft mud that reeked of manure mushed up between my fingers. I whipped my hands back and forth to shake it off, but I couldn't get rid of it. Soon, I found a small door, opened wide enough for me to squeeze through without the hinges scraping.

The only light came from the far end of the barn, where two large doors opened out into a pen. As my eyes adjusted to the dark, I made out four or five black-and-white mottled cows lying on their sides in a thick mat of straw. At intervals, a cow lifted its head as if in a dream, licked its fat lips, sighed, then lay back down. A hayloft filled to overflowing ran down one whole side of the barn. Ladders stood at either end.

The odor of sour milk and manure filled my cheeks with watery saliva. I was obsessed with the need for something, anything to nourish me, anything. My eyes wandered the dark corners of the barn and spotted them. There, beneath the loft sat two fat milk canisters made of tin with rounded caps. The thought of milk, something I'd not seen in more than a year, overwhelmed the last of my caution. I hurried toward the canisters, my shoes clomping across the dirt floor.

I tilted the first canister, but it was empty. Then the second, and heard a light, soft slosh. The lid's clasp clicked as I popped it open and placed it on the ground. I lifted the light canister and poured out the milk, filling half of the bowl-like lid. When I dropped the canister it made a hollow, tin thud, but I was more concerned with not spilling my precious gift. Kneeling, I dipped my mouth into the slightly sour milk and drank.

Thank you for this, Mama.

The milk ran down my throat and entered the empty cavity of my stomach in a cool stream. Cramps throbbed and then eased as I drank and drank, feeling the creamy, sour nectar circulate through the tissues of my body, filling me in a way that half-rotted potatoes and carrots and bread could not.

Mama, I hope you are well cared for, wherever you are.

I rested back on my heels and tilted the tin cap above me, spilling the last drops of milk into my hungry mouth. My eyes adjusted better to the dim silvery light. My heart beat in a gentler rhythm.

I am well cared for, neshomeleh, but I miss you terribly. Hurry to me, my love.

A mule, his eyes crusted with what looked like dried snot, huffed in a stall. His straw bedding made a dry scratching sound as he shifted his hooves.

I will, Mama, but I'm so tired.

Chickens cooed, a cow lowed, and a nightingale's fluted song carried in from outside.

Sleep, sleep, beautiful child / free from worry and pain—

A serene weariness fell over me. Each rung of the ladder squeaked like a mouse as I climbed into the loft, and the hay rustled as I curled my body into it, spread Mama's blouse over me—and then the coat—and drifted into sleep.

● ● ●

"What are you doing here?" A brown-haired boy no more than ten or eleven stood above me. His eyes were brave little slits, and his chin jutted out so that his mouth formed an angry pout. "You're not supposed to be here. Get out!"

My eyes darted to the ground to see if his father was near, but I heard only the cows in the pen and the snot-eyed mule pacing in its stall. My nose ran from the frigid air, but the rest of me was warm beneath my coat and held by the straw as if by two cupped hands. "Please, don't tell anyone."

He threw his shoulders back and grew his voice to its fullest belligerence. "No! I know you're a Jew, and you're not supposed to be here!"

I threw the coat off me, leapt up, and pushed him into the straw. From outside the barn, a male voice called out, "What is it, Maksym?"

I shoved the blouse in a coat sleeve with the empty scarf Mama used for my bundle, and I flew down the ladder.

"A Jew, Papa, a Jew!"

The man walked into the barn from the pen. "What?"

I ran out the small door on the side of the barn, past a wide-eyed woman carrying a basket of laundry. My legs carried me past the house and onto a gravel road. I turned to see the father level a gun at me, heard the bang of it fire, and a bullet broke through the air above my head.

Mama, please help me.

My body loosened even as my mind tightened, and my temples throbbed. I knew another bullet would come. A vision—like an impulse—of the bullet tearing into my flesh, knocking me down, and leaving me dead tightened my chest and jolted my legs into a run.

I'm sorry, Mama.

Bang! Then the popping of a bullet as it sped through the air past my right shoulder. My vision narrowed, so there was only the dirt and gravel of the road. My breathing and my pumping heart sounded in my ears as if their vibrations traveled through water. Everything external was colorless and distorted. I didn't *feel* anything.

Hide, Musia, hide—

My legs propelled me forward in short, fast strides to a rhythm of their own making. My lungs inhaled and exhaled.

My arms, even the one holding the coat, pumped as if they alone would help me take flight. My muscles contracted and expanded without thought or intention. Blood circulated from heart to brain to legs to arms to muscles to heart and so on. These motions and movements, the machine of me, operated beyond my ability to control or influence their workings. It had an unreal quality. The synchronous pieces of the mechanism raced down the gravel road as if it were a flickering image from an aged movie reel projected into my mind's eye.

The forest is too far, Mama. Hide where?

Past the few dilapidated clapboard and stone houses I watched myself run. Ahead of me spread a wide swath of cut and harvested fields, home to pheasant and partridge, but no longer a deep sea of chin-high golden wheat. The road arced and left the beaten-down dirt yards of the village, and a low ridge of hedgerow rose on either side of me. The father and his boy must be behind me, but they were no longer within sight.

There, Musia, the stones.

Panic propelled my body, but instinct drew me toward a small pile of stones, the collapsed remnants of an abandoned well. I tossed the coat in ahead of me and then plunged into shadow and soft sand.

I looked up into a bright blue illuminated sphere, expecting the faces of the boy and his father, gun in hand, to look down at me, a rabbit caught in a shallow pit. My fingers pressed into the cold, damp sand, its grains rose and fell around my fingers.

What now, Mama?

Remember Alice in Wonderland?

Yes.

And the Mock Turtle?

Of course, 'The master was an old turtle we called Tortoise because he taught us.'

I lay down in the sand and draped the coat over me. My fingers dug beneath the coat, and like a turtle I threw handfuls of sand on the coat and around its edges, then waited in the dark for the two hunters to find me, or not. The world for that moment was quiet except for the heaviness of my breathing. Afraid the father and boy would see the sandy bottom of the well rise and fall with life, I inhaled, held the breath, then exhaled.

I remember Papa reading that book to you, neshomeleh.

Voices came from the road.

I remember, Mama.

"I don't see her," said the boy, his breath quick and light.

—and he read to your friends—

"She must've run into the woods," said the father, his breath heavy and hard.

I remember that too.

"Too bad," said the boy.

I can see their little faces. Helena and Tauba and Rena—

"Yes, too bad," said the father.

I loved them, Mama.

"The Germans would have given us money?" asked the boy.

—and Gerda and her tousle-haired baby brother Julian—

"They would," said the father.

I loved them too, Mama.

"I'm sorry," said the boy.

—as well as Zofia with her bright blue eyes—

The father's voice was kind, forgiving. "I'm sorry, too."

—and my neshomeleh sitting at her Papa's feet, listening to him read.

Tears bubble from my eyes.

I miss Zofia so much.

■ ■ ■

The whimpering of the ghetto's starving children kept me awake at night. Lying on my stomach in my slat bed, the backs of my thighs and bottom in too much pain to roll over, I heard their soft, quiet weeping drift up through derelict floorboards.

I didn't know these children, but every day one or two of their shrouded bodies lay on the street for the burial committee formed by the *Judenrat*—their heartbroken mothers forced to decide between laboring to feed their remaining children or watching as their child was carried off to the pit where the committee took all the bodies.

By late autumn, there were so many bodies: children, men, and women. The starved, diseased, beaten, executed, as well as those whose lives ebbed from sheer hopelessness—they lie crumpled on the streets like human litter for sad-looking men—aged beyond their years—to pick up and haul away. These corpses were often not put out until after their week's ration was collected, the body stiff and bloated from the delay.

Soon, there were more bodies than material to cover them, their expressionless eyes and parted lips facing up to the sky, waiting for the committee and their place in the pit.

Each morning, Mama, Tchiya, and the others left for their labor, and Hannah helped and cared for me. I never knew if a *łapanka, Sonderaktion (*a "special action" as the Germans called mass roundups), or the simple act of murder would claim Mama or Tchiya. The anxiety of waiting made it difficult to sit still.

As soon as I'd healed enough from the SS officer's beating, I went outside to rejoin my friends.

"Where's Julian?" I asked Gerda.

Nobody answered. Tauba and Rena looked down to their shoes, and a delicate sorrow drifted through Gerda's eyes.

"Follow us," said Zofia.

"Where to?"

"You'll see."

Gerda, Zofia, Tauba, Rena, Helena, and I walked through the streets, keeping our eyes and ears open for any sign of danger that could come in the form of a *łapanka, Sonderaktion,* or a single black-uniformed Ukrainian guard. Out of boredom, they often killed anyone they found on the street during the day, men and women, young and old, and left the body for the committee.

We came to a pale brick wall that separated the ghetto from a small, poor neighborhood of mostly Poles. The market district was a few blocks beyond it, toward the center of Horochów. The wall ran down the middle of what had been a narrow side street girded by apartment buildings with short stoops. Now the street had become two alleys, each the mirror image of the other: one free and one the ghetto.

As we walked down the alleyway, a boy of about twelve emerged from one of the many heaps of rubbish. When we marched into the ghetto, plentiful evidence suggested the Germans had forced the former residents out of this part of the city and built the walls in a rush. Small piles of unusable bricks, battered furniture, baby prams, clothes, pots and pans, books, kitchen waste—anything they couldn't carry or discarded in their haste—lay scattered on the streets and in the tenements. What we couldn't use, we pushed into piles and left to deteriorate.

Without any furniture or beds, people tore lathes from horsehair-plastered walls to make beds and dumped the plaster out of windows into alleys or streets. Anything left in the apartments that the new residents couldn't put to some purpose they discarded to make room in the overcrowded, single-room dwellings.

"The wall isn't very thick, and they didn't build it into the ground," said the boy, arms crossed, looking every bit the proud engineer. "We've built a tunnel, like a rabbit hole, to the other side."

Zofia shook my arm. "We can sneak in and out!"

"Where is it?" I asked.

The boy looked up and down the alley and then gave a quick click of his tongue.

"Over here," said another boy's voice from beneath a mound of plaster, broken lathes, rags, pipes, and other assorted junk.

Zofia led me to the mound, where the wan, dirty, gentle face of a boy of about ten peered out of the rubbish, like a mouse in its nest.

"Do you want to go and see if we can get some food?" asked Zofia.

I looked at Gerda and the other girls.

"You go," said Gerda. "If there's too many of us, we'll get caught."

The older of the two boys stepped forward. "Be careful. They'll probably kill you if they catch you."

Whether I go or stay, I'm dying.

All of us ate only a thin soup at night. We lived in a state of slow starvation, and our lives revolved around food. Our play centered on food. Our conversations were about food, and each day we stepped around the bodies of those who'd died of hunger. Our hands, arms, and legs trembled from hunger, and our clothes hung loose from thinning bodies.

Gerda's eyes and face were sunken and hollow, her hair thinning. My eyes drifted to Tauba, Rena, and Dinusia. We shared the haunted look of people starving to death, some of us faster than others. The Germans forced larger families with young children to split their rations or stop feeding those for whom it was too late. I knew why Julian was no longer by Gerda's side.

The opportunity to get food tugged far harder at me than the risk of death or Mama's anger for taking such a risk. I shook my head to say yes, I understood the danger, then looked at Gerda. "We'll bring something we can share."

"Wait," said the older boy. "Your coat, leave it here. We have a hiding place."

"The star," said Zofia, pointing to the gold star sewn onto the coat.

We slipped through the small tunnel and pushed aside a board to come up behind an assortment of stacked boards, bricks and empty crates that were used to hide our door to the outside. Workers had left all these items when they built the wall. None of it looked out of place. We walked to the corner of the building and looked down a wide, open street into a neighborhood. It felt as if we'd fallen through

Alice's rabbit hole. On our side of the wall was dirt, an utter lack of anything green, rubbish piles, death, starvation, and hopelessness. On this side were strips of grass, burned by night frosts to an olive-tinged green. Trees, leafless except for a few amber survivors, lined the street, and a breeze blew dried leaves skittering across a sidewalk free of corpses and rubbish heaps. A woman in an overcoat, her hair tucked into a scarf, pushed a pram toward the market. Other women and older men moved past open windows or sat looking out into the street, watching their happy, healthy children play.

Zofia turned to me and teased my hair with her fingers, then teased her own so that it looked less stringy and unwashed. "Here," she said. "Pinch your cheeks so they redden. We have to look like we didn't just sneak out of the ghetto."

I pinched my cheeks and followed her to a building, where we walked up and knocked on a door. In Polish, Zofia asked if we could have some food. The woman closed her door without a word. We knocked on another, and an old man said, "You don't belong here." We went to another building, and the woman answering the first door swore at us, but the next gave us each a potato and a carrot. "Leave and never come back," she said, shooing us away from her door. We each hid our potato and carrot in the bodices of our dresses.

We continued like this until we'd managed a few more potatoes and two eggs. We slipped through the tunnel and emerged back into a gray place of death. Relief at returning safely and my pride that I could help Mama and Tchiya was tempered by a desire to return to a world of food and color and life. The boys were gone, so we covered the tunnel entrance with trash and debris and gave a share of the potatoes and carrots to the girls but kept the eggs for ourselves.

"Look, Mama, Tchiya." They both stared at the carrot, potato, and egg nested in the blankets on my bed.

Tchiya looked around the room and whispered, "Where did you get that?"

I hesitated for a moment, and Mama stepped closer.

"Musia, where did you get this? Did you steal it?"

"No, Mama."

Mama looked toward Mrs. Zelinski, who was lying in bed while Hannah heated a thin broth for her and Janusz to eat. Mama asked me again, "Where did you get this?"

"Does it matter, Mama? I didn't steal it from anybody, and, look, there's an egg. An egg, Mama! When was the last time we've seen such a thing?"

"I know, Musia, but food like this doesn't just fall out of the sky."

Janusz stood, "I need air."

Mrs. Zelinski looked at him. "Don't go outside, Janusz. They'll take any man or boy they find."

Mama watched them.

"I'll be all right." He put his newsboy cap on and walked out the door.

Words came from deep in my throat. "They are gifts from me. Tchiya is not well and we need them."

"Don't put this on me," Tchiya said, her eyes narrow, tired, and angry. "I have to go to the toilet."

Mama watched her walk out and frowned. Her words came out like a train engine with a full head of steam. "Where did you get these?"

Mrs. Joselewicz rolled over, and her exhausted eyes fell on me. "Just tell her, Musia, for goodness sake." She turned and went back to whatever waking dream occupied her.

My body tensed, and my face warmed. I motioned for Mama to lean close. "I snuck out."

Her head pulled up; her lips were pale and thin. "Out of the building?"

I looked hard at Mrs. Joselewicz's back. "The ghetto. Some kids made a small tunnel. It's brilliant and brilliantly hidden, and I snuck out of the ghetto. A couple of Polish women gave these to me."

"You were alone?"

"No."

"Who was with you?"

"It doesn't matter." Tears welled in my eyes. *Why won't she accept this gift?* "Please, Mama, I want you and Tchiya to have these."

Mama touched the egg as if it were fragile as silk. "You must promise me you will never do this again."

"But, Mama—"

She leaned in to my face and placed her hand on my shoulder. "Promise me."

"I promise."

I'd lied to Mama before but never about something so important.

The next day, Zofia and I went farther toward the market to avoid begging from the same people. Beyond our hollow eyes and our clothes that hung from our bodies, we looked odd walking about in the cold wearing short-sleeved summer dresses. At the first door we knocked on, a man threatened to set his dog on us. A woman slammed her door. Others swore at us, called us dirty Jews and pigs and said we should go back to the ghetto, where trash like us belonged. One woman gave us each a potato and shut the door without a word. That night, I snuck the extra potato into our soup.

For the rest of that week, Zofia and I snuck out, as did Gerda, Tauba, Rena, and Helena, as well as any other kids willing to take the risk. We were on the cusp of starvation and death, and this gave us hope. However, with so many of us wandering the outside, it was impossible to find food near the wall. We had to go into the market, where Ukrainians and Poles maintained an uneasy mix—one a friend to Germany and the other its enemy.

Working in groups, or even pairs, carried greater risk. A single, begging waif angered those disposed to hate us, but a squalid gang hunting around the shops of Horochów would cause them to seek out the authorities.

My first day at the market, women looked at me as if I were a dirty mutt. One woman asked, "Why should I give you anything?"

"Because my family is starving," I said.

"Well, if you weren't Jewish, you wouldn't be hungry, would you?" She turned and walked away, a sack of food over one arm.

The next day I took a gold ring with a ruby in it out of the hem of my coat—the last of Mama's jewelry—and put it into a pocket on the front of my dress. At the market I did my best to blend in, to become just another child waiting on a parent, but no matter how much I teased my hair and pinched my cheeks, my sallow complexion, dirty hair, and loosely draped dress gave me away. Each woman I approached ignored me or told me to get back into the pigsty with the rest of the Jews.

Frustration and hopelessness ate at my spirit, and I sat— shrunken and tired—by the stoop of a shop. Four graying women, all of them dressed nicely and burnished by the unique cruelty of wealth, walked out of the shop. Each carried a cloth sack heavy with food, and I could make out the outlines of sausages, apples, carrots, potatoes, and bread. Without thinking I asked, "Please, may I have some food?"

The women looked at me, lips pursed and eyes demure. The tallest and thinnest of them curled the edges of her lips into a prim frown.

"I'll pay," I said.

One of the women tilted her head. "Oh, don't even."

She looked to her friend then to me, her eyes veiled. "What could *you* possibly have?"

I handed her the ring. "It's gold with a ruby."

She brought the ring close to one eye and perused it like a jeweler. "It's fake."

"No, ma'am, it's real. My father gave it to my mother."

She turned the ring in her fingers. "I'll give you an egg."

Her friends let out small, affected laughs.

"Is that all?" I asked.

"Maybe a carrot," she said looking down at her bag.

One of the women looked around nervously. "For goodness sake, don't play with her. What if the police see?"

The woman's terse frown ebbed, and her eyes betrayed the slightest concern. "Two eggs and that's it."

I took the eggs and put one in each pocket and quickly walked away from the market. I hated those women, but I was proud to be able to give these beautiful eggs to Mama and Tchiya.

Without looking, I turned down the narrow alley. As I neared the entrance to our tunnel, the husky voice of a man called out. "Stop!"

I turned to see a black-uniformed guard running toward me. He grabbed my arm and shook me, his fingers digging into my skin. "Where are you going?"

I tried to twist out of his grip, but he shook me harder, then threw me against the ghetto wall. I cowered against the bricks, breathing in small, quick gulps, and he stood over me with his nostrils flared, clenching and unclenching his hands.

"Where are you going?"

Fear choked in my throat.

"Why are you here?"

I had no answer for him.

What do I say, Mama?

His eyes scanned down my body and stopped at the bulge in my pockets. "What do you have there?"

Death was close. I thought of my lie to Mama and it burned in my chest.

He pulled his revolver from its holster, cocked the hammer, and pointed the barrel at my nose. "Hand them to me."

I reached into my pockets, pulled the eggs out, and placed them in his outstretched hand. He dropped them in front of me so that they smashed. With the gun pointed at my head, he pushed my face down into the mess, then pressed his boot on the back of my head. "You're a lying,

Jewish scum," he said as he ground my face into the smashed eggs. Warm blood, mixed with the broken eggs, stained the pavement.

My body trembled, and I let my eyelids fall closed, waiting for the gun to fire and the bullet to tear through my skull.

Why won't he just kill me?

Guilt and shame overwhelmed me. I hated myself. I had lied to Mama, and I did it because I believed I wouldn't get caught and killed; I believed I was smarter or luckier or better than the others. The backs of my thighs and my bottom still ached, and my torn skin had barely healed from the beating by the SS officer. And yet again, my life rested on the impulse of a cruel man. The anonymity of the burial committee and my lime-dusted body dumped in its pit was as much my future as any other's.

We all balanced on a thinning membrane between life and death.

Please, please let me go home. I just want to go home. I don't want to be here anymore.

Tears mixed with the slew of blood and egg that bubbled up around my nose as I tried to breathe. He lifted his boot.

"You are to get back where you belong and never show your face here again. Understand?" He latched his fingers around my arm, jerked me to my feet, and walked me to the ghetto's entrance. All he had to do to get the guards to open the gate was a quick whistle and nod of his head, the kind of thing that would get any resident of the ghetto killed. He walked me a little way in then pushed me down to the ground and stood over me. "The Germans are at war with Jew scum like you, and they won't stop killing every Jew you know—your friends, your family, all of you—until they've rid the world of your disgusting race."

I tried to crawl away from him, but he grabbed my throat and forced me to look into his bulging eyes, each a dot of blue surrounded by infinite white mapped by thin, pulsing veins. I closed my eyes, and he slapped me.

"Look at me, Jew bitch."

His body shook with rage. My heart ached with helplessness, and the air felt thick so that I couldn't take enough of it in. Flecks of his warm spit sprayed against my bloody cheeks, and his hand tightened around my throat. I withdrew into an unknown, internal place where sensation became watery, dreamlike.

I'm spreading my wings—

"Go tell the rest of your nest of rat Jews the Germans are killing you to create a perfect society. You are the last Jews alive on this earth."

He threw my head down hard onto the pavement. The fetid gray ghetto dissolved my fantasy of flight. He walked toward the gate, straightened the lapels of his coat, and tilted his cap to just the right angle. The guards at the gate smiled.

Blood and yellow egg mucous smeared my dress. I touched my face; the scrapes on my cheeks and nose felt rough on my fingertips and stung like fresh, deep burns. But I was alive.

When I walked into our small room of an apartment, Hannah looked up from Ania. "Oh my God, are you all right?"

"No."

"Watch Ania while I get some water." She picked up the basin and left the room. Her clubfoot made a soft, fleshy sound as she limped down the hall. Ania pulled her blanket up to her mouth and sucked on it. "I don't like living here," she said.

"I don't either."

Her eyes drifted up to the ceiling. "I think we're going to *Him* soon."

"I don't know where I'm going,"—*God is not here*—"but don't be afraid"—*I am a liar.*

"I'm not afraid."

"Why not, Ania?"—*I dishonor Mama and Papa.*

"I look for God every day."

"Do you find Him?"—*My soul is heavy with sin.*

"No, but he is here."

"Why?"—*Please, Mama, forgive me.*

"Because Papa said, 'God is abundant, and God fills the world.'"

Hannah came back into the room and washed the blood and egg from my face. "I'm so sorry, Musia," she said each time I winced. She wiped at the stains in my dress, but all she could do was soften them. Then she held a small mirror up to my face, and I didn't recognize the florid, scabbed face looking back.

"Mama is going to be very mad at me," I said.

"You're alive, Musia. That counts for something."

"But I've disappointed her again."

"She's a kind woman." Hannah stood and took Ania's hand. "Let's go wash. Your mama will be home soon and want to see her smiling, clean girl."

I dabbed salty tears from my eyes and let the pain ease my emotional burden.

Mama and Tchiya came home with the others, and Mama's eyes flared when she saw I was hurt. "How did this happen? Who did this to you?" Her clothes hung from her pinched body. Not long ago her body had brimmed with womanly curves that filled her dresses. I had wanted to look like her, to be like her.

No more lies, no more disappointments.

"I snuck out of the ghetto and bought two eggs with the gold and ruby ring you gave me—" I began.

"You did what?" Tchiya said.

"Tchiya, please." Mama turned her reddened eyes to me and listened as I told her everything except the guard saying we were the last Jews in the world. I didn't want to scare Ania or the fragile Mrs. Zelinski. And then I rested my hands in my lap. "I guess he is one of the kind ones. He could have killed me, but he didn't."

I don't know how you could love me, Mama.

She rubbed her eyes then looked at me, eyes red and tired,

brows knit in worry. "You must promise me you won't sneak out again."

"They're starving us, Mama."

She placed one hand flat on her lap and held my shoulder with the other. "We'll make do. I promise."

"Yes."

"Yes what?"

"I promise not to sneak out again."

"And you have to tell the other kids the guards know you've been out. They'll be looking and watching for you."

"I will."

Then Mama wrapped her arms around me, and I burrowed my face into her bosom. "Do you forgive me?"

"I love you and am abundantly able to forgive my *neshomeleh*."

"That's it?" asked Tchiya. "You're not going to punish her?"

Mama lifted her head to look at Tchiya. "It's been enough, don't you think?"

Tchiya stood and scowled at Janusz as she walked into the hallway. Mama's eyes followed her. Janusz left as well, the stairs creaking beneath their footsteps.

Mrs. Zelinski rushed to the door. "For God's sake, be careful, Janusz. They're taking men every day." When she turned and closed the door, her eyes burned a mark in my forehead.

The next morning, I rushed downstairs and to the door but paused before opening it. *łapanka, Sonderaktion,* and the threat of idle murder all seemed so real and close.

Are we the only Jews left?

I stepped onto the stoop and into cold, clear air. Two doors down, a small child lay shrouded in her mother's thin cotton scarf with petite blue and pink flowers on it. Across the street a woman lay with her legs emerging from a burlap potato sack. Near her, an elderly man was half buried beneath a thin layer of debris so that his legs, feet turned out, protruded from rotting horsehair plaster.

What will death feel like?

My eyes wandered to the end of our street, and there, just past the end of the pavement, a woman Mama's age lay sprawled in the dirt, blood pooled around her face, her neck torn by a bullet. She had died near the bulrushes and arrowroot, both of which were brown and desiccated by late autumn air.

A dream?

On the roof of the building across from me were three guards.

Or nothing?

Two had their rifles slung over their shoulders; the third held his at the ready, his eyes on me.

I'm so afraid.

The membrane between life and death thinned.

Where does Ania's faith come from? What does she see that I don't?

The guards believe I am a Jew bitch, member of a disgusting race. I dared not look to the water and the stubbly fields beyond. They'd shoot me for such a thing.

That morning I told Zofia what had happened to me, although she had already seen it in the bloody scrapes and bruises on my face.

"Please don't go out anymore, Zofia."

She pushed an errant lock of her stringy hair behind an ear. In her eyes was the girl who'd held the injured baby rabbit that sent me rushing to Papa, but hunger had withered her body. "I don't know, Musia."

Tears watered my eyes, their salt stinging as they rolled down my cheeks. "Please, Zofia, promise."

She crossed her arms over her coat and looked down at the ground. "I will."

A day later, Gerda knocked on our door. "It's Zofia."

We walked to the main square. Lying on her back was Zofia, her arms stretched above her head and a carnation of blood blooming on her chest. Grief, disgust, and confusion festered in my belly and spread into my limbs as an uncontrollable shiver.

She's still afraid. I can see the fear in her eyes.

Her once sparkling eyes and white-as-milk cheeks were the same slate blue as the sky. Her face looked up into the clouds, lips parted, her eyes wide with fear and shock. Her hair draped around her face like an amber halo.

She can't be gone.

The same guard who'd caught and beaten me stood beside her, a revolver in his hand. When he saw me, he smiled. "No one is to touch this Jew bitch."

That night the guards marched the laborers past Zofia. Her mother broke from her group and fell onto the body of her daughter, but a guard hit her in the back of her head with a club and ordered the others to drag her home. Mama was one of the women who helped her.

Mama came into our room and drew me into her. "She's not suffering anymore, neshomeleh."

"She looks so afraid, Mama."

"My love, the Zofia we know and love is beyond fear and pain."

"That scares me even more."

"She's in a place where the cruelty of these people can no longer touch her, neshomeleh."

"But what if it's only darkness?"

"Remember, God is abundant and fills the world."

"But God isn't here."

"Neshomeleh, I am here with you, and Tchiya is here with us, and we carry our love with us. God is in that; he is abundant within each of us and within our love."

"I loved Zofia, Mama."

"I know. I did too."

"She was only eleven."

"I know. It's a horrible, horrible thing."

"I'm sorry, so very sorry, Mama."

"You have nothing to be sorry for, Musia."

"I've lied and hurt you. I don't want to die without you forgiving me."

Her fingers caressed the soft hairs on the back of my head. "I forgive you, my love."

The next morning Mama, Tchiya, and the others marched to their work past the main square and Zofia's body. I helped Hannah with Ania, but I didn't go outside. I couldn't bear to see Zofia's body again.

The women and Janusz returned home that night, exhausted and lost in their hunger. No one said a word, and we slept with the windows wide open despite the coldness of the night, to rid the room of the smell of rot. I slept with Mama, my body curled into hers.

The next morning the speakers crackled, "Everyone is to report to the main square immediately. Everyone is to report to the main square immediately." I held Mama's hand as we walked and squeezed it a bit harder when we neared the square. By now, I knew the process through which a body decomposes, and I trembled at the thought of seeing Zofia lying in her dried blood.

In the middle of the square was a wooden frame with three nooses hanging from the wood crossbeam. A long wooden bench stood beneath each noose, and Zofia's body lay beside one of the newly constructed posts for the gallows.

Guards with rifles surrounded us, and a German SS officer I'd never seen before stood beside the gallows. Four Ukrainian guards led three young Jews—one girl and two boys—into the square, their hands tied behind their backs and their faces taut with fear.

"Oh my God," Mama muttered.

Three women let out a wail at the sight. "Please, hang me, not my child," one of them yelled, and a Ukrainian guard struck her on the back of her head with his rifle. She collapsed unconscious, blood trickling from her scalp.

The SS officer spoke in Polish as guards lifted the teens onto the bench, placed a noose around each neck, and tightened it. "We caught these three trying to escape. Apparently, there are those of you who think you can leave without a pass. I hope after today there will be no more confusion."

The SS officer stood to the side of the gallows, and one of the guards stepped forward. "No one can look away or close their eyes. Anyone who does so will find themselves up here next!"

Air was like dust trying to pass through my dry mouth. Vomit rose from my convulsing stomach, and I curled and uncurled my toes to distract from the sour burn in the back of my throat. "I don't want to watch, Mama. Please, please don't make me," I cried.

Mama placed one hand on my shoulder and the other on Tchiya's. "Be brave my loves, please be brave."

A few women prayed, and others sobbed as the guard picked up a sledgehammer and knocked the bench over. We didn't look away or close our eyes as the two young men and the girl's feet flailed in the air, and the girl jerked her legs seemingly to tighten the rope around her neck, to bring about the end of this misery that much sooner.

The three hung in the air, choking, struggling, their bodies fighting death.

The second boy's feet, legs, and body shuddered. The girl's struggle slowed as did the other boy's, their bodies shuddered, and all three swayed gently, their eyes bulging and the tips of their tongues poking out between their slack lips.

The SS officer stepped forward, his hands held behind his back. "They will remain on display, as will the girl, for the next week, and they will be replaced by anyone who tries to leave without a pass. There will be no work today, so you can think about your choices."

Some stayed to pray, but Mama, Tchiya, and I walked away. Out of sight of the soldiers, my stomach convulsed in painful retches. There was nothing to vomit other than thick, acidic bile.

Mama placed her hand on my back, "I'm so sorry, neshomeleh."

Tears flowed over the scabs on my cheeks, and I closed my eyes as spittle ran down my chin. "I want to go home, I want to go home, I want to go home ..." I would have done almost anything to remove the image of those swaying bodies as well as the many other people the Germans forced us to watch die in that square.

• • •

Lying on the bottom of the well half-covered in sand, I was sure the man and his son were gone. I rolled onto my coat and stared up into lavender-gray light.

Mama, I must have fallen asleep.

You did, neshomeleh.

The damp cool of the sand rose through my coat, my belly ached with hunger, and my body shook from cold. I stood and dug a hole in the soft sand and peed into it, covered it up, then sat with my coat wrapped around my shoulders and rested my butt on its hem.

I need to get food.

Yes, neshomeleh.

I looked up at the slick river stones stacked to form the well's wall.

But first I have to get out of this well.

The Forest Nymph

The fingernail on my middle finger cracked then tore off. My other hand tightened its grip on a slick well stone, but the sudden shock of pain and shifting weight of my body pulled me away, and I fell. My back landed hard on the sand, and my head snapped back. I stuck the bleeding finger in my mouth and felt warm saliva on stinging flesh and a jagged bit of nail against my tongue. All my fingernails were brittle and broken except my ring finger, the stub of which was raw and bloody, a bit of bone protruded through the skin.

Above me was a rounded roof of india ink speckled by starlight. The air was damp and cool so that I shook with an unrelenting chill. The night was silent other than a slight breeze blowing over the top of the well.

Keep trying, Musia.

But I keep falling!

My eyes searched for a route: places where an errant rounded edge projected from stones stacked flush, one atop the other, with a thin layer of mortar between them.

You were always my little woman of the woods, neshomeleh.

I know, but this is too hard, Mama.
Running, playing, climbing—
I remember, Mama.
—always with your little penknife.

I sat up and pulled my coat from my shoulder and took the penknife from a pocket. The smooth, cream-white handle shone in the starlight, and the weight of it in my palm was reassuring.

Papa gave this to me
Yes, he did.
I remember you didn't want him to.
You were so young; five, I think.
Six, Mama.
And what did you do five minutes after he gave it to you?
Cut myself whittling a stick.
That's right, but you didn't cry.
I didn't want you to take it from me.

The penknife has been in my pocket for years. It had carved willow branches by the creek near our home. It bounced in my pocket while I played with Zofia and our friends on the estate of Horochów's last *Szlachcianka,* an aged woman who was an echo of lost Polish nobility. I'd carried it to school, hidden in my book bag, and refused to lend it to anyone, worried they would lose it or let it be taken by a teacher. In the ghetto, it connected me to Papa. It sliced potatoes and other small items I'd snuck into our soup at night. It was there for Mama when she mended our clothes or helped remove a large splinter from Ania's hand.

The larger of the two blades wasn't easy to open. Embedded in the knife's hinge was grit and lint, tangible proof of my love for this small thing, so that it squeaked like a little mouse when I swung the blade out.

I used the tip of the blade to etch loose mortar from between two stones until there was space for the toes of one foot.

Where are you, Mama?

The blade etched another space for fingers.

I'm right here, neshomeleh.

Then toes.

Have you fallen—

Then fingers.

—off the edge of the world?

And toes.

No, neshomeleh. I am seeing you in every dream and loving you with every breath.

I'll find you soon.

I climbed back down the ladder of stone I'd carved with my little knife and picked up my coat, checking to be sure Mama's blouse and the scarf were safe. Then I shook the coat to feel the weight of my few gold coins and the brass key to our home.

I want one more hug, Mama.

My arms wait for you, my love.

My bleeding finger stung so much my eyes watered. The finger next to it, the stub, was sore and bloody too, but not as painful as the missing nail. The skin on my hands looked withered; its bones ached from the cold. I climbed up the well's inner wall, digging out each rung of my ladder with throbbing hands, and finally crawled over the top.

The air was sharp, and above me a moonless haze of stars spread across the sky. Rolling onto my side, I listened for the sound of people or a dog but heard only the tender whisper of distant trees bending to the wind. The faintest hint of light glimmered in the eastern horizon.

Every muscle trembled. The knot in my belly twisted, making the agony of starvation worse. It took all of my will to coax my muscles from lethargy to cooperation. I pushed my body up onto my knees and felt something hard, rough, and cold beneath one hand. Half buried in the dirt beneath a stone was the rusted blade of a small spade. I wiggled it loose and tucked it into the sleeve of my coat with Mama's blouse and scarf.

Aching, I walked from the stones, across the road, and into a field of cut wheat. Bitter air flowed over the stubble, and the chill of it permeated my clothes and dimpled my skin. I put Mama's blouse on, wrapped the scarf around my neck and shoulders, put the other items in my coat pockets, and pulled it around me like a shawl, but still the wind blew through.

A crow cawed and landed near another black-eyed bird at the far end of the field. It was a lonely sound, and I wished for Mama to be with me, for this to be a dream.

You can't wish this away, Musia. Put your wishes in your pocket.

Yes, Mama.

Remember your dream at the river?

With Papa and the birds?

Yes, and he opened the cage, and the birds circled and flew away?

He said they were Tzadikim—

Yes—

—and I cried because you and I needed one.

—and Papa said they are needed elsewhere, neshomeleh.

I pulled the coat tighter around my body and stepped from the bristly field into woods. My socks were wet, and my toes were numb. Each step worried me as it rustled the first of the dead fall leaves.

Then he said I have to find my own way, alone.

My dear girl, you are never alone.

No? Then where are you?

I'm with you.

No, Mama, I'm alone.

I pushed through a cluster of small, gangly saplings, and most of their broad leaves fell to the ground. The knot in my stomach tightened, and the cramping wouldn't ease, even with my arms wrapped around my belly.

I'm going to starve, Mama, or some farmer or soldier is going to find me and kill me just like Zofia or Ania or Buzio.

Don't talk like that, Musia.
I want to lie down and let go, Mama.
Find your way to me.

On I walked, farther into the forest and into the night, arguing with Mama. In one moment I wanted to allow my soul to slip from my body, but then anger and rage propelled me forward through spider webs, sharp branches that poked into my face and skin, and mud that seeped into my shoes and wetted my socks and feet.

No! I need to find you. My body needs you, Mama. One last hug, just one last hug.

Stinging thorns, like cat claws, tore into my arms, legs, and face.

In the darkness and lost to my anger, I'd walked into a tall thicket of briars. Pain and rage boiled, and I screamed out in a pitch so high it reverberated through the top of my scalp into the roots of my hair. I twisted and shook my arms and body to free them from the briars but only heard the tearing of the coat's fabric and felt the burning sting of thorns piercing my skin.

"God! Why do you do this to me? Kill me or let me find Mama!"

Musia! Stop!

"No! No! No!"

Tears poured from my eyes and each thorn prick increased the volume and intensity of my cries until utter exhaustion and pain left nothing but despair. I tilted my head back and stared—my eyes blurry with tears—up through a canopy of broadleaved trees into low, billowing clouds. A drop of chilly rain fell onto one cheek, then another on my forehead.

Lowering my head, I searched for some way through that wouldn't tear my coat and clothes more than I'd already done. The briars held no berries, but most of their broad, serrated leaves—blotched brown and yellowed by autumn— remained. The patch was thick and offered no obvious way through. My anger had allowed me to walk far enough into it without noticing that turning back didn't look better. Any direction I chose promised more thorns.

Rain fell with a steadier rhythm; its pitter-patter sounded off briar leaves, and each drop that landed on my shoulders seeped through the fabric. Knees shaking, my body, almost of its own will, lowered me into the darkness of the briars. Thorns tugged on the coat and my skin, then let go as my knees touched the raw, wet earth. I did my best to pull all the thorns from my skin and clothes, but there were so many. Then I took the small spade and etched out a shallow grave to cradle my body.

I wrapped the coat around me so that most of my body would not lie on the ground, pulled Mama's blouse up over my nose to breathe in her faint scent, and held my tummy with one arm. The cramping knot wouldn't ease, but it was enough to let sleep overtake me.

■ ■ ■

I woke off and on through the night to the sound of rain drops splattering the briar leaves. Shivering, I curled my knees into my chest. In a state between wakefulness and sleep, memory slipped me into my bed in Horochów. Rain drummed on the roof, and the quilt tucked over my head was warm and snug, the house quiet and dark.

With the first gray light of dawn, the rain moderated to a chilly mist. I couldn't stop shivering. An image of burrowing into a hayloft crossed my mind, but the stinging, torn fingernail reminded me of the risk.

Cramps felt as if an invisible hand were twisting my belly. And thirst burned in my throat. I raised myself up onto my knees, the coat wrapped around my shoulders, and licked the moisture from a leaf, then another, and another until I felt a tickle on my tongue and bit down. There was a soft crunch and the innards of whatever had found its way into my mouth squirted out. The taste was bitter, but I swallowed, and my stomach accepted this new food.

I used the tips of my fingers to pull leaves toward me until I found an iridescent green beetle and sucked it into my mouth. I looked on more leaves and then searched the ground, where a slug pulled its body over the peaty soil. I plucked it up and tried to swallow it without chewing, but it stuck in my throat. I coughed it back up into my mouth, chewed it, and felt its gooey innards and flesh slip down.

The knot in my stomach eased. I brushed away dead leaves and twigs to root around in the dirt for more. An earthworm squirmed, and I ate it and then another. A white grub curled into a fetal ball, and I popped it into my mouth. Every morsel was bitter and gritty, but the cramps eased, as did the penetrating chill. A cornucopia of bug life was all around me, and I scrounged for it, happy to have something to eat.

With food, my energy returned. I gathered my belongings and crawled through the brambles, which was easier than trying to walk through them. Thorns still poked my knees and hands and tore at my clothes, but I emerged out the other side with only a few new scratches.

The gray ceiling lightened, then broke, and sunlight mottled the forest floor. As I walked, the air warmed, but the holes in the soles of my shoes beneath the ball of each foot grew larger. My clothes were still damp; the coat itched and was heavy with moisture. I wanted to stop and let the sun dry my clothes, my skin, warm me to my soul, but with every passing day the forest thinned, the dead leaves around my feet deepened.

Where are you walking, neshomeleh?

To you, but I'm tired.

Beneath the spindly, gnarled branches of a small tree, hazelnuts lay in small piles. Some were chewed by squirrels, but many were whole. I bit into the shell of one, and a sharp twinge of an exposed nerve radiated out from my tooth. For months my teeth had been hurting, and my gums bled. With the penknife I carved the shell from the nut and ate it like a little chipmunk, my eyes and ears listened for danger.

I ate more nuts and worms and any other little creatures I found. After filling my stomach, I used Mama's scarf as a sack to carry as many nuts as would fit in it. And on I walked, the sun warming and drying me as the day passed.

When night came, I dug a little hole beneath a tree, wrapped the coat around me, and despite the cold I slept a dreamless sleep. In the morning I ate a few hazelnuts and foraged for bugs. The air was cold, and a thin sheen of frost coated the edges of fallen leaves, and crystals of ice had formed in the light dirt. Any creatures I might eat were hidden away in the warmth of their little homes.

It's going to be winter soon, neshomeleh.

I know, Mama. Are you warm?

Yes, very, so come to me my love.

I am, Mama. Maybe today.

I packed my belongings and wrapped the coat around me.

Cover your bed, Neshomeleh.

Why, Mama?

Remember the Szlachcianka's Gajowy who cared for the Szlachcianka's estate?

I remembered Zofia and I often saw the *Gajowy* as we played in the woods on the old noblewoman's estate. Though she was the last of a dying class, her land was immense, with streams, ponds, and forests managed and protected from poachers by the *Gajowy*. I bent down and spread leaves and twigs over my tiny grave. If this forest had a *Gajowy*, he would hunt me down like any other poacher in his woods.

The sun lit the forest, and I felt secure in its light. Beneath beech trees I found nuts still held within their soft-spined husks and ate them. Later, as I walked, acorns fell like rain from their oak mothers and slapped against leaves before thudding into the ground. I ate them, too, and packed a pile of them into my little satchel made of Mama's scarf. As the day passed, the sun warmed the ground enough to release a few worms. I thought of trying to get a squirrel, but they were far too quick for a half-starved girl to capture.

At each small stream, I stopped and took a deep drink and rested for a moment. For days my head had itched, and I'd picked a few nits from my hair. I'd had lice in the ghetto; everyone did. Mama, Tchiya, and I spent many nights combing them out of our hair, which helped, but we never got rid of them. Within a day or two, the itching became unbearable, and we spent another night combing nits out of our hair. If they got bad enough, they drove you half mad with itching, and scratching at them formed pustules they congregated in to feed on the puss, blood, and soft skin. The only way to treat them was to shave the person's head, which had happened to Janusz and Ania.

At one stream, I dunked my head beneath the cold water and held it for as long as I could. I hoped to drown the little buggers, and when I lifted my head there were a few floating nits. I brushed out my hair with my fingers as it dangled over the water and more nits were floating. I brushed the surface of the water with my hand, then dunked my head again. After a few times there were no more nits in the water, but I knew they would be back.

By late afternoon I reached a place where the forest skirted the edge of a long, wide field made brown and barren by fall harvest. Dense blackthorn grew along the border of the field and forest. I could crawl to it and remain hidden. The field sloped down to a wide, slow-moving stream fringed by tall grass and sallow-thorn laden with orange berries. A large village of clapboard houses and barns and bulbous spires of an Orthodox church spread out from the stream's far bank. A dirt road ran through the village and disappeared in either direction into a hedgerow twisting through a patchwork of fields. Beyond the village, cows grazed in a pasture, and the land spread out into a rolling jigsaw of stubbled hay and wheat fields.

I lay down, so I could look through the blackthorn into the village. Smoke rose from chimneys, and brown garden plots stretched behind each house. A man made his way toward the cows in the pasture, followed by a young boy. A woman threw chicken feed to a clutch of hens. Another man hauled sacks of potatoes from a weathered wooden cart into a potato cellar. These cellars dotted the land around every farm village and looked like low mounds of dirt and grass with stone-framed entrances and wooden doors. The man carried the sack through the low door, then emerged with it empty to fill from his wagon again. Inside, I knew there would be wooden bins filled with potatoes.

My eyes strained to see a sign, any sign, of Mama's tall, angular frame. I did this for what felt like a long time, so long that I became lost to the idle pleasure of watching these people in their routines. But there was no sign of Mama.

Remember your fourth birthday, neshomeleh?

I do, Mama.

And the pink wool outfit with a hat that tied under your chin and mittens to match that Papa and I gave you?

They were beautiful.

I remembered it was cold, and a pristine snow covered the ground. There was only Mama, Papa, and Tchiya. I received a puzzle, books, a few games, and the beautiful pink winter clothes. Mama pulled the tights up over my pudgy little legs and tied the laces of my winter shoes. She helped me put the cardigan on and did up the shiny, pink buttons. Last were the coat, hat, and mittens.

"You look beautiful in pink, my little love," she said, then Papa led me out our door and down the street. The snow had stopped falling, and I held Papa's hand as we walked in the silent reverence that follows a snowfall. We made our way to the path that followed the river, only a few kilometers from where Mama and I later hid as we tried to escape the ghetto. Wavy borders of ice lined the edges, but a gentle current kept the middle clear. On the other side, the spires of the

Orthodox church glistened gold in an early winter sunset. It was beautiful.

In our home, many of the conversations between my parents were about emigrating to America. My grandmother, Papa's mama, had left after the death of my grandfather. Then Papa's five sisters went one after the other. Of his family, only we remained. Before he was taken away, my father had filed and refiled papers at the consulate. Mama, Papa, Tchiya, and I had joined him for a few of these trips to answer questions, and Mama and Papa warned me to be on my best behavior.

Looking across the river in my pretty new pink outfit, I asked, "Papa, is that America?"

He smiled. Wrapping me in his long, strong arms, he picked me up and held me tight. "No, my little neshomeleh, but I wish it were."

After the consulate visits, when we arrived home and peeled off our outside clothes, he took me into his library and showed me how far away America was on his huge globe.

Over the next few years, politics and the topic of emigrating to either Jerusalem or America was part of every discussion, of every dinner, of every gathering in our home. I didn't realize what it was all about. My world was school, my friends, and the woods and fields around our house. The political discussions of Hitler and the Nazis, the threat of war, and the fear it aroused in Papa and Mama and their Jewish friends scared me. I didn't want to have anything to do with it.

We submitted papers and went for more interviews. Grandmother and my aunts sent letters assuring the authorities we would have a place to stay and the ability to make a living for ourselves, but none of it came to anything. Then in the spring of 1939 the University of Lwów offered Papa two tickets to the World's Fair in New York.

"Please, Simcha, take yourself and one of the girls," Mama pleaded one night. "Once you're there with your family, they will have to let us come to you."

"No, Fruma."

"But, Simcha—"

"I'm sorry, no. I've asked the university for another two tickets. I'm sure they will let us all go; why only two tickets for a family of four?"

The university said no.

We traveled to the consulate that summer to fill out more papers, deliver more letters, and appeal for permission to emigrate, but left with only vague assurances. Then came September 1. Hitler invaded and took the bulk of western Poland; Stalin took the eastern third. The border between Nazi Germany and Soviet Russia ran a few kilometers from Lwów and Horochów.

We no longer had any hope of emigrating.

...

I crawled away from the blackthorns and continued to walk. At night, I found a place to dig a little grave and slept till dawn, then walked again. I had no plan, no route or bearing, just the thought that if I walked, I would find Mama—or find other survivors who'd seen Mama, or I would see her in a village, living as a Ukrainian or Pole.

This became my routine for the next few weeks as the season ebbed from the golden light of autumn to early winter's slate gray. The forests stretched on for kilometers and kilometers, broken only by immense brown fields of wheat, hay or potatoes. When I reached a field, I'd find a safe place for a little grave and wait for nightfall. Then I'd eat what food I'd managed to scavenge from the ground and set out for the next forest. Often, I could see that forest across a patchwork of fields, and it seemed close but— because of the night air or the moonlight or perhaps it was my eyes—as I walked, the forest seemed to move farther away. Sometimes I'd make it into the trees as light shone over the horizon, and I'd have to find a good spot for my little grave.

Every so often I smelled smoke and knew it was coming from chimneys in a village. Other times recently cut clearings or some other evidence told me people were in the woods. Fear of being caught and killed made my heart race, but the desire to find Mama and safety drove me toward each village or cluster of homes in the woods.

My senses were attuned to the sight, sounds, and scents of the forest, but I was aware too that the forest was transforming with the change of seasons. Fewer leaves meant the scent of wood smoke traveled deeper into the woods. Without leaves, sound echoed a greater distance, and I could see farther.

It was a hunter's season.

Anyone could see you, neshomeleh.

I must find you.

Careful, my love, careful.

From hiding places, I would look for Mama but never saw her. Then I would sneak away, satisfied to perhaps have heard a human voice or watched people tending to their lives.

Sometimes one village looked exactly like another, and I wondered if I walked in a wide circle. If I wanted to find Mama before the depth of winter, I had to be sure I didn't walk the same ground over and over. I remembered Zofia telling me that moss only grows on the north side of trees, and that became my imperfect compass.

One morning I woke to a thin layer of wet snow. I'd become used to being damp, but this was different. The air was so sharp and cold it bit into exposed skin, and a trail of footprints in the snow followed me. My wet feet ached as if made of stone because my shoes were falling apart. I removed the laces and shoved leaves into the shoes to cover the holes, then wrapped and tied the laces around the shoe to hold the sole and upper together. This worked for a while, but the leaves either broke apart or fell through the holes. With my knife I cut young twigs from a balsam tree and layered them in the shoes, then wrapped and tied the laces around the shoes again. This worked quite a bit better, but still my feet were wet and cold, and every few hours I had to replace the balsam twigs.

My fingers were red then white from cold. As I walked they warmed but never enough to chase the chill away. When I used the knife to cut balsam branches, the skin on my hands was so cold it stung.

Eat something, Musia.

I'm doing my best, Mama. Please stop.

I chewed on balsam bark and needles, which were bitter and dried my mouth. Nuts on the ground were wet and would soon rot, but I collected and ate what I could. Squirrels bounced through the trees and forest floor around me, and on a couple of occasions a rabbit darted from beneath a bush. More often I found their tracks, as well as those of deer and other animals. I thought of killing a small animal with my knife, but I was drowning in a sea of damp cold, and hunger hollowed me.

Soon each step was more like a stumble. Words slurred through my lips, and an unstoppable shiver rattled my body.

Cold and hunger winnowed my thoughts to the need for warmth and the need for food. There were no other needs, no other desires, no planning, strategizing, just the constant focus on escaping what was killing me by placing one foot in front of the other.

Sing with me, Musia.

I don't think I can.

Yes, please, sing this with me:

> *Soothing songs and*
> *poems I weave because*
> *my soul longs for you.*
> *My soul desires the*
> *shadow of your hand,*
> *to know every one*
> *of your secrets—*

That's too sad, Mama.
Yes, my love. What about this:

> *I have a pair of goats,*
> *That rock the children,*
> *Ah! Wonder of wonders,*
> *How the goats rock*
> *the children—*

I smiled, remembering Mama singing this song when I was a little girl fussing over my food.

> *I have a pair of bears,*
> *That clean the house,*
> *Ah! Wonder of wonders,*
> *How the bears clean the house,*
> *And the goats rock*
> *the children—*

You forgot the roosters, Mama. You always forget the roosters that gather the kindling.

Ah, yes, my love, I always do.

Early one evening a faint tendril of wood smoke whispered to my nostrils. It tickled a memory of home, and I followed it, mesmerized.

Well before I reached the edge of the woods, I could see through bare branches a broad field leading to a clutch of farmhouses and barns. I lay on my belly and crawled like a snake through dead leaves and loamy dirt to the edge of the woods. From there I looked through bare blackthorn and autumn-browned thistle into the houses, like some woodland creature in one of Papa's books. Smoke rose from chimneys, and the sounds of men poking away at last-minute chores echoed from a barn and the far side of a house. A beaten and pocked dirt road led from the homes slantways through a field, disappearing over a rounded hilltop.

The back of a barn faced the woods. Between me and it lay a potato cellar.

Wait for dark, Musia.

I will, Mama, I will.

That night there was no moon, only near-perfect darkness. The metal latch to the potato cellar gave a slight scratch, and the door creaked on its aged hinges. With the door closed, darkness was total, but the air, though cool and damp, was warmer inside.

Feeling the black space in front of me with my hands, I found my way to a bin and grabbed a large, hard potato. Then I sat with my back against the bin's short, wooden gate. The dirt-encrusted skin peeled easily with my knife. The potato crunched like an apple when I bit into it and tasted sweet and starchy.

My eyes became somewhat adapted to the darkness, and I could make out shadowy forms of the bins and walls. It was too cold to take my coat off. There was only one way in and out of the cellar.

What if someone comes, neshomeleh?

A warm pulse of worry fluttered in my chest.

It's late. No one will come.

But what about morning?

Mama, I'm warmer here than I am in the forest. And I'm eating.

I ate what I could of the potato, then wrapped as many as I could in Mrs. Voitenko's scarf. I sat back down with my legs stretched out, my back resting against the hard wood of a bin and pulled the collar of Mama's blouse to my nose. Her scent had faded even more.

One hand patted the heavy, brass key to our home and penknife in the breast pocket of the coat, and I tilted my head back to sleep. Around me, fat and lazy rats nudged through potatoes, and one scurried past my feet. Without opening my eyes, I curled up my legs and covered them with the coat. Sleeping with rats was something I'd long grown accustomed to.

...

Musia, wake up, my love, wake up!

My eyes opened to darkness. Soft dawn light pinched through cracks in the potato cellar's door.

You have to go, neshomeleh!

I know, I know, Mama.

My legs uncurled, and a startled rat wiggled from where it had been tucked into my coat for warmth. My hands held my cramping belly, and I watched the darkened form of another rat run along a ceiling beam.

Potatoes aren't enough, Mama.

Musia, you must go.

The penknife's blade squeaked, mouse-like, as it opened. My body kept still, and my eyes wandered through the dim landscape of the small cellar. The scratching of rats surrounded me, and I caught the outline of one from the corner of my eye, but I waited. Outside, a crow cawed, and another answered. Through the door's seams, the outside world brightened, but I remained still.

Musia, you need go!

I won't survive on nuts and potatoes.

Musia!

A moment more—

A rat poked its head from a bin and sniffed the air. My body tensed as the rat eased out from the bin, then I leapt. One hand pressed its body into the floor. The rat screeched, its body flailing, legs scratching at my hands. Its head twisted to bite at my fingers with its long front teeth.

Its screams sickened me, and my muscles stiffened with fear and disgust as its body coiled and legs thrashed in my hand. I stabbed at the rat's neck but missed, and the blade hit the ground. I stabbed again and again at the rat, but only cut it. Its thrashing and shrieking intensified.

Its neck, Musia, slice its neck!

I'm trying to, Mama!

I bore my weight down on the rat's body and with a careful thrust, stabbed the blade into its neck and sliced out at an angle. It shrieked from pain and fear, its blood dribbled onto my fingers, and I stabbed its neck again.

The rat's so loud, Musia! Run, please run, before someone comes.

The dying rat flailed in my hand, and my eyes turned to see the first copper light of dawn filter through the door. My imagination conjured an image of a man's body standing outside, ready to throttle me as I'd done to the rat.

I let go of the still little body, picked up my potato-laden bundles with one hand, and opened the latch to the door, listening for any human sounds. All was quiet, so I picked the rat off the ground and stooped outside the cellar into the waxing daylight and cold, metallic winter. Blood was on my hand from the rat and a small cut.

I stepped away from the cellar and ran across the field in the growing light.

"Stop! Stop!"

I turned to see a stout, stub of a man standing by the corner of the barn, a pitchfork in his hand. He wore wool pants tucked into tall barn boots and suspenders over a black sweater that bunched at his waist. Anger furrowed his brows.

His eyes caught mine, and I stopped. The weight of his potatoes, and I suppose his rat, weighed on my arms and the coat.

"Who are you?" He signaled with the pitchfork for me to come to him.

Don't go to him, neshomeleh. Run, please run!

"A forest nymph!" I turned, pushed through the thistle and blackthorn, and ran into the woods.

• • •

Over the next few weeks, I wandered from forest to forest, using tree moss as my compass. I set a course north and then east, believing Mama wouldn't have gone too far in any one direction or hidden in a farmhouse or small village. When in a forest, I walked during the day and did my best to keep my various wounds clean in small streams. Lice picked at my skin and fell out in droves when I dunked my head or found the courage to strip and hold my entire body in the water, but I could never get rid of them.

When I had to cross fields, I waited for night. Sometimes a village or copse of farms bordered the fields, and I hid as close as I dared to look for Mama. If a potato cellar was near enough, I snuck into it and filled my bundles and pockets with potatoes. Rats, often fat and lazy, were reliable inhabitants, and I got better at killing them with my hands and knife, though I never got used to the muddy flavor and softness of their raw flesh.

Winter took firmer hold, and the temperature remained below freezing each night and most days. The sun rarely came out, and many days were full of wet snow or rain or both. A determined shiver rattled my body, and I stopped through the day to replace the balsam twigs that made up more and more of my shoes. The ends of my toes and the heels and balls of my feet were calloused, the skin hard and broken, the toenails soft and cracked, and all of it ached or stung as I walked. My thoughts often stuttered, and my body felt stiff and clumsy. Potato cellars gave me a chance to dry out a little and have a warmer night, but my sleep was anxious and shallow.

A few times I came upon bodies. Their skin looked soft, as if it were melting from the bone, and black. Their mouths and eyes were bone, putrefying flesh, and expressions of horror.

Don't look, neshomeleh.

I had to be sure Mama wasn't among them.

Another day voices of men drifted through the woods, but I ran from them before I could see who they were and what they were doing.

With the cold, foraging in the forest was harder. Bugs were rare, and acorns and beechnuts that had fallen in abundance during the fall lay rotten on the wet earth, though I ate them when I could. Hunger sometimes impelled me to put something, anything, into my mouth to chew on. Gnawing on bark and twigs helped, but neither was enough to stop the cramps when they came. One day, after eating nothing but bark—I'd run out of potatoes two days before—I found owl dung, furry from the rodents it had eaten, and ate it. It was disgusting, but the pain subsided a little, and this, with fox dung, became my last-choice option.

And I walked and walked, day after day, until I entered an immense forest. As I left the field of frozen stubble I'd crossed in the dark, it was as if the air pressure had changed. The forest closed around me; its atmosphere and quiet was unsettling.

I dug a little grave and, covered by the boughs of a few pine trees, slept through the day. At night I wandered farther into the forest and stopped when I found another pine stand beneath which I could dig another little grave. Morning came, and my eyes opened to three deer pulling at the little buds at the ends of the pine branches. Their eyes were nervous, and they ate with a deep sense of caution. When I sat up, they darted away. I tried to eat one of the little buds, but the flavor was sharp, and it dried my mouth.

For two days I walked without any sign of a break to this forest—no villages or farmhouses, just kilometer after kilometer of hardwoods and occasional stands of pine. Nuts were scarce, as was any other food. I watched other animals to see what they ate, but the cold limited their number, and most—squirrels, foxes every so often, and rabbits—ran the moment we saw each other.

It snowed one night, a dry, fluffy snow that hung in the trees and covered the ground. The air was bitter cold the next morning, and it took all my will to get my muscles to cooperate.

Excited birds chirped, and my eyes followed the noise to a tall, leafless bush. Hanging from its limbs were bright red, withered bunches of berries; some were covered by caps of bright white snow. Little blackbirds chirped as each landed on a branch, plucked a berry, then flew to another perch to eat it.

The berries were sweet at first, but turned sour, with a sharp aftertaste. I waited a moment to see what would happen. My cramps eased, so I ate more and put some in one of my bundles and kept walking. A few hours later a deep, sharp cramp, different from those caused by hunger, started in my belly. I thought to walk through it, but within a few minutes the cramp was too painful to walk.

A tall spruce, its branches dusted with snow, was the only place I could dig a little grave and hope to hide. As I dug, I vomited red berry juice. The cramps eased, then their intensity built, and I vomited more red juice plus seeds and yellow bile.

I tore into the earth with the rusted metal shovel blade. I threw up again, then dug some more. Finally, the hole was deep enough for me to lie in with my knees curled up to my chest. I dragged what branches I could to my hole and used them to cover me like a mouse in its burrow.

Tears ran down my cheeks from pain, and I vomited through the night.

Mama, was I so bad that you had to leave me at the river?

Oh, no, my love, no.

Then why did you leave me?

Because I love you, neshomeleh.

But I failed you.

I wanted to die, to be done, to be free, but the pain and vomiting continued into the next day and with it came the liquid opening of my bowels. I ate snow for water, but it made me shiver. I chewed on spruce needles, but they dried my mouth, and I had to eat more snow. Around me, my tracks roiled the snow, which was stained first red, then yellow from bile and fluid stool.

Large, fluffy clouds rolled past the stars that night, and I fell into a dreamless sleep.

Sunlight poked through the cover to my little grave the next morning, and something shook the spruce branches above my head so that snow fell onto me and ran down into the collar of my coat.

"Mała dziewczynka, obudź się." My eyes turned toward the voice of a man speaking Polish, telling me to wake up. His boots were large and leathery, wrapped in brown wool cloth up over his wool pants to the tops of his calves. He squatted onto his haunches, a gun in one hand and two dead rabbits tied together by twine hung over one shoulder, and he wore a thick, brown wool coat. An ammunition belt was strung across his chest.

"Are you the *Gajowy?*" I asked in Polish.

A smile broke across his whisker-stubbled face. "No. I'm the man who killed the *Gajowy."*

A Warm Fire

"**W**hy did you kill the Gajowy?"

The man's eyes relaxed. "He deserved what he got."

He cradled his gun in one arm and wiped his aged, sun-reddened cheeks, then looked at the snow around my little grave. "I wasn't sure what I'd find beneath this tree."

My neck and chin ached from tension, and I kept my hands on the ground beneath me to steady my shaking. "What do you mean?"

"There's a lot of blood and shit in the snow."

"It's not blood. I ate some berries that made me sick."

A laugh huffed from him, but his lips did not smile. "Are you alone?"

"Yes, I'm looking for my mother. Her name is Fruma."

"Fruma what?"

Don't tell him.

Why, Mama?

He'll know you're Jewish.

What if he can help?

What man with a gun will help a Jew?

"Perlmutter, Fruma Perlmutter," I said.

Musia, you bad girl!

I had to.

He'll know you're a Jew.

I'm dying anyway, Mama.

"No, I don't know her. You're a Jew?"

Say no, Musia!

The cramps from the berries had lessened, but cold, hunger, vomiting, and the watery running of my bowels had hollowed me. "I am."

Musia!

He looked out into the forest then to me. "Get up."

. . .

We walked to where another man—much younger, with black hair, a beard, and haunted eyes—stood in a small clearing with a rifle cradled in his arms. Sunlight reflected bright white off the wet snow into his squinting eyes. "Who is this?"

The older man carried his gun in one hand and adjusted the rabbits slung over his shoulder. "A Jew."

The young man raised his rifle and aimed it at me. A low *pkewww* left his lips, and he smiled.

Neshomeleh, ask them their names.

Why, Mama?

If they know you, maybe they won't shoot you.

I wrapped my arms around my belly to fend off the ache of hunger and looked to the older man. "My name is Musia."

"What makes you think I want to know your name," he said.

The younger man slung his rifle over a shoulder and looked through the woods.

"It's the polite thing to do."

The man scratched his chin. "My name is Paweł, and the boy is Tymon."

"Hello," I said to Tymon.

He turned from me. "We have to go."

Paweł pushed my shoulder to get me to move. The three of us, Tymon in the lead and Paweł behind me, crunched on dry snow and pushed through small pines, thick brush, and low-hanging branches laden with powdery snow that clung to my wool coat. I hugged my reddened and tender hands in my armpits to try to warm them, but I often had to push snow-covered branches from my face. My feet were also numb from snow leaking through the leaves and twigs I'd used to patch my shoes. Snow kicked up above my socks and beneath my dress onto exposed skin.

Before long, my body was shaking with cold, exhaustion, and hunger, and my legs had stiffened, making it difficult to lift my feet. The distance between Tymon and me grew, and Paweł urged me on with a terse word or a slight push.

The toe of my shoe caught on a branch hidden by snow, and I fell. I tried to break my fall with my hands, but I was too weak and landed hard on the rusted shovel blade in my coat. I turned onto my side and held my hand against where the blade had dug into my chest.

"Get up," Paweł said.

Tymon walked back toward us, and I heard the solid, metallic click of the rifle's bolt as he loaded a round. I turned to see him raising his gun.

"No," said Paweł.

"She's too slow."

"We may need her."

"For what? Look at her! She's dying. The best we can do for her is kill her now."

Paweł looked down at me, and his eyes softened as they met mine. "When was the last time you ate?"

Ask them to just leave you, Musia.

My body shuddered. "I can't remember."

"How long have you looked for your mother?" Paweł asked.

"Since August."

"You were in a ghetto, weren't you?"

"Yes."

He looked to Tymon and then back to me. "Have you seen any soldiers in this forest?"

Tymon's hands were white from squeezing the gun. "Yes," I lied.

"We're going to risk our lives for a Jew?" Tymon asked.

"She can tell us about these soldiers." Paweł reached into a large pocket in his coat and handed me a chunk of bread from a paper wrapper. From another pocket he handed me a small piece of dried meat. "Eat this, and we'll talk about the soldiers near a warm fire."

He looked to Tymon. "You go ahead. We'll be along."

Paweł leaned his gun against a tree branch and sat next to me and lit a cigarette. The bread was dry and the meat so hard my gums bled, and my mouth ached, but the food soothed the pain in my belly. I finished, and we sat, quiet, as Paweł smoked.

Paweł shifted his weight as his rifle slid from the tree branch and fell into the snow. His head turned toward the gun.

Run into the forest, Musia!

My body coiled.

No, Mama.

Don't you want to find me?

I do, but—

Then do what I say!

No, Mama.

Paweł looked back to me, his eyebrows furrowed. I released the tension in my limbs, and his eyes softened. He coughed and spit a brown glob into the snow a few feet from me, pressed his cigarette deep into the snow and stood. "Let's go," he said, wiping snow from his gun.

My hands and feet burned with cold, but the shaking had subsided, and my legs were stronger. He walked behind me, and I followed the tracks left by Tymon. We passed through thick, hardwood forest and then into a thinner forest of pine. Vertical stripes of snow clung to the trunks of the mast-like trees, but if I turned to look behind at Paweł, I saw only gray bark mottled by dark green lichen that grew like rime ice. Daggers of sunlight cut through the trees to the forest floor. The snow was a bit deeper than in the hardwoods, but we had less brush and fewer fallen trees to pick our way through.

After a couple of hours, the forest sloped upward, and blue sky was visible through the tree trunks. In the distance was the gentle patter of a stream and the faint scent of a wood fire. "Stop here." Paweł stepped a few paces ahead and called out, "Just dear old Paweł, boys. All's well." A man's head and upper body appeared at the crest of the rise, and he waved to us.

At the top were two trenches with two men in each. At the edge of one trench was a machine gun mounted on a flat tripod and aimed down the slope. In the other, two men held German machine guns strapped over their shoulders. Looking out into the distance, I saw on either side dim outlines of more trenches with men watching the woods.

"Two hares and a Jewess," said a young man with round glasses and barely a wisp of beard as he pulled his hands from the machine gun to blow on them. "We can eat the rabbits, but what the hell do we do with the Jew?"

Paweł looked back at me. "She's seen German soldiers."

"SS?"

"I don't know yet."

Paweł and I walked down the backside of the hill into a dale where a stream wound through. We followed the stream for a few minutes, and the scent of wood smoke grew until it filled my nostrils. A few moments more and we entered a camp of tents pitched among the trees. Small huts that looked like potato cellars were dug into the hillsides that rose up either side of the little valley created by the stream. Men and a few women huddled around four or five fires. Farther into the woods, beyond the tents, was a line of about ten tarpaulin-covered supply carts and a paddock fenced in by rope and pine boughs. Horses foraged from the ground or leaned their long, brown necks past the fence to pluck what they could from the trees with their lips and teeth. In among the trees and wet snow, the whole place looked like a fairytale.

They're brave to have fires and live like this, Mama.

They are not friends, Musia.

"Who are you?" I asked as Paweł led me toward one of the earthen huts. We sat on a couple of logs set beside a small fire pit with a few charred pieces of wood in it.

He smiled. "Hunters."

My eyes drifted to the rabbits hanging from his shoulder.

"Rabbits, yes," he said, "but also Germans and anyone helping them."

"I don't like the Germans, either."

"I'm not surprised. So did you really see soldiers?"

Lie to him, Musia. He's looking for a reason to keep you alive.

He'll know.

I turned my eyes from Paweł, ashamed of the lie I had told. "No. Only farmers and dead bodies since I left the ghetto."

"That's what I thought."

The men and women looked from their fires as we passed, and the shadow left by the yellow Star of David burned on my chest. "Please don't shoot me."

Paweł frowned. "We don't kill children."

There aren't any children here, Musia.

I know, Mama.

How could there be no children among them?

I searched Paweł's eyes for the truth. "Where are the children?"

His frown deepened, and he looked away from me into the forest. "I don't know."

Musia, look at their hard eyes. They'll kill you.

I don't think Paweł will let them.

Neshomeleh, this man is no friend.

You don't know that, Mama.

I hugged my arms around my chest and looked to Paweł. "Can I stay with you?"

No, Musia, come to me, find me. My darling girl, safety is with me, with Tchiya.

I'm not giving up, Mama.

I feel you letting go.

For the first time since you left me I'm not alone.

I didn't leave you.

I disappointed you, and you left.

No, neshomeleh. What I did was out of love.

Paweł scratched his bristly chin. "You would have to contribute a weapon."

Musia, he can't keep you safe.

In the forest, I'll die.

I pulled the penknife from my coat, opened it, and thrust the blade toward him, but my hand and arm quivered, and the blade was pathetically small. Paweł's eyes narrowed. "Put that away. You look ridiculous," he said, then stood. "I'm sorry. We have a rule. We don't take anyone who doesn't have a weapon."

"Please."

"Stay the night by my fire and have some food, but no." He walked away with his rifle and the rabbits. Tears filled my eyes. For a moment, I hadn't been alone. I could have been part of something with other people. Instead, I was cast away, unwanted, part of nothing. I belonged only to Tchiya and Mama.

I miss you so much, Mama.

I miss you, too, neshomeleh.

I don't want to die out in this forest.

I know.

How would you ever know where I am or what became of me?

...

Paweł returned without the rabbits and told me to follow him. Without a word he led me through the camp to the woods.

"Paweł?"

"Yes."

"Are there any other Jews here?"

He stopped to look at me. "No. Why?"

"I'm looking for my sister Tchiya too."

He rubbed the back of his neck. "There are no Jews here."

He led me into the woods, and I thought he might turn on his word and send me right away into the cold, darkening afternoon. Above the pine crowns lay a bleak, slate sky. Though I was with people, loneliness tightened my chest with greater force than ever before.

In my mind I heard Mama warning me to run, to leave this man and his people, that he was leading me into the woods to kill me or hurt me in some other way. I hated him for his rejection, but I wanted warm food and a fire, if only for one last night.

I pulled the collar of Mama's blouse up to my nose, but nothing was left of her, only the lingering tang of vomit and dirt.

Paweł brought me to the edge of the pine woods where the forest began to return to a mix of hardwood, brush, and pine. "Grab what dead wood you can," he said and began pulling fallen branches from the snow-covered ground. Both of us filled our arms, and we walked back to the camp where he built a fire from logs stacked next to his little forest home while I watched.

"Where are you from?" I asked.

He looked up. "Warszawa," he said then blew on the budding flames.

"What did you do?"

His eyes tensed. "I taught economics at *Warszawa Szkoła Główna Handlowa.*"

"You were a professor?" I remembered Papa, his fine suits, pince-nez resting on his nose, groomed and stern in his library, but saw none of that in Paweł.

"Yes."

"My Papa was a professor at the university—"

"I don't want to talk, Musia." A small flame took hold and hissed as moisture in the wood burned off. He stood, said, "Don't let the fire go out," and walked into the heart of the camp.

I sat on a log close to the fire and fumed at his cruelty. Lice became more active in the warmth and bit at my scalp and skin. I dug my fingers into my hair, armpits, and crotch to scratch at the lice like a stray dog. In my threadbare coat and clothes, I looked every bit the outcast from the world of people.

You're a lovely girl, Musia.

I'm an unwanted girl.

Not to me, not to Tchiya.

Where are you both?

Soon I would be cast out into the forest and begin the slow process of dying ... again. I knew I had to go back toward the people who had killed us in the ghetto and who had killed us in the haystacks. If I could make it to a village or set of farms tucked into some small vale, there would be potato cellars and haylofts to hide in and steal food from. I had to be near people.

I pulled the coat tight around my body and remembered winter in the ghetto and how the cold, guards, work, starvation, and *łapankas* were a grindstone turning us to dust. We had no wood for heat, the food rations grew smaller, the stench was unbearable and inescapable, and the number of ill people grew larger. Bodies littered the streets until they became bloated and obscene. A single *łapanka* took the men of the *Judenrat's* burial committee, which left the duty of hauling bodies to the pit to emaciated women. It was more than they could ever keep up with.

My friends disappeared or withered until there were only empty spaces within which a person once lived. Zofia was the first, followed soon after by Helena and Julian. Guards beat Tauba to death, and German SS snatched up Gerda and Rena in a *łapanka*. Each loss hurt as much as the one before and woke within me once more the realization that it could soon be my turn, or worse, Mama or Tchiya's. I was terribly, terribly afraid that one day, any day, the Germans would take them, or the guards would beat them to death, and my dreams reflected this intense anxiety. In the most intense and real dream, I was wandering naked through the ghetto seeking Mama and Tchiya but unable to speak to any of the ghost-like people wandering the street. I screamed and screamed, but no sound emerged. I was alone and helpless.

In the ghetto, fear grew and became tauter with each death. My stomach ached from fear and hunger, my temples pulsed with the sensation that death was nearing my family, and acidic vomit rose and burned the back of my throat, sometimes lasting for hours.

Loss and fear took its toll on others as well. Death came not just from a bullet, beating, or illness, but also from despair. Some walked into a sniper's bullet or lay down in the street and slipped away. By morning, they were another of many frozen corpses waiting for the pit.

And the decrees by the Germans never ceased. Each day brought some new demand. They reduced rations. They required us to bring them money or gold or any other valuables they could think of. They used the decrees to twist the knife a little deeper because they knew we had nothing. When we couldn't meet their demands—there was no way we could—they required the *Judenrat* to bring them some number of Jews for a *łapanka.* There were terrible arguments as the *Judenrat* sat in judgment to decide whom the Germans should kill. Of course, the *Judenrat* had no choice—the quota in lives had to be met—so they sought out the enfeebled and sick.

This is why they selected Hannah. One day, the Germans ordered all Jews to turn over a quota of jewelry. I felt the weight of the coins and last of Mama's jewelry in my coat and asked Mama what I should do.

She held her finger to her lips and moved toward me. "Quiet, Musia." Mrs. Zelinski looked up at Mama, but Mama ignored her. "Remember, rainy day, these are only for a rainy day, nothing else."

"But the Germans—"

"Will do whatever they are going to do no matter what."

"But maybe if we—"

Mama looked to Mrs. Zelinski, whose dull, bleary eyes stared at us, then turned to me and placed a hand on my cheek. "No, neshomeleh. We need them far more than the Germans do."

The next day, as Mama and the others worked, the same tall, lean man with round tortoiseshell glasses who had seen Hannah that first day in the ghetto knocked, then entered our small room. He was much leaner than before, and his glasses were held together with string and bits of tape. His face was gaunt and eyes hollow, but he wore a long, warm, military-style wool coat. Behind him were two other members of the *Judenrat,* equally as gaunt, wearing similar coats. Behind them, three black-uniformed Ukrainian guards loitered in the hallway, rifles slung over their shoulders and batons dangling from their belts.

The man looked to Hannah, who was sitting on her bed playing with Ania. "Hannah Zelinski, you are to come with us."

Hannah's eyes fell.

"She's waiting for her mother and too young to work," I said.

The man looked at me. "You're not on our list yet. Hannah, come with us now, or the guards will come drag you out." The two *Judenrat* members' heads bowed.

I opened my mouth to speak, but Hannah held her hand up and said, "Musia, don't worry. I have to go." She placed her hand on Ania's back. "It's all right, Ania"—her eyes turned to me—"Musia will play with you." Hannah put her coat on and limped to the door. She turned to me and said, "Tell Mother I love her," and then she left with the men.

I didn't know what to do. Who do you go to? Who do you ask for help? How do you stop the murder of a single girl when each day there are countless more bodies in the street and the Germans take whole families to kill?

I pulled Ania close, and we cried and waited for the others to come home.

Mama was the first to walk through the door. I ran to her, my face burned red by tears, and wrapped my arms around her body, taking in the scent of her and her warmth.

She held me close and asked, "What is it, Musia?"

"They took Hannah."

Her body tensed. "My darling girl." She patted my back and asked me to stay with Ania while she waited for Janusz and Mrs. Zelinski in the hallway. I pulled Ania close to me, and soon we heard footsteps on the stairs.

"What is it?" asked Mrs. Zelinski. Her voice was raw and cracked.

There was a delicate murmur and then a ragged, croupy moan, "No, no, no ..."

Rosa and Belen came into the room. Their once lithe teenage bodies and dewy skin were gaunt and pocked with bruises from beatings and sores from lice. Behind them, through the door, I saw Mama holding Mrs. Zelinski close. She tucked her face into the nape of Mama's neck, and her body heaved with each sob.

Rosa said, "What happened?"

"Hannah's gone," I said.

Belen held her younger sister's hand and led her to her bed, where she held her as they both wept. "They're going to come for us all," Belen said, her eyes dark with anger and fear. "I heard a German say they are going to get rid of our disgusting race."

"Stop it," cried Rosa, snot bubbling from her nose. "Please, just stop."

Ania started to cry. "Is Mama going to die?" Her eyes were big and brown and wet.

I leaned toward Belen and whispered, "Don't talk like that."

"It's the truth."

Rosa looked at her sister. "I don't care if it's true. Right now, we are here, together, and Mama will come home, and that's all I want to think about."

Belen lowered her head. "It's better to know."

"Not tonight, it isn't," Rosa said.

Mama walked through the door holding Mrs. Zelinski. "Is Janusz home yet?"

"No, Mama, not yet," I told her.

"That's all right. I'm sure he'll be here soon with Gilda," Mama said, referring to Mrs. Joselewicz.

Mama guided Mrs. Zelinski to her bed, where she sat with her fingers woven into her curly hair, staring silently at the floor. There was no ration that night, but Mama took three potatoes and a pot down to the kitchen to wait in line to boil them into a simple soup. While she was gone, Tchiya arrived, and I told her the *Judenrat* had selected Hannah for a *łapanka*.

"Figures those cowards came while we're at work," she said.

Mrs. Zelinski's eyes looked up through her tangled, oily mass of curls to Tchiya. "Have you seen Janusz?"

Pain and worry formed at the edges of Tchiya's eyes. "No. Why?"

Mrs. Zelinski's gaze returned to the floor.

"He isn't home yet," Rosa said.

"Have you seen our mother?" Belen asked.

"She was behind me with Ania's mother, but they stopped to talk with Mrs. Berman." Mrs. Berman lived two floors below us and often issued forth whatever news and gossip she managed to collect during the day. Much of what she passed along was untrue, but she was right enough times to worry people whenever she spoke.

At this news, Belen and Rosa's bodies eased. A happy spark lit Ania's eyes. "Mama," she said.

Soon, the door opened and Mrs. Cukier and Mrs. Joselewicz came in. Ania leapt from my side and wrapped her arms around her mother's waist. Mrs. Cukier's hand trembled as she placed it against Ania's back.

"Is Janusz home?" asked Mrs. Cukier.

Mrs. Zelinski looked up through her curls, her eyes wide. "No. Why? What did Mrs. Berman say?"

Mrs. Cukier's eyes fell to her daughter, and she brushed the hair on the back of Ania's head. "She said the Germans took all of the men and boys in his group."

Mrs. Zelinski pressed the palms of her hands into her eyes as if to hold back a flood of tears and rocked back and forth rasping, "No, no, no, my babies, no, no ..."

Tears fell from Tchiya's eyes, and she dropped onto her bed and curled her legs into her belly, her back to us. Her body shook in time to her weeping.

"Where's Hannah?" asked Mrs. Joselewicz.

"She was taken too," Belen replied.

Mrs. Cukier sat on her bed, pulled Ania into her lap, and held her close.

Mrs. Joselewicz sat beside Mrs. Zelinski and placed a hand on her knee. "Let's hope they're together."

Mrs. Zelinski said nothing, but her eyes closed, and I felt her heart breaking. There was nothing we could do. We all knew where Janusz and Hannah were going, perhaps already there, maybe already dead. That they die together was the best we could hope for.

Mama returned with the soup and looked around the room. Tchiya and Mrs. Zelinski lay in their beds sobbing, and the rest of us sat with our heads lowered and eyes vacant. I lifted my eyes to hers. "Janusz is gone too."

Mama wiped her eyes with the back of her hand. "We need to eat. Mrs. Cukier?"

"You don't have to share," Mrs. Cukier said.

"I know, but I want to. Please." Mrs. Cukier accepted some for her and Ania as did Mrs. Joselewicz, Belen, and Rosa. When Mama came to Mrs. Zelinski, she said no.

Mama sat on Tchiya's bed and rubbed her back. "I'm sorry, my love."

Tchiya lifted her head. "Why?"

"Why am I sorry?"

"No, why are they doing this to us?"

"I don't know, my love"—she set the pan on the floor and looked at me as she rubbed Tchiya's back—"but I do know that despair will take us before the Germans do."

I turned my eyes away because I knew despair had crept into our hearts.

The next morning the air was bitter cold, and the sun was still below the horizon. Mrs. Cukier tucked Ania in with me and then left. Tchiya lifted her body from bed and stumbled into the hallway. Mama watched her then leaned down and whispered into my ear, "Take good care of Ania, neshomeleh, and never forget that I love you."

My chest tightened. "Where are you going?"

"Nowhere, my love; I'll be home tonight, I promise." She kissed my cheek and waved as she left the room.

Mrs. Zelinski tossed the covers from her bed, sat up, and swung her feet to the floor. Her eyes were bloodshot and dark; puffy folds curled beneath them; her face was ashen and gray. Her shoulders shivered, and she pulled her coat tight around her body. "Goodbye, Musia." She shuffled out the door and down the hallway.

In the evening, Mrs. Berman knocked on the door and poked her head in. Her voice was quiet to the point of somber. "Mrs. Zelinski's dead."

"How do you know?" Mrs. Joselewicz asked.

"Her body's lying in the snow by the river."

We burned the wood in the Zelinski's beds for warmth and picked through their belongings. It wasn't much, but it was all they had left to give.

● ● ●

"I told you not to let the fire go out," Paweł said, walking out of the darkness and handing me a watery bowl of stewed rabbit and potato. He placed some tinder and a few logs on the coals and blew on them until flame burst from the tinder and caught on the wood. He grabbed another log from the pile of wood, dropped it on the ground near me, and sat on it with his legs crossed and his body slouched around his bowl of stew.

In silence, we ate, and then he lit a cigarette and smoked with his eyes intent on the fire. When the flames ebbed, he stood and placed a log or two on the fire then sat down again.

Out in the woods, among the tents and log and dirt huts, people sat near fires. Every so often, a set of glowing eyes glared up at me, but no one approached our fire. They spoke among themselves and laughed, and Paweł sat silent as a stone.

"Why won't you talk to me?"

"I have nothing to say."

"If I ask you a question, will you answer it?"

"Depends."

"What do you have to live for?"

His eyes turned to me, and the fire reflected off them. "To kill Germans."

"That's not enough."

He thought for a moment, then started to say something, but stopped and turned his attention away from me back to the fire.

"There are people who need me," I said.

"Good." He didn't look up.

"They love me, Mama and Tchiya."

Paweł tossed his cigarette into the fire. "Don't tell me that."

"Are there people who love you?"

He pulled another cigarette from his pocket and lit it.

"Do you have a family?" I asked.

He spit into the fire and bowed his head so that his eyes stared down into his lap. "I suppose these people"—he nodded toward the fires among the trees—"are my family now."

"Paweł—"

"Stop it. I've fed you, and you're warm. Go find your family in the morning because you can't stay here." He stood. "Don't let the fire go out if you want to stay warm. I won't get up to help you start another."

"Dobranoc i słodkich snów," I said as if he were Papa padding out of my bedroom in his slippers after tucking me into bed, but Paweł walked into his hut without a word.

Kindness won't work on him, Musia.

I know, but it's polite to say goodnight.

The night closed in around me, and the air grew colder, sharper. I scooted closer to the flames, pulled my knees close to my chest, and wrapped the coat over my legs. After a few minutes, Paweł came out and threw a wool blanket at me. "You can sleep on this."

I cleared snow away from the ground then laid down with the blanket tucked around me. The fire burned warm, and my stomach was full, but in the morning, I would begin dying again.

I'm waiting for you, Musia.

Dobranoc i słodkich snów, Mama.

Goodnight to you, my love.

Kasia

I woke in the middle of the night to the hiss of snow landing on embers. The wood had burned to cinders as I slept, and my body shivered beneath the blanket Paweł had thrown out to me. I placed fresh wood on the embers and blew up a flame, then sat with the blanket wrapped around my shoulders and held my hands over the budding fire to gather its warmth.

The forest beyond the glow of my little fire was a shadowbox fantasy of statuesque pines with little orange galaxies of embers floating within a crystalline mist. Except for the hiss of the fire and the delicate pit and pat of snow falling in the woods, the camp slept beneath the protective watch of sentries scattered among the trees.

Tears welled in my eyes. Come morning, Paweł would send me out into the woods. My mind created elaborate scenes of my corpse lying beneath a cover of snow, my expression frozen in despair or pain as I'd seen on so many bodies. I wanted to hope that Paweł's heart would change, that he couldn't send a little girl, even a Jewish girl, out into the woods to die, but hope was an indulgence, a conceit and denial of the reality I'd lived since the day they took Papa away.

My thoughts were broken by the whinny of a horse that carried through the woods in a dull echo.

There are wagons, neshomeleh.

I wiped my eyes and looked toward the paddock at the edge of the camp. The snow was too thick and the night too dark to see anything other than islands of gentle, orange embers.

Watch for shadows moving around the embers, my love.

All was still.

Walk just beyond the edge of light among the trees.

Only a faint wheezing came from Paweł's hut, no sign of movement. I crept to the fringe of light and passed through into darkness, moving toward trees and snow with the blanket wrapped over me, like a dark, woolen ghost. Powdery snow came up to my calves and deadened the sound of each step to a thin whisper. My eyes adjusted to the dark, but still I brushed against pine trunks and almost tripped over a fallen branch. With each misstep, I paused to look for shadows moving among the embers, then continued until I reached the paddock and the wagons.

Lifting the tarp of one wagon and reaching into it, I found a long, warm, woolen coat. I dropped it on the ground and went deeper beneath the tarp, finding more warm clothing: woolen socks, mittens, pants, and a shawl. Deeper in the wagon were pairs of boots tied together by their shoestrings.

I pulled brown wool pants on over the skirts of my dresses and used a shoestring to tie two belt loops together, so the waist was snug. Then I rolled the cuffs up, so they wouldn't drag. My tattered socks peeled off like dead skin and were replaced by two pairs of warm wool socks. The boots I pulled from the wagon were two sizes, but they were warm, and the leather was good.

I ran my hand over the breast of the coat and noticed no shadow was left from a yellow Star of David. The coat fell to my calves, and the shawl covered my head, the ends draped around my neck like a scarf. Everything felt so big—I must have looked like a bedraggled waif dressed in her father's clothes.

I dared not leave behind the coat Mama gave me with its valuables. Paweł's blanket worked as a sling to carry the coat, extra socks, and the rusted shovel blade. The penknife and brass house key as well as Mama's and Mrs. Voitenko's scarves were tucked into the inside pockets of the coat with the coins.

I rolled the tarp down and left my worn socks and shoes in a heap.

Paweł will chase you, Musia.

He hunts Germans, not Jews.

You don't know that.

Let him chase me then.

He'll kill you for stealing.

What choice do I have if I want to find you, Mama?

I moved to another wagon. This one held food supplies, potatoes and loaves of bread that were hard and frozen. I had no idea why the people in this camp had dug shelters for themselves, but not a root cellar. I took a half loaf of bread and some potatoes, then put the mittens on and hoisted the sling over one shoulder.

Mama, this will keep me going for a little while.

Yes, my love.

Fern-like snowflakes settled on my eyelashes and melted on my cheeks and filled my footprints as I crept away from the paddock into the woods. The boots were large and awkward, but also sturdy and warm. Each step made little, creaking mouse sounds, but the snow swirled in a slight breeze and fell in a dense lace curtain. Somewhere in the woods, lookouts hid in their trenches, ready to shoot. I stepped, then listened, then stepped again.

The ground rose. Rather than seek its crest I sought to walk its shoulder, where there was less likelihood of a trench. Step then listen, step then listen until I leaned into the side of the hill, its top an unknown distance away, and heard a muffled cough. I closed my eyes and listened for any human vibration on the wind.

"Bądź cicho," a man's voice shushed in Polish.

The voice whirled with the snow but seemed to come from above me on the hill.

"Tak, tak," a man's voice responded.

Another step and I listened for any sign they'd heard. Nothing. A step and I listened. Trees rose above me into the falling snow, and below was a gently gurgling creek. A step and eyes closed to listen, one step after another, until the hill sloped downward under my feet. A cough sounded, but snow, trees, and growing distance muted it. More cautious steps, and the distance grew until each step followed in quicker succession, and the need to remove myself from these woods was greater than the need for silence.

Every so often I stopped and opened the coat to let heat out but closed it as soon as my skin felt cool, then continued to trudge through the snow until sweat and exhaustion forced me to stop again. After a few hours, the snow eased, and a slate gray light lit the forest. Before long the tall, straight pines gave way to oak, beech, balsam, and denser underbrush. Pushing through it was tiring, and I had to stop more often to rest, but I dared not dig a little grave to sleep in. If Paweł and Tymon came after me, they would catch me up. Although new snow dulled my tracks, they would find me.

My eyes squinted in the white and gray light, and I kept my body moving forward. To where, I didn't know. I only knew I had been right earlier: I needed to be near people. I had to find a town where there would be people, food, and perhaps Mama.

■ ■ ■

The caw of a crow echoing through the forest is the voice of loneliness.

For two days, I walked. The snow that was once light and easy to manage became compacted beneath its own weight and, I suppose, the weight of heavy, freezing air. Each step burned in my legs and lungs and wore at my body and spirit. Bread provided some succor, as did nibbling at a potato, but the old feelings of despair and shame strengthened as the distance and effort to reach Mama and Tchiya grew.

A crow's cackle sounded, gray as the forest, and a breeze rattled thin branches above my head. Tears dribbled down my cheeks, and the salt stung their chapped skin. My knees shook, and a sharp pain cut into my chest. Sobs broke from my lips, my throat constricted and quivered with each gulp of air, and I dropped onto the snow with the thought that only death would bring relief.

This isn't what I taught you, neshomeleh.

What is THIS, *Mama?*

The defeat of love by despair.

A stream of steamy air spread from my mouth, and I closed my eyes. An image passed through me of Mama, her face drawn, her eyes pitted by exhaustion as she tucked me into bed. I complained of hunger and argued that the Germans and the guards were never going to give us peace. She smiled and said, "Despair cannot take root when there is love, and I love you so much."

...

I woke to a darkening sky, my body stiff from cold. I ate some bread and gnawed at a potato, which chased away the ache in my belly. A light snow began to fall. I welcomed it, as it would help hide my tracks. With only the needs of my body as a clock—eat when hungry, sleep when tired—I stood, shook the snow off, and began to walk.

"I love you, Mama," I said to the sky. My despair lightened, but guilt was a more tenacious emotion. It clung like blight, and the only way to kill its growth was to find Mama and be forgiven.

Through the night I pushed through the snow and woods until the sun began its early morning glow. Weariness overtook me, and I found a balsam tree to dig a little grave

under and covered myself with branches. Sleep came easily;
I didn't care if I was found.

My eyes opened to deep metallic gray and a whiff of
wood smoke on the air. Brushing myself off, I walked in its
direction, listening for any signs of people in the woods, but
my footsteps and the tuneless caw of crows were the only
signs of life.

At the top of a small rise, the edge of the forest was close
enough for me to stay in the trees yet look down upon a
cluster of four farmhouses and small, bent barns tucked into
a swale at the crook of three low, sloping hills. A road of
packed snow ended amid the farmhouses and disappeared
up and over the hill to my right. A snow-covered field
separated the village from the forest, and broad, wide
fields spread from the gray buildings into the horizon. At
the border of the nearest field, beside a barn, a mound
indicated a potato cellar. I assumed its door faced the house
it belonged to.

Smoke rose from chimneys, and when a person—always
a woman or young girl or boy—left a house to walk to a
barn, my eyes widened, and loneliness pricked at my heart.
I wished to live in a warm home, safe from murderers
and death, free from fear, like the people bundled against
the snow walking to tend to their cows, a horse or two,
chickens, and perhaps some pigs. I imagined root cellars
beneath their houses filled with canned vegetables, berries
and jams, eggs, and cured meats and sausage wrapped in
burlap against the chill. For the pantry my mind conjured
flour, sugar, salt, and spices—thyme, nutmeg, mustard, and
rosemary—jars of potato *zupa* and bread and cake.

That was our home, neshomeleh.

I know, Mama.

We had so much, my love.

I miss it all.

As the light waned, the sound of a motor rose. A boy
ran from a barn into his home, and women looked from

doorways or windows and then withdrew inside, shutting them. A German military car with a canvas roof, knobby tires, and a black cross with white borders bounded over the hill pulling a black trailer covered by a tarp. The car bounced along the packed snow until it reached the center of the village and stopped. Four SS soldiers—one of them in an officer's uniform—eased out of the four thin metal doors. Thick leather belts with pistols in holsters were wrapped around their gray-blue wool coats, and each carried a machine gun, their fingers on the triggers as their eyes scanned the houses and then the fields and woods.

Don't let them see your eyes, Musia.

I lowered my head and listened for staccato bursts from the guns, ready to leap up and run if they came for me.

"Hallo," one of them called out. *"Herauskommen!"*

With those words, my body went cold. My eyes drifted over the snow and stubble of the field, into the village. A door opened, and the soldiers instinctively aimed their guns at it. An elderly man with a long, gray beard held his hands out in front of him and stepped from the house. He wore a dirty brown tunic and wool pants, but no coat.

A soldier walked toward him and patted his hands over the old man's body to search for a weapon. The old man raised his hands a bit higher and said something to the German. The officer shook his head and said something I couldn't hear. The soldier searching the old man stepped back and let the barrel of his gun drift downward.

The old man held his hands out in supplication. His eyes were fearful and his mouth slack. As he pleaded, the officer listened with his mouth set in a frown, then interrupted the old man with a wave of his hand and his head shaking no.

The three soldiers began to search through the nearest barn, taking small tin milk canisters and bundles of what I thought might be eggs. Then they went into the potato cellars and took sacks of potatoes. They loaded it all into the trailer. When they finished, the old man held his head in his hands, and the Germans left him standing in the center of his small village.

I waited for the car to pass over the hill and the sound of its engine to evaporate into late afternoon gray air before I crawled down the rise and disappeared back into the forest.

They won't stop hunting, Musia.

I know, Mama, but this was different.

Why?

The Ukrainian was scared.

I walked well past dark beneath a star-streaked sky. The air was crisp and cold, but the energy of plunging through snow and brush kept me warm until my legs tired from the effort. Another balsam tree, another little grave, and I slept, covered by a thick layer of wool and branches.

The next morning, I woke to sun breaking through the leafless canopy and shining into my eyes. I had a breakfast of near-solid bread and a frozen potato, then walked and searched for Mama and a village.

Day by day and week by week I walked through the forests during the day and crossed the fields between them at night. I ate what ground forage I could find, but to survive I relied on sneaking into the small villages that dotted the landscape. Each was a mirror image of the last with a handful of houses, barns, and potato cellars tucked within rolling hills to protect them from winter winds sweeping over stubbled, snow-covered fields.

During daylight I watched from the forest for danger or for any sign of Mama. The villages held women and children as well as the elderly but scarcely any men, which eased my fear of slipping into a barn or potato cellar at night to look for food or warmth. Unfortunately, inside the barns and cellars I found little food. There were hardly any cows and chickens and rarely any pigs or other livestock except for a plow horse or two. Milk tins often only held a few drops, though every so often I drew milk from a cow's teat and lapped it from my hand. If the hay in the loft was deep, I burrowed in like a nit to sleep and made sure to leave before sunrise.

If the barn was too close to the house or too far from the woods, I tried a potato cellar. Again, there were precious few potatoes, and I felt guilty taking more than a handful or two. Even the number of rats decreased, but not so much that I couldn't kill and eat one with my knife.

Beyond soldiers and men, dogs were a threat. The slightest noise raised their ire, and they bit me and nipped at my heels as I ran away. Their barking woke people who shouted curses at me, the dark figure racing across a field toward the forest, and sometimes bullets whistled past and thudded into muddy snow. No one chased me into the forest, and even the dogs stopped at the forest's edge. Perhaps they were afraid a gang of partisans or Jewish criminals—one of the epithets shouted at me—lurked just beyond the edge of light in the darkened forest.

Each adventure into a barn or potato cellar was a trauma, and on many days I didn't have the will or energy to slip into a village or even to walk. For days I would lie in my little grave daydreaming and speaking to the animals—foxes, birds, deer, squirrels, rabbits—that came near. Their wide, dark eyes showed little concern for the ragamuffin lying beneath the boughs as they picked around for food.

I daydreamed of Mama and our home and sitting with her and Tchiya and Papa at our dining room table, sharing just one more meal as a family. Occasionally these fantasies straddled the realm between dream and reality, and I could almost smell Papa's pipe and Mama's perfume and sense the texture of chicken and spiced, boiled potatoes and steamed carrots with thyme and basil, or hear Tchiya practicing the piano or her violin as Mama brought food to the table and Papa called for her in his stern voice.

I sang to myself and spoke with Mama. Memories came cascading from an unseen and unknowable well within me, and I cried.

Fear was ever present but subsided as I hid in my little grave. Only hunger, thirst, and indescribable cold could dislodge me from my retreat to confront the terror of venturing near people.

Though I could find food and warmth near people, the people themselves meant biting dogs, hatred, soldiers, bullets, capture, and death. Other than the animals of the forest, anything alive and connected to humans was my enemy. And yet more terrible than anything was the pain of being alone. Days and weeks went by without hearing a human voice. Imaginary conversations with Mama tumbled from my lips as I stumbled through the underbrush and snow, but aural hallucinations of voices in the woods threw me from fantasies into a state of abject fear. As much as I yearned for the comfort of human contact, the thought of seeing another person terrified me.

And then one day, as the forest transitioned into spring with ferns unfurling and buds easing into leaves, footsteps disturbed my conversation with Mama. Without a thought I dropped to my knees, and my eyes searched through dappled green forest. A squirrel hopped through dried leaves, and birds sang in trilling chirps, but there were no more steps. Bent low, I walked again, then heard the steps behind me in the woods.

That morning I'd left a village with some potatoes after drinking my fill of soured milk from a tin, and I wondered if this was someone coming to get me. Hunched over, I stepped quicker, but my feet crunched on leaves and broke dead twigs as the wool coat and bundle caught on thin, green-flecked branches of young trees and bushes. A bear couldn't be louder! So I stood to my full height and hurried toward the darker, safer forest. The pace of the steps behind increased and drew closer, until a soft, female voice called out in Ukrainian, *"Vitayu, stij!"*

"Tak," I replied, and turned to see a young woman of about eighteen stepping through the undergrowth. She wore large, wool pants that could have been those of her father or an

older brother. Over her dirty, white blouse was a black cardigan buttoned to the hollow of her neck. Her eyes were a lovely hazel, and she wore her light blond hair in a thick braid.

"I'm Kasia," she said.

Her smile warmed and worried me in equal measure. The only people who'd seen me since the partisans were Ukrainian farmers, and they wanted nothing more than to see me dead.

Lie to her, Musia.

What if she wants to help?

Don't tell her your name.

"I'm Talia."

"Are you alone?"

Lie to her.

She'll know, Mama.

"Yes. I'm looking for my mother."

"What's her name?"

No, Musia.

"Fruma."

Musia!

"Fruma what?"

"Perlmutter."

Oh, Musia, I cry for you.

Kasia's eyes drifted down to the bundle that lay by my feet then back to me and any tension melted from them. "You're a Jew."

Lie, Musia.

"Yes."

"You can trust me. I hate the Germans too."

Neshomeleh, she's lying.

Shush, Mama.

"Have you seen my Mama?"

Her eyes drifted from mine, and she shook her head no. "You're the first Jew I've seen in a long time. Are you sure you're alone?"

"Yes, why do you ask?"

"It just doesn't seem possible a young girl like you could have survived alone all winter."

"I've been lucky."

She smiled. "You must be."

"Why are you here?" I asked.

"What do you mean?"

"I don't know. There aren't many people wandering the forest."

"I was at the school in *Rivne*"—she used the Ukrainian name for the city rather than the Polish *Równe*—"but the Germans took my Papa to work in a factory, in Hamburg, I think."

"I'm sorry."

She looked from me as sadness softened her features. "They took all the men in our village except for the older ones. Then they took our crops and food for their soldiers in Russia."

"They stole everything my family owned."

"Where are you from?"

"Horochów."

She nodded. "They would have taken my brother, Slavko, but he ran into the woods and hid there for days until it was safe to come home. Without Papa, I had to come home to help with the farm, and that's what I do. I tend the cows in the morning then at dusk, and during the day I work in the fields with Mama and Slavko."

"I'm sorry."

"So now you know why I hate the Germans too."

Musia, ask her why she's in the woods.

Quiet, Mama.

Kasia's eyes searched through the forest to be sure we were alone, then she came close and placed her hand on my shoulder. "I know what it's like to be a hunted animal. Come with me to my house, and we can hide you in our barn and give you food."

She's lying, Musia. I swear to you as your mother that she is lying.

Where are you and Tchiya, Mama? Are you in a barn? Fed? Warm? Are you even looking for me?

That is such a terrible thing to say. I love you more than my own life, Musia—

I disappointed you at the river.

Enough of that, my love.

"What do you say, Talia? Will you come?"

"What if soldiers come? They'd kill you and everyone in your village if they found me."

Kasia's eyes narrowed as she took a moment to think.

This girl is lying. You know that, don't you?

She hates the Germans too, and she has food, a place for me to hide, to be safe.

None of it is true, neshomeleh.

This would be over, Mama.

This? What do you mean this? Your life?

No, Mama. Being alone, wandering the woods, slowly dying.

The only thing that will be over is you, Musia. She will turn you in, and they will kill you.

Kasia's face relaxed. "Talia, there's an abandoned house in the forest near our farm. You can hide there. I'll bring you warm clothes and food, and you could even have a fire without anyone seeing. Maybe after a while you could help with the cows, and no one would know the difference." She smiled. "We could be friends."

Don't go, Musia.

"I don't know."

"Please, Talia. I told you, I hate the Germans too. We have to trust each other a little, right?"

No, Musia.

"Will it be just you?"

"Yes, of course, just me."

"I'll meet you there tomorrow. I have to get some things from a hiding place first."

Her smile brightened. "Even better, bring your things. I'll be sure to bring clothes and food, as much as I can, the biggest feast you've seen in a long time." She then described how to find the abandoned house and said we should meet in the middle of the day, as close to noon as I could figure. Then she hugged me and left to gather her cows.

Why do you get so upset with me, my love?

Because guilt doesn't leave room for anything else.

I walked deeper into the darkening forest where I'd dug a little grave beneath a large pine. There I ate a soft potato, its rancid juice spilling down my chin, and the last of an uncooked rat I'd killed a day or so before. The thought of warmth and food, real food, was wonderful. I hoped Kasia was sincere, but perhaps Mama was right.

Fatigue outpaced my troubled mind, and I passed into a dreamless sleep.

The first sigh of morning light woke me, and I picked up my possessions and wrapped them in a neat bundle.

Leave them here beneath some leaves, Musia.

Why?

Kasia was lying.

Why would she?

Why would a stranger offer help you didn't ask for?

In my heart I knew Mama was right, but I wanted her to be wrong. I tucked the bundle beneath the pine boughs and hid it with a covering of pine needles and leaves. There was no way I would walk away deeper into the woods without seeing if Kasia really did want to help me. I followed the directions she'd given and shortly after sunrise arrived at the abandoned house, which was no more than a foundation and toppled stone chimney.

A hint of wood smoke carried on the air, which meant her farm and village must be near. Around the foundation of the old house the land was flat, with thin trees growing where a yard used to be. A small, tumble-down barn of rotted wood sat back farther in the woods. I saw a slight rise deeper in the denser forest, and that's where I lay down behind a fat beech tree. I buried myself beneath branches and leaves.

And I waited.

The dirt was soft and cool. I dug into it and found little white larval balls and popped them into my mouth. Light from the east fanned out through a canopy of budding leaves. The forest warmed, and winter wilted in the presence of spring. I rested my chin on the back of my hands, and my eyes became heavy as images leapt into my mind's eye like a slow turning kaleidoscope—Papa and Mama working in our garden, smiling, and Tchiya helping them. Spring for me was always a release from the claustrophobia of winter, a time when I could go back into the woods behind our home and the streams, fields, and forests of the *Szlachcianka's* estate.

But, as always, memories of family, especially of Tchiya and Mama, drew me back into the ghetto, where a colorless spring had ebbed into the perpetual gray. Bodies clotted the streets and overwhelmed the exhausted, sick, and starved women of the *Judenrat's* burial committee. The skin of the dead darkened and softened in the warming weather, and the stench permeated every breath of air and drowned the fetor of our bodies, clothes, and little rooms.

During the day, the ghetto was quiet, a ghost city of corpses, and then in the evening the workers, now entirely women, shuffled down the streets, praying their remaining children would still be alive and not died or taken in a *łapanka* during the day. In our apartment, Rosa and Belen were gone, both taken while they worked. When Mrs. Joselewicz had come home that night and word sifted through the dying community that her daughters were gone, only despair remained in her sallow, jaundiced face and eyes.

"I'm sorry," Mama said as she handed Mrs. Joselewicz a bowl of thin soup. She took it and brought the bowl to her lips to sip but didn't look up or acknowledge Mama.

Through the winter and into the spring a dry, wheezing cough nagged at Tchiya until one evening, a couple days after the Nazis took Rosa and Belen, she returned home sweating from fever and was unable to catch her breath. Mama tried to hand Tchiya a bowl of soup, but she pushed it away without a word and rolled over on her bed to sleep.

Mama set the soup down and rubbed Tchiya's back. "It'll be all right, my darling girl."

Tchiya's fever grew worse, as did the cough, and sweat snailed down her temples and the back of her neck. Mama placed precious slices of potato on Tchiya's forehead to bring down the fever and then sat beside Tchiya, afraid to remove her hand from her back, as if life itself flowed from Mama's body into Tchiya's.

"She can't work in the morning," I said.

"I know," Mama replied.

Tchiya shifted her weight and lifted her head. "We need the food."

I sat up. "I can work for her."

"Musia, it's lovely of you to offer, but no."

"Why not? We need the food, and no one will notice."

"You're brave to offer, my love, but you're too young. We will make do."

Frustration simmered within me. We were starving to death and needed the food ration or else Tchiya would die, yet Mama treated me like a child.

"Nothing will happen, Mama," I said.

"I'm sorry, neshomeleh, but you were beaten—"

"That wasn't my fault."

Frustration and anger lined Mama's mouth. "I'm not saying it—"

"And it was so long ago. Why won't you trust me?"

She turned her eyes down and took a slow, deep breath. "I do trust you, but you were nearly killed."

"But—"

"And it was just a few weeks ago that the German beat you, Musia."

"That is a long time ago, Mama. And I know better now, I do."

Mrs. Cukier pulled Ania closer to her, and Mrs. Joselewicz turned away on her bed. The beds of Rosa, Belen, Janusz, Hannah, and Mrs. Zelinski were gone, burned for warmth.

"Musia—"

"Oh, why won't you trust me?"

Tchiya rolled over and placed her pale hand on Mama's lap. "If I'm not there for the count, they will come look for me here. If they do that ..." her voice trailed off.

Mama rubbed her forehead.

A coughing fit consumed Tchiya for a moment, and then she rasped, "The guards in the warehouse aren't very strict. As long as the headcount is correct they're satisfied."

Mama lifted her eyes to Tchiya.

"All I do," Tchiya said coughing, "is knit sweaters for the soldiers in Russia. Musia can do that. Right, Musia? You can do that?"

"Yes." I'd spent my life watching Mama knit for our family.

"Are there Germans?" Mama asked.

"The guards are all Ukrainian, and the Germans never go there."

Mama looked up to the ceiling. "I need you, Simcha, so much." She patted Tchiya's hand and looked at me. "Be careful, neshomeleh. You and Tchiya are more precious than you'll ever know."

Tchiya and I fell asleep to Mama's gentle voice singing,

Sleep, beautiful child,
sleep free from worry,
a star is singing,
the trees rustle,
blow out the candle my love,
sleep is on its way to you

The next morning Tchiya gave me her pass, and I met with the young women at the main gate. A couple of them asked about Tchiya, and I told them she was sick. They said not to worry, the guards won't care and there are never any SS. The gates opened, and I took a deep breath as I stood in line to show Tchiya's pass to the guard. He looked at it, then me, and paused for a moment, but waved me through.

My muscles were stiff with fear and early morning cold, but the same girls walked with me to the warehouse where they worked. Outside, a diesel generator coughed at irregular intervals; inside the lights flickered. The warehouse was cavernous, gray, and cold. The lights hummed. Laid out on the cold cement floor were a series of square wooden tables with chairs on each side and bundles of wool piled in the center of each table and beside each chair.

Two girls led me to Tchiya's seat, then sat at their own chairs. Two wooden knitting needles worn smooth by Tchiya's busy hands rested where she'd left them the day before, and a half-finished scarf waited for her return.

Eight or nine guards paced down the aisles between the tables and watched over us. There was no talking, no communication of any kind. Any girl thought to be taking an eye off her work had the back of her head slapped. When they could, Tchiya's two friends looked up to encourage me with their eyes and nodded to say I was doing well. They were kind, but at twelve-years-old I couldn't work as fast. A guard saw me fumble with the needles and frowned but didn't say anything.

By midday the knitting was going better; I'd finished the scarf and begun another, and the girls no longer looked up from their own work to check on me. The world reduced itself to the buzz and flicker of the lights, the cough of the generator, the texture of coarse wool on my fingers, and the clicking of fat, wooden knitting needles. It was soothing, and though I worried about a *łapanka*, at least I was away from our fetid little apartment.

At midday the guards let us take a fifteen-minute break, no lunch, just sitting with our hands in our laps, and then the yell of a guard telling us to get our Jew fingers busy.

By afternoon the sun slanted in through a set of windows up near the metal roof of the warehouse, and I took a moment to stretch. Just as I dipped my head down to continue knitting, a sharp bang on one of the doors echoed through the warehouse. We looked up, and the guards eyes widened, and their bodies tensed. Two of the black-uniformed guards raced to the door as a group of five Germans burst in. They wore gray-green uniforms with the SS insignia on their lapels. Four of them—tall, lean young men—wore side caps and carried blunt, ugly machine guns with the leather straps slung over a shoulder. The fifth—a muscular, compact man whose puckered lips looked as if he'd eaten something sour—wore an officer's hat with a silver eagle above a death's head insignia. He carried a pistol in a holster attached to a wide leather belt.

The officer's puckered mouth produced a stream of loud, angry words, but the only one I could make out was *Inspektion.* We kept our eyes on our work, and the guards stood at attention as the officer dressed them down. When he finished, the guard nearest him turned and yelled, "Keep working, Jew maggots!"

I leaned toward the girl next to me and whispered, "Is this a *łapanka?*"

"Shush." Her eyes remained on her needles.

Behind me a guard yelled, "Shut up!"

Fear tightened in my chest and burned the back of my neck as I mouthed, *I won't let you down, Mama, I won't let you down ...*

The guards were stiff and silent while the Germans walked through the rows of chairs and tables. Their hobnail boots clacked on the cement floor, and the sound of it grew louder as the officer came closer. Tap, tap, tap. The generator coughed, the lights flickered, one hundred knitting needles clicked to an innate rhythm, and my mind detached from the anchor of my body. The cold, gray warehouse, slanted rays of sunlight reflecting off the far wall, the threat of death—it was an unimaginable and horrific place only a brief walk from the chestnut-lined street and beautiful home I once shared with my family.

Tap, tap, tap … *faster, work faster*, I thought. But no matter how hard I tried, I couldn't make my fingers do what I wanted, what I needed them to do. The eyes of the girl across from me darted up and then back to her work, and the metallic tap of the officer's hobnail boots stopped. The muscles in my neck stiffened beneath his glare, and I knew the eyes of each guard and German soldier were focused on me.

In my hands, the needles were clumsy and clicked to an irregular rhythm like tuneless notes in an otherwise harmonized orchestra. The beating of my heart escalated until it felt as if it would leap from my chest, a vertigo-like sensation distorted my vision, and fear contorted into panic. My shaking fingers dropped stitch after stitch or the tip of the needle failed to find the next loop, and with each mistake and attempt to fix it, the officer's nasal breathing grew in its severity until he bent his body so that his face was above my head. *"Schneller, du untermensch!"*

Warm droplets of spit sprayed against my neck, and the sudden breath of violence startled me and caused a needle to drop onto the table. The rattling sound of it reverberated in my ears and distorted into a clanging that echoed throughout the dull gloom of the warehouse.

"Stricken schneller du Judenscheisse!"

My trembling fingers pinched at the needle as it rolled on the tabletop.

His boots tapped on the cement as he moved his body to stare down on my face. He was so close that I smelled his sweat on the wool of his uniform. *"Schneller Judenschwein!"* Anger twisted his face, and little bits of frothy spittle formed at the corners of his lips, which betrayed the slightest shimmer of a smile. Then he slammed a fist down onto the table, and the needle jumped from my panicked fingers.

"Du Jude hündin!" he screamed and spat in my face, then grabbed the needle just as I reached for it and plunged it into the first joint of my ring finger.

· · ·

Lying in the soft dirt as I waited for Kasia, I held the stub to my eyes. It was forever irritated, and I remembered Mama's increasing panic as infection blossomed in the oozing stump and feverish chills shook my body. That I did not die from the infection was a miracle, but the skin and bone and tendon and nerves refused to heal. I was not so naïve or girlish to wonder if I would ever feel the warmth of a man placing an engagement and then wedding ring on it. Life did not have a future. It was only surviving from moment to moment and dreams of Mama, Tchiya, Papa, and food.

From the direction of Kasia's farm, I heard footsteps crunch on small twigs and dried leaves. My breathing slowed, and I kept my eyes as low to the ground as I could. From the far side of the tumble-down home, movement among the branches resolved into Kasia's pretty face and blond hair. She paused and turned to look behind her, said something, then came to the edge of the foundation.

"Damn," she said, then turned and called out, "The little bitch isn't here."

From the woods emerged a tall, lean young man. His dark, oily hair fell in a straight line across his forehead, and he wore a tunic and wool pants tucked into his boots. In his hand was a small pistol.

"You should have made her come to the farm with you yesterday," he said.

"I tried, Slavko, but she wouldn't do it."

"That's because you weren't friendly enough. You should have given her food."

"I didn't have any."

163

"Well, you screwed this up. Between you and the Germans we'll be lucky if we don't starve."

"Maybe I can find her again."

Slavko looked through the woods and rubbed his nose with the back of his hand. I lowered my face into the dirt and imagined my body becoming a leaf on the forest floor. "Maybe," he finally said.

"I'll find her and make sure she comes this time."

"We need the money, Kasia. There aren't many Jews wandering around as there used to be, and who knows how long this God damned war is going to last."

"I know. I'm sorry. I'll find her, and we'll get the reward. I promise."

"Careful of the partisans," he said, and then his footsteps on the leaves and twigs faded into the woods.

My eyes looked up through the leaves and debris at Kasia. She watched Slavko fade into the trees and then walked past the stone chimney, and her steps faded too as she disappeared into the forest to hunt for me.

I'm sorry, neshomeleh.

I am too, Mama. I miss you so much.

I miss you too, my love.

I lay in the dirt until well past dark, wiping tears from my eyes.

Paranka

Every so often a breeze carried the honey-lemon scent of linden trees in early summer bloom into the ghetto. We raised our nostrils to this fleeting perfume, and images of cream yellow blossoms dangling beneath wide, heart-shaped leaves reminded us that life continued beyond the gate and river. In quiet moments, when the lindens blessed us, our former garden and its menagerie of budding flowers and pear and apple trees on the precipice of bearing fruit came to me in gentle wellsprings of memory.

And as quickly, these images dissolved into gray-brown death.

The uncountable thousands who had walked into this world less than a year before were less than half their number. I imagined a place somewhere beyond the walls where German soldiers and Ukrainian guards piled the bodies like a human garbage heap. Within that mass of twisted arms and legs, broken hearts, shattered dreams, and wasted promise was my friend Zofia, her beautiful blue eyes consumed by rot or rats. And with her, mangled and lost to the world, were the Jewish friends I knew from home and then from this place—Helena, Tauba, Rena, Gerda, and her younger brother, Julian, as well as the boys who had dug the hole to the outside and guarded it so well.

Tchiya, Mama, and I lived, but we had no brains; we had only hunger and the painful craving to eat, no matter what. We had no reason to hope, only the certainty of death and the instinctual desire to forestall the inevitable. And yet Mama was the author of our will to live, the narrator of our love for each other and the ability of love to preserve and impel our intention to live—if not for ourselves, for someone else.

She sang to us each night as if we were still newly born, and she made up stories where the endings were fresh with life and its joys. Whether she carried despair and the knowledge that death was approaching, we didn't know, but she transmitted her love to us, and somehow it worked. It did not deliver us from despair, but love held it at bay and transcended hope, death, and cruelty.

As spring slipped into summer, even the pungent aroma of linden trees couldn't overwhelm the stench of rotted corpses and the fetid reek of the walking dead we had become. Nor could Mama's stories, songs, and love hide the growing signs that a horrible change was soon to come. First, rumors drifted through our diminished community, rumors that were slowed only by the death by beating of Mrs. Berman. Then the number of guards increased, followed by visits of small groups of SS soldiers. They walked through the ghetto all dressed up in their blue-gray uniforms and shining leather boots, spitting at us and ordering the Ukrainians to beat any Jew that didn't grovel before them in the gutter.

"We have to do something, find some way out," Mama said one evening. Her eyes were dark and shrunken and her hair thin and gray. Starvation and beatings had eroded her once celloesque curves so that her dress fell and swayed from her shoulders as if hung from a clothesline.

Neither Tchiya nor I said a word.

"We must still have friends on the outside; there must be a way ..."

...

Early summer in the forest was much different from the ghetto. The sun shone bright, and the world beneath the canopy was a splendid green. Wildflowers bloomed violet, honeycomb yellow, scarlet, and lavender. There were fiddleheads for a while and then dandelions, watercress, maple seeds that spun down from above, larva and bugs of all sorts, snails, and more to forage from the forest.

The villages and farmland came back to life, even though the Nazis took the men who worked these fields. I watched from my perches in the woods as women, children, and old men tilled fields, some with tractors working wide, long expanses, and others with horse and plow for more modest plots. The scent of manure rose from the dirt and carried into the edge of the forest, and to me there was a sweetness to it that brought back visits with Mama to the farms near our home.

With renewed life came renewed dangers. The villages were more active later into the evening, making it difficult to slip into a barn or potato cellar. The Germans still took more than could sustain life on these farms so that I measured milk by the drop. Potatoes were tiny, wilted, and filled with sour juice. Often, fear kept me from the farms, and hunger forced me to eat fur- and bone-permeated scat from owls and foxes as well as seedy, dry droppings from bear and deer.

There were also more people in the woods. Farmers cut and hauled wood from the edge of the forests ringing their land while, deeper in the woods, partisans and their hunters killed each other, leaving the bodies to rot and be torn into by rats, wolves, ravens, and other carrion eaters.

No longer did I feel safe in the woods. Nor did I travel by day. I existed within a middle ground between the darker forest and its edge, a band of woods where I hoped farmers dared not go and hunters of humans were afraid of ambush and death. The shovel blade was my savior, and I used it to dig my little graves beneath the angles of large boulders or deep beneath thick, low-hanging pine boughs. I covered myself with all manner of bracken but slept with fear and never deeply.

But still, the need to find Mama or Tchiya was overwhelming, as was the need to hear any human voice not directed at me in anger or hate. When the compulsion of hunger and loneliness drove me from the woods, I paused beneath farmhouse windows opened to the night's air to hear sparse words and phrases shared among scared and stoic families before sliding into a barn or cellar. As often as not, a dog would rise at the scent of me and bellow out his alarm, leaving me to run for my life back into the forest.

Adding to my discomfort were the lice infesting my body. Pustules caused by their bites marked my skin, and I scratched out flakes of dried blistered skin and scabs from my scalp and hair until blood reddened my fingers. One night, as I stumbled through a thick stand of broadleaved trees, I growled as my fingers dug into my itching, inflamed scalp. Then I lifted my eyes to a mosaic of glinting pinholes more beautiful than the ornate ceiling of any synagogue I'd ever seen: the stars.

With the back of my hand I wiped tears away as my body, scalp to toes, twitched with crawling, biting parasites. The deep, stuttering rhythm of an owl sounded through the trees, and beneath it millions of crickets chirped to a cadence that rose and fell like a slow breath. And just beneath that was the soft, steady tempo of a stream that sounded in my imagination like the babble of a thousand *Shedeem*, the sprites in Papa's fairy tales.

I stumbled down a knoll where a shallow stream cut through it and followed the gurgling water until the forest floor leveled and the stream dropped into a broad, rock-rimmed pool. I pulled each possession from my clothes and the wool blanket sling, laid them on a wide, flat rock, and then stripped naked. In the moonlight, my pale legs and body shone light blue, marked by burgundy-colored ulcers and mottled scrapes and bruises.

The pool's surface was ink-black and reflected the firmament of glinting pinholes. I dipped one foot in and watched its marred whiteness disappear into cool black up to my knee. The rocks at the bottom were oblong and slick with moss so that I didn't trust standing and let my body flow into the water. It was cold and soothed my skin. I submerged my face so that my hair flowered out around me, and I wished for every nit to drown.

For a moment time paused, the world went far away, and pain and fear and loneliness and sadness for Mama and Tchiya and Papa lifted. I was a child allowing my body—a body conditioned by starvation and abuse to remain in a state of suspended girlhood without any hint of the woman I could become—to savor cool water.

And yet, as good as water always felt, my skin crawled with nits and the stinging itch of their bite. Lifting my head from the black water, I reached for my penknife and began to cut my hair down to the scalp. The blade was now dull and worn; the process of cutting slow and tedious and more like pulling root-and-branch rather than cutting or shaving. Every few minutes I dipped my head beneath the water and came to the surface to watch knotted, greasy strands float away from me.

After what seemed a long time, I lowered my scalp beneath the water for one long, final soak and did my best to wipe away any remaining nits. From the flat rock beside the pool I hunched down and dunked my clothes in the water for a good long time to drown the nits, or at least get them to release from the fibers and float away.

I wrung the clothes out then hung them from tree branches, ate my last potato, scavenged bugs from the ground, and ate a handful of peppery watercress growing along the edge of the stream. After the dampness left the clothes, I put on my pants and Mama's blouse, folded the remainder into my satchel, and kept walking.

The bundle was heavier, but a breeze whispered through the trees, and for a time the biting and itching subsided. My only complaint was that my scalp became dry and irritated, and when I rubbed it, I felt patches of dried blood where the knife had scraped the skin or pulled out small clumps of hair.

As dawn rose in the eastern sky like a divine, waking eyelid, I sought out a place for my little grave and found one beneath the angle of two large rocks. I built a wall of twigs and leaves for cover, laid the coat I had taken from the partisans on the ground, and folded it around me. Sleep came, and I drifted away into a world of dreams.

"Prokydaysya!"

My eyes blinked open, and through my cover of leaves and branches, I saw a pair of shining black boots.

A hand reached in, grasped my shoulder, and shook me. *"Prokydaysya!"* he said in Ukrainian.

"Paweł?"

"Ni," and he shook me hard. *"Vypovzaty,"* he said and then in Polish, "Crawl out."

My legs and body were stiff from hunger and walking the night before. I was also exhausted and assumed it to be about midday. Like a doe gaining its feet for the first time, I crawled out from the nook and stood before a man of medium height with black hair, beard, coffee-brown eyes, and thick, caterpillar-like eyebrows. He wore a brown shirt with the sleeves rolled up past his elbows and wool britches tucked into new, knee-high, black leather boots. A rifle was slung over his right shoulder, and a horse whinnied from deeper in the woods.

"How old are you?" he asked in Polish.

You're a child, Musia.

"I'm only ten," I lied.

"Hmm, where are you from?"

Tell him you don't remember, neshomeleh.

No, he'll never believe such a ridiculous lie.

"Horochów."

He raised his eyebrows, which seemed to pull the rest of his sluggish face up. "You're quite far from home. What did you do? Did you run away?" He smiled as if he'd said something funny.

Tell him you are going to relatives.

This lie felt pathetic, but I said I was going to my aunt's farm for the rest of the war.

His glare meandered over the dried ulcers and blood that mottled my shaved scalp. My eyes fell away from his, and I raised my hand to touch my bald head.

He hitched the rifle up his shoulder. "You look like a Jew."

Do not trust him, Musia.

I know, Mama.

Mama's threadbare blouse hung loose from my body and exposed my girlish breasts. I wrapped my arms around my chest. "I have to pee."

His eyebrows lifted his face again. "You're not going to try to run?"

"No. I have to pee, and I want to cover myself."

Don't run, neshomeleh. He'll shoot you.

Trust me, Mama.

He smiled and said very well. Reaching into my den, I pulled the coat Mama had given me from the satchel and wrapped it around me, then walked into the woods where he could hear but not see me. I squatted to pee, and my shaking fingers tore into the lining of the coat. At first I felt nothing and a feverish tingle of panic swept up my spine, but then I touched something solid, metallic. I withdrew one of the three gold coins from the coat's lining and pressed it into my palm.

"Are you the *Gajowy*?" I asked as I stepped from the trees.

His eyes narrowed. "*Tak*, I'm the *Lisnika*," he said using the Ukrainian term. "And you're a Jew, no?"

You're Polish, Musia. Tell him that.

"Polish, I'm Polish."

His eyebrows rose again, and the corners of his mouth lifted with them. "I can see the shadow where you tore the star from your coat."

I looked at my chest and there, burned into the fibers, was that faint memento of the Nazis.

His brow wrinkled, and his horse brayed. "It's time to tell the truth. Even if you were just a God damn Pole, a little Polish girl wouldn't have a shaved, bloody scalp. Your sow mother wouldn't leave you to wander the woods alone, and you wouldn't wear the coat of a Jew."

I lowered my head. He walked to me. His body was an arm's length away. "There is no aunt, is there?"

"No."

"And everyone you know and ever knew is dead."

I raised my eyes to his. "No."

"No?"

"No. My Mama is alive."

Don't fight with this man, Musia!

"Where is she?"

"I don't know."

His eyebrows relaxed, and he smiled. "Do you think I'm a bad man?"

"I don't know yet."

He laughed and rubbed his mustache and beard with one hand. "I'm not. And I'm going to do you a favor."

Don't believe him, neshomeleh.

I know, Mama.

"I'm going to take you to the police, good Ukrainians."

"How is that a favor?"

"Come now, look at you. I don't know who's been hiding you, but you'll never survive out here alone."

"I'd rather take my chances in the woods."

He smiled again. "A little girl like you will never survive."

I looked away from him into the woods.

"I'm taking you to the authorities, and they'll decide what to do with you."

I pressed the gold coin deeper into my palm. "Of course, they'll kill me."

"Not necessarily."

I turned my eyes back to his and held the coin out in my fingers. "This is worth far more than what they'll pay you for my body."

He looked at the coin and then at me, and his lips thinned. "I could have both."

A shiver ran down my spine and without thinking I stepped from him, reared my hand with the coin back near my ear, and shifted my body to aim at a thick patch of forest. "I'll throw this where you'll never find it."

His eyes brightened, and he scanned my body, then looked toward the woods. When his eyes returned to me, my hand shook. He squeezed the leather strap of his rifle. "You'll die in the winter."

"I'll find my Mama before that."

"No, you won't."

I jutted my chin out and looked into the woods. "Better freeze or starve than a bullet in my head."

He was quiet as he stared at me. I steadied myself to throw the coin if he attacked.

He reached out and gestured for me to give him the coin. I looked into his eyes, and his eyebrows lifted his face into a smile.

"Give me the coin, and you can go," he said.

"Yes?"

"Yes, but you know you won't survive the winter."

I placed the coin in his hand.

He began to walk toward his horse but turned and swung the rifle from his shoulder, so the barrel aimed at my chest.

Liar.

"I don't want to see you in this forest ever again."

I nodded, and he turned and left.

...

I didn't mark time by months or weeks or even days. Life compressed into moments bracketed by sunrise and sunset as well as endless kilometers of forests and the semi-liberation of emerging from a darkened wood into a field of waist-high, immature wheat as an estuary of stars shimmered above. Sometimes I sat in the middle of a field and listened to the sharp, violin-like chirping of crickets fold in with the deep bass notes of owls and mournful arias of wolves and distant hounds. Joining this orchestra was the reedy sound of wheat tassels brushing against each other in a low breeze.

By day I slept, careful to cover myself and leave no trace in the woods lest another *Gajowy* was prowling about. When a garden or barn was particularly kind to me, I spent days with my hoarded food and remained shrouded in my grave between the deep forest and the villages and fields. Birds settled in the dried leaves around me to pick at bugs and pluck up materials for their never-ending remodeling of their nests. One morning I wandered from my den into a thicket of stunted, leafy young trees, and as I squatted, I noticed a nest in the crook of a branch and heard frantic peeping. Looking into the nest, I saw three tiny, moist chicks with bright yellow beaks raised to receive food. A fourth was picking its way out of a brown-speckled, powder-blue egg. In the branches above, Mama and Papa trilled their anger at me, but I stood my ground and watched the miracle of that vulnerable life as it was born.

If you can survive, I can too.

That night as I slept in my little grave, gunshots woke me. I sat up. With my eyes closed and ears like radio antenna, I listened to the single pops of rifles and then the sustained staccato rattle of a machine gun. Dense forest dulled the shots, but I knew they were not far. For a moment my heart and mind returned to the river and the volleys of bullets that had passed over our heads as we hid in the bulrushes.

Images flashed like a frayed movie reel through my mind's eye: Mama's eyes and face, fearful, expectant, and Mrs. Cukier's body slumping dead, with Ania's corpse held to her bosom.

My eyes tried to bore through the trees for any sign of light from a fire, and my antenna searched for sounds of engines or nearing humans but found neither, just the blunt crackle of guns for a few minutes and then silence. I reached out for more leaves and branches and did my best to submerge my body into the ground, but it wasn't enough. Death had followed me into these woods, and there was nothing I could do. I wanted to run away, but to where, in what direction? The woods, for all I knew, were filled with soldiers looking for me. Was it the Ukrainian *Gajowy* I paid off who had sent these murderers into the forest, my forest? Who were they killing? Was Mama one of them?

I pressed my body into the earth and fought to control my breathing, which came in hard, rapid gulps choked by despair.

I'm not with those poor people, neshomeleh.

No, Mama?

No. I'm not with them. I'm not with them. ...

These words repeated in my mind until each breath came slow and deep and pacified the panic and despair. Crickets, owls, and the baying of wolves as well as the scurrying of small creatures finally broke the tense silence of the woods in the immediate wake of the shooting. Their music was like a balm, quieting the tension in my muscles.

I lay awake until morning. Throughout the day I dared not move, much less leave my nest, worried that soldiers were searching the forest for Jews and partisans such as Paweł. The sun warmed and then heated the forest so that my skin became salty and wet, and my stomach ached with hunger. Thirst dried my throat, and I dreamt of the stream at night, floating in its cool water. Believing I was trapped and that any movement would draw gunshots and soldiers, I had no choice but to drink what I could of my own urine.

By the next morning I had to move from my little grave and search for a brook in the woods, perhaps even a garden spreading out from a farmhouse, brimming with ripening carrots, cucumbers, tomatoes, and other vegetables we could only have dreamed of in the ghetto. I swung the satchel over my shoulder and stumbled out into the woods, following the moss on trees, believing it would guide me north and past where the shooting came from. But sound in a forest during high summer is a funny thing. It seems not to travel in a true path but to broadcast out in an apron, wending among the trees in large, confused arcs and nonsensical angles.

Direction, too, is deceptive.

Or maybe in my heart I needed to be sure Mama was not among those I had heard murdered.

The sickly-sweet scent of death surrounded me, and then I found the first body. It was a young woman in a thin dress, with bare feet, lying face down in dried leaves and wildflowers. A ring of dried blood stained the back of her dress around where the bullet had caught her. I didn't touch her, but something was different, something I couldn't quite place at first. Through the trees lay a clearing with more bodies: men, women, children, lightly dressed for the heat of summer, all dead and lying in a row, piled one on top of another, all of them shot in the chest. Death grimaced across their faces, and bloat bulged open the eyes of some so that they gawked up at the sky, while others looked as if they were sleeping. Their arms and legs were twisted around the bodies piled on and beside them, making it hard to tell where one person ended, and another began. The children were the most painful to see. Their bodies looked like pale, grotesque dolls. Not a single body wore shoes.

Go from here, Musia.
I'm looking for you, Mama.
I'm not with these people, neshomeleh.
How should I know?
They aren't Jews.

I looked closer and noticed the bodies were all thin but not starved, and their clothes, though bloodied and worn, did not look as if they'd been living and hiding in the woods.

They're Polish, neshomeleh.

They could be from Horochów?

Yes, my love, they could.

Flies wandered across the faces; their straw-shaped tongues flecked into dried blood and probed pale, waxy skin. Bees drifted around the bodies and hovered above bright yellow buttercups; miniature, violet bell-shaped flowers; and flowers with white petals and pollen-laden florets at their hearts. Birds fluttered from branch to branch and warbled their warnings and songs in equal measure, and two yellow-and-black butterflies with light blue on their swallow tails danced in the air.

I walked from the clearing until I found a brook, thin from long days of summer sun, but ample enough to drink its cool water and let it flow over my body.

Summer was cruel and beautiful, frightening and sweetly fragrant, unnerving and melodic, and it was giving way to the imminent, malevolent season that was winter.

• • •

The sun dipped a bit lower in the horizon each day and chilled air seeped into the nights, which filled me with dread that winter was advancing, and I'd not found Mama, nor was I prepared for the cold. Days, weeks, and months of walking through brambles, mud, and over rocks had torn and tattered my shoes and clothes. The soles of the boots I had stolen from the partisans were separating from the leather tops, and I held them together by tying strips from the wool satchel around my feet.

With autumn, rain fell harder, colder, and more often, and the woods remained damp and cold for days afterward. This only hastened the disintegration of my shoes as well as my socks, which had holes in the toes and heels, even though I wore two or three pairs at a time. My clothes suffered as well, and the only piece that was whole was the partisan's coat, because I kept it—and the coat with my valuables—in my satchel, safe from thorns and somewhat protected from rain.

On the nights I found a quiet village and managed to outwit the dogs and sneak into a barn or potato cellar, there wasn't much for me to steal or scavenge. The Germans and Ukrainian police were using this area, which Papa described as the breadbasket of Europe, as a larder for the German army in Russia. Gardens were desolate, as were the vast fields of wheat and hay. Starvation, cold, and fear were no longer only for Jews, but also for Ukrainians and the handful of Poles who remained in the farming communities dotting the landscape.

Out of necessity, these people entered the forests to forage for food and kill whatever animals they could. For me, this meant the woods were more dangerous than ever. I had no choice other than to hide as deep in a forest as I could go, often remaining hidden for days until the hunger, thirst, cold, and loneliness were intolerable. More often than not, I ran from dogs frothing with anger and the hateful calls of the people I attempted to steal from. Of course, if I managed to enter a barn or cellar, I found precious little to eat.

And then, one morning I woke to a veil of falling, silver-white crystals that enveloped the forest floor and collected in the nooks of branches and pine boughs like soft eiderdown. It was beautiful and frightening.

There isn't a wish strong enough or a prayer powerful enough to send winter away, neshomeleh.

It's a lot without you, Mama.

Don't let despair get in, my love.

I love you, Mama.

That's my girl.

Snow fell and swirled through the woods all day and into the night. I tucked my limbs into my belly like a cat sleeping on a warm quilt, but my body shivered from cold as well as fear of winter and the thought of death. Every so often I pushed up through the cap of snow covering me in my little grave and hopped around the trees to warm myself, then dug through snow for nuts or food of any sort. My teeth ground on sticks and dried leaves, anything to cast away the unpitying pain of hunger.

A small potato, soft and warm from cradling it against my body, was the only store I had, and I parceled each bite out through the night. In the dark, covered by falling snow, chills shivered up my spine, and my eyelids were heavy with the overwhelming desire to sleep. Dreams flickered past, and in them Mama's voice urged me, "Blow out the candle and close your eyes, beautiful child."

No, Mama, I'll never wake up.

And the dream burst with a flash of terror, and I pushed up through the snow to hop and warm my body and chew on bark and pine needles, anything to ease the pain and stay awake. Tears coursed down my cheeks, and I called out for Mama to please come, to please save me, to let my body bury itself in her warmth and her sweet fragrance.

I am near, Musia, always; I am near.

Anger welled in my chest, and the beat of my heart, slow and steady, ran like a machine fired by great, huge shovelfuls of fear and desire to live. When these fuels ebbed, I always had the enduring memory of Mama's hands warming my cheeks and her round eyes and bulb of a nose, just like mine, inches from me while she said, "I love you, Musia."

"You say it too much."

"I don't want you to forget, ever."

This is what carried me through the night and into the next day, but as the snow tapered I had to move. My footprints littered the snow around my little grave, and if I stayed, exhaustion, cold, and hunger would wrap their bilious fingers around my throat. Death hovered over my shoulder like a dark angel as I trudged through calf-high snow and pushed through dense woods to where the brush thinned. Through thinning trees, I saw fields spreading out past the horizon and a small collection of farmhouses and barns.

From my usual perch at the edge of the forest, I watched smoke rise from chimneys and heard the soft lowing of cows, but not much in the way of human activity was visible. With winter, there was less for the Germans and the police to take. It was now up to the people—women, boys, girls, the elderly—to survive. That night I made my way to a small mound and found the entrance to a potato cellar beneath the snow. Inside was a meager amount of potatoes. Even the rat population had declined. I ate a soft, sour potato and still managed to kill a rat with the penknife. Its raw flesh tasted like the smell of bog grass, but the hunger pains waned, and sleep passed over me as a silent shroud.

With the remains of the rat and a handful of potatoes I disappeared into the forest the next morning and found a den for my little grave beneath the overhang of a large, flat rock. For two days I napped during daylight but remained awake through the night afraid the cold would take me. Again, hunger, exhaustion, and cold forced me from my modest sanctuary into the forest until I came upon a single farmhouse and barn. A dog barked with its tail stiff in the air and eyes set on the woods where I hid, so I left when a woman called for the dog to be quiet.

On through the woods I went, always trying to head north until I reached a farm and a cellar or, if I was lucky, a barn for a night. Sips of milk, perhaps potatoes and a rat, which I became adept at trapping and killing, followed by sleep for three or four hours until sunlight, fear, or both woke me.

This was my life, searching for Mama, food, and shelter in ever deepening snow and cold until one evening, after what might have been two or three weeks, a wind descended upon the forest and left in its wake a still and brutal cold beyond anything I'd ever experienced. As I lay with my legs pulled into my chest. an uncontrollable shiver took my body. Trees cracked as if rent apart by a wicked ogre.

Mama, I'm going to die.

No, Musia, walk now. Find a farm, someplace, anyplace other than in this hole in the woods.

With my belongings and every stitch wrapped around me, I trudged out into the forest. The snow was deep and hard but not hard enough to support my weight. With every footstep my disintegrating boots crunched down through a layer of ice into powdery, crystalline snow. Sweat trickled down my back and froze in the fibers of my clothes so that they were stiff and cold against my skin. My lungs burned with each breath of bitter air, and my legs burned with each hard-won step. Before long, breaking through the crust over and over again scraped my shins until they were raw and bloody.

The desire to allow sleep to carry me into death was almost overwhelming. Despair welled and surged like a black tide within my starved and aching belly, but I tamped down each wave with the desire to live, if not for myself, for Mama. *I love you, Mama, I love you, Mama …* and the warmth of her heart beat within mine, my consciousness fixated on one simple task—one step, and another, and another until the first bloom of morning light glowed before me and revealed, through thinning trees, a snow-covered field and the outlines of a farm.

I leaned against the fat trunk of a weathered grandfather of an oak and looked out upon a large farmhouse and barn surrounded by a handful of outbuildings. An icy, snow-packed track ran parallel to the edge of the forest, and a thin, frozen waterway snaked through rectangular fields on the far side of the farmhouse, twisting north and south for as far as one could see. To the east, ever more rectangular fields girdled by angular wooden fences and hedgerows formed a white patchwork hemmed at the far horizon by a thick band of gray and green, the edge of yet one more immense forest.

Scattered here and there were the outlines of other farms tucked into dells and other contours, quiet in the darkness, without a single light blinking across the landscape.

The field glistened in orange-tinged predawn light, and the snow was unbroken, clouded glass except for a foot-trail that ran in a straight line up its center. The farmhouse and barn were quiet; not even smoke curled up from the wide stone chimney. My breath fanned out in small puffs, and the frozen sweat embedded in the backs of my clothes sent shocks through me when it touched my skin. Not a single bird called to the oncoming daylight, nor did the lowing of a cow break the silence. Not a soul moved within the sting of the coldest air I'd ever felt.

I took the path through the field. It was as wide as a large person, and the snow was broken into crystals like loose sand. The halo of dawn breaking over the horizon cast me as a brown, golem-like figure moving across a plain of pure white. I pressed my chin to my chest to fight the cold, my eyes lifted to see ahead. My ears were antennas listening for the growl or bark of a dog, though I didn't know if I would run or lie down in supplication.

Fortune was upon the golem.

Rusted metal hinges creaked as I opened the narrow, wooden door on the side of the barn and crept in without so much as a titter from a dog. After a few moments, my eyes adjusted to the dark interior, cavernous and cluttered with tools and equipment stored away from the elements. A row of stalls lined the far wall, and above them was a loft so full of straw that it spilled down onto the floor, where boots and hooves had trampled it into the dirt-coated floor. Two plow horses occupied two adjacent stalls, standing motionless except for shivers that rippled down their bony, muscular flanks. Their breath rose like steam from their nostrils, and neither seemed to notice or care that I'd entered their home. The other stalls were empty, but three milk tins sat in a corner beside a large set of doors that opened out to what I believed was a paddock. When I opened the tins, they were empty and dry. I squinted in the dim light but saw no sign of food of any kind, other than straw. Without any thought of a plan, my body heavy with fatigue, I climbed into the loft and burrowed into the straw.

Damp with sweat and shivering, my eyes drooped, and sleep took me.

• • •

My eyes opened to the bewildered face of a young woman. She wore a floral scarf wrapped over her hair and tied beneath her chin. She had high cheekbones, a full mouth, a pale complexion, and eyes as wide and as blue as a cornflower.

She pressed one finger to her lips then disappeared.

Run, Musia.

Beams of bright sunlight cut through gaps in the barn's plank walls.

It's daylight, Mama, and it's so cold. Just let me sleep. What comes will come.

I pulled more straw over me, rolled over, and closed my eyes, but the side door to the barn opened and with it came the voices of a man and young boy complaining of the cold in Ukrainian. They fed and watered the horses with melted snow then banged around their equipment. Outside of the barn, the lowing of two or three cows and the muted babble of chickens blended with the lilting voices of a woman and two girls as they moved about tending to the animals.

A third man entered the barn, and I could tell from his withered voice that he was much older. Behind him followed the throaty breathing and rhythmic pad of two dogs. He asked for work, but the man said no, it was too cold, and he should go back in with *Babyusa,* Ukrainian for grandmother.

Before long, the man and boy as well as the woman and young girls retreated from the cold into the house, and I smelled wood smoke from the farmhouse chimney.

Now, Musia, you can get away.

To where, Mama?

She's going to turn you over to the Germans, just like Kasia.

I'd never make it across the field into the woods. And then what? Freeze to death? Look for another barn? No. What comes will come.

Through the long, quiet day, sleep came like an intermittent warm breeze, and worry fluttered away. *At least I've had a couple of hours of peace,* I thought.

Mosaics created by light and shadow lengthened, then ebbed as darkness fell over the barn. The scent of a warm fire lingered, and as the air became even colder, a quiet settled over the animals and the house. Life suspended its ceaseless labor to observe warmth in all its forms, but I remained cold and alone, and the insistent pain of hunger deepened. I pulled my penknife from my coat and kept it ready if a mouse or rat should come close.

A door to the house opened and shut, followed by the sound of lone footsteps on crisp snow. The side door opened, and an oblong rectangle of light passed into the barn. My heart beat so heavily in my chest that I worried someone could hear it in the silence. The person hung a lamp on a peg or nail and the bottom rung of the wooden ladder to the loft creaked under their weight, as did the next and the next.

"*Ahov?*" a young woman whispered in Ukrainian.

Lay still, Musia.

"*Dziewczynka?*" she whispered in Polish.

Shhh, Neshomeleh.

No, Mama.

"*Jestem tu,*" I whispered in Polish and sat up to reveal myself. Kneeling in the straw was the same girl from the morning, with the same scarf, wearing a dirty, brown wool coat that fell to her knees. Cradled in the crook of her arm was a rusted pail. "Are you going to kill me?"

Her eyes widened, and in their deep blueness I saw Zofia. "Here." She held the bucket out to me.

I looked at the bucket then to her. "Please don't give me to the Germans."

Her top lip formed an exaggerated cupid's bow that thinned when she smiled. "I won't." She looked toward the door and listened for any human sound, then turned back to me and nudged the pail forward. "This is for you," she whispered.

I tilted forward and looked into the pail to see a small, red-checkered towel. When I pulled it up, I found a fat slice of brown bread and a ceramic bowl covered by a plate. The young woman took the towel from my hand and spread it out in front of me on the straw, then laid the bread on it. With her fingertips she lifted the bowl out and placed it on the towel, then removed the plate. As she did this, steam rose up into the frigid air. My eyes opened wide and my cheeks warmed.

"It's not much," she said.

"It's beautiful."

She reached into the pail and handed me a large spoon. "My aunt made the broth from chicken bones, and there's potatoes and boiled egg in it."

Afraid that my trembling hands would spill the soup before it reached my lips, I leaned over the bowl, dipped the spoon into the soup, and scooped it into my mouth. It was salty and had an earthy flavor of baked onion and potato and was so hot that it burned as it slid down my throat into my stomach. The bread was dense, a bit stale, and heavy in my fingers. When I dipped it into the broth it softened, and its milk-sour and nut flavor reminded me of all I had taken for granted in Mama's kitchen.

"Is it good?" she whispered. A smile smoothed her cupid's bow.

My eyes rose to hers, tears dripping from them. "It's beautiful."

She watched me eat and then collected the bowl and towel and placed them in the pail. A house door opened, and she held her hand out for me to be quiet.

"Paranka!" an older woman called out.

"Is that your name?"

She pressed her finger to her lips and whispered, "That's what they call me here." She looked to the side door of the barn and then to me. "Are you all right?"

"Almost human."

She smiled. "I'll be back in the morning." And then she climbed down the ladder. She paused by the side door to look back up at me, then closed the barn door behind her. After she left, I climbed down the ladder, aware that the door could open, but the urge to go to relieve myself could not be ignored. At the bottom, I slinked into one of the plow horse stalls, did my business, then mixed it into the straw as the nervous horse rocked back and forth.

I climbed back into the loft and laid down. My body floated in a sea of straw and the scent of wood smoke and the sound of muted laughter from the house dissolved into dreams.

■ ■ ■

Early morning sunlight cut like darts through cracks in the walls and lit errant objects: the rusting tines of a hay tedder, a plow blade, scythe blades leaning in a heap, wooden hay rakes. There were more implements than people to work them, and I realized this farm was not immune to the world. These people had felt their share of loss.

A house door opened and closed followed by the creak of the side barn door. I looked over the edge of the loft, and there was Paranka with the same pail. She climbed up into the loft and pressed her finger to her lips, then leaned her mouth to my cheek. "Everyone is awake, so no noise."

I nodded and watched as she laid out the same small towel and placed a small corner of bread and dried fruit on it. She then handed me a tin cup of milk, which I drank right away.

"Eat quickly," she whispered.

When I finished, she wrapped the cup in the towel and placed both in the bucket.

"Thank you," I said.

"Shhh." And she left.

Throughout the day the farm was an organic machine orchestrated by a well-worn routine. The barn was never empty, nor was the paddock or yard. The house door groaned as it opened and rasped as it shut. Infrequent laughter and frequent calls in Ukrainian for Paranka to come help with a chore interrupted the periodic silences. To my ears, it seemed she was never in the right place at the right time. If she worked outside, they wanted her cleaning inside. If she was cleaning inside, manure on the dairy floor needed shoveling and a new bed of straw laid down. There must have been hay for the animals hidden somewhere from German and police confiscators.

Maybe the trail into the woods told a piece of that story, as well as the story of how they protected what I'm sure was a modest amount of food, which Paranka so generously shared. I wondered how generous the others would be if they knew I was hiding above them in the loft. Would they turn me in for the reward?

By early afternoon the deep cold eased, but the air was still raw and crisp. Sun beating down on the side of the barn through the day warmed the straw, but with people always present I was unable to move. The straw was a nest, and I was its mouse, hiding from the eyes of people and afraid that even the slightest movement would draw a wary eye. Paranka was the first person in more than a year to treat me as a human being, but in my mind and heart I believed I was a small girl, frail and weak, at the mercy of others and with death hovering, chasing me, hunting me, waiting for me to leave the shadows and enter the light.

The cold bled into my bones so that they ached from the marrow out and stillness stiffened my muscles, especially those in my legs. It was a painful labor for me to remain motionless, but more so to remain quiet. Of all my torments, loneliness was the fuel to my fears and anxiety. There wasn't a voice to inhibit my imagination, which often was like a wild child rampaging within me. There was only the voice of Mama. Now Paranka had come, yet my life depended on not reaching out, not standing in the midst of this cold, airy barn and saying, "I am here, and I am human too!" I was a drowning person unable to call to the stranger with caring eyes who stood at the water's edge, because a mob would throw stones and shoot guns at me.

You trust her, Musia?

Yes, Mama, I do.

What will you do if the police come?

Run, Mama, always run.

Night came and with it a deeper, harsher cold. My ears pricked at any sound that might be Paranka coming to me. Animals moved in their stalls, a cow—maybe two or three, I had no idea—lowed, and the chickens tittered in their roosts. The sound of a rat running through the straw or across the floor of the barn was as loud to me as a human sneaking past. I heard gnawing and the call of crows out in the fields and perhaps a squirrel or two snatching up any fallen bits of food for their nests.

Time moved at an unknowable pace. Was it hours or minutes since the sun had melted into the horizon? Was it so late that she wouldn't come to me or too early for her to smuggle herself to me with food? Tears of exasperation dripped down my cheeks, their salt stinging as they ran.

But then I heard the soft groan of the door and gentle click of the latch, followed by footsteps. An aura of light entered the barn and in its midst was Paranka with her pail. This time she brought water to drink and steaming potatoes for me to eat. She held her finger over her lips as I nibbled bits of a soft potato from a fork, and from her coat she pulled out a set of flannel pajamas. They were careworn, but an exquisite sight.

"Put them on," she whispered.

The last of the potato dropped into my mouth, and I stood for the first time that day to take my clothes off. The smell was awful. My skin and the fabric of my clothing in places had become one so that the two almost tore apart. Naked, except for my underwear, and covered in ulcers, cuts, and bruises, I stood before Paranka. In the soft glow of lamplight, tears fell from her eyes.

"There is almost nothing left of you," she said, wiping her eyes.

My chin fell into my chest, and I grasped my hands in front of my belly, trying to cover myself.

"I'm sorry," she said, then urged me to put the pajamas on.

They were soft and warmer than any of my other clothes. I didn't want to cover them with a coat or the blanket I'd used as my satchel, but the cold would not relent.

"My name is Musia, and I'm Jewish."

Paranka smiled. "I thought you were either Jewish or Polish."

"Why couldn't I be both?"

She wrapped her arms around her chest. "Why are you here, alone?"

I sat back down into the straw. "I've lost my Mama, and I'm looking for her. Have you seen any other Jews?"

"Only dead ones."

An image of Mama's body in a heap of corpses flashed through my mind.

Paranka's eyes widened, and she leaned forward. "I'm sure your Mama wasn't one of them."

"Good. I don't think she was either."

"Where are you from?"

"Horochów."

"You're a long way from home."

"Where am I?"

"Wołyń," she said, using the Polish name for the region to the north of Horochów, "a bit north and east of Równe."

Równe and Łuck are the two largest cities in Wołyń, with Łuck being about one-hundred kilometers west of Równe. I must have walked between these two cities, or perhaps north and then around Łuck, which is about fifty kilometers from Horochów.

"Where are your boots, Musia?" I showed them to her, and she shook her head. "The dogs sleep indoors, and you are here. Where's the justice?" She picked up the pail and started for the ladder. "Be still, Musia. I'll be back tomorrow as soon as I can."

The next morning the sun rose as before, and the straw warmed, and the people moved about their business with laughter, often calling for Paranka to do this or that or to ask why isn't she here or there. As seemed the routine, they all went inside around midday, and the scent of wood smoke rose.

It wasn't until that night that Paranka returned to the barn with her pail. Inside it was a tiny piece of cheese, something I'd not eaten for two years, and dense, warm bread. From her coat she handed me a pair of warm boots. Their soles were almost worn smooth. Inside them were two pairs of thick, wool socks.

"Thank you," I said, wiping a tear from my eye.

"I want to help, Musia."

"Why?"

"I'm hiding too."

"You're Jewish?"

"No, Polish—well, half Polish and half Ukrainian. My mother was Ukrainian, but she fell in love with my father, a Pole, and after they married they lived in Lwów. I was born not long after, and then two years later my sister came."

"My Papa was a professor at the university," I said.

Her eyes looked down and then to me. "Was he killed in Lwów?"

The word *killed* jabbed my chest. "No. Why?"

She wiped her eyes. "You've seen so much, Musia."

"What do you mean?"

She turned to the door and then looked at her hands in

her lap. "I shouldn't say anything." Her eyes lifted to mine, and golden light from the lamp reflected in them. "But when the Russians came to Lwów, they arrested many people, Poles and Jews, but most were Ukrainians, thousands of them, and they put them in Brygidki prison in Lwów."

"Why?"

"I don't know. My mother said because they were enemies of the Soviets, but they never said why. They just took people."

I nodded.

"And then one day everything went crazy. It was madness. There were Russian soldiers everywhere, destroying whatever they could as quick as they could because the Germans were coming—including the prisoners." She paused to take a breath. "They killed them all. Some they shot, some they beat to death, and others they threw grenades in their cells and then left the bodies."

"Were your parents in the prison?" I asked.

"My father was."

"I'm so sorry."

She wiped away tears with the back of her hand. "When the Germans came to Lwów, they found the bodies in Brygidki and drove around in trucks with loudspeakers saying that it was the Russians who had killed all those people and that the Jews helped them and that all Jews are Muscovite reptiles who've sucked our blood for centuries."

"What? That's not true, it can't be! Certainly not my Mama and Papa."

She tucked her hands beneath her arms to warm them. "I believed it at first; everybody did. We were so angry and so disgusted that when the Germans rounded up Jews to bury the bodies, we didn't say anything. And then when the SS took them away, we knew they would kill them, hundreds of them, but we didn't say anything. We were just so angry."

"I can tell you my Papa had nothing to do with this. He wasn't even in Lwów when the Germans came. It's all lies. You have to believe me."

She looked to the door, bit her lip, then looked back at me. "I have to go; they'll notice."

"Wait, no." I wrapped my fingers around her forearm as she reached for the checkered towel. "You believe me, don't you?"

"I have to go, but yes, I do. After the Germans built the ghetto in Lwów, I saw our neighbors, friends of mine and my parents, good people I grew up with, called *pigs* and *murdering Bolsheviks* and starved to death and murdered. I knew it was all lies, lies to keep us angry, to make us silent."

She crawled to the ladder, and I leaned toward her. "What about your mother?"

She looked up at me, and her pale face shone in the flickering light. "I'll tell you later, and you can tell me about your Mama."

"Paranka, am I safe here?"

"No one's safe, Musia."

And she left.

. . .

After I heard the door to the house close, her story, the lies and killing and hatred and fear overwhelmed me, and I saw how small I was—a squashable mouse hiding in the loft.

The next morning came dull and gray. As I listened to the people work, the slate darkness in the barn felt forlorn, and I wondered how long I could hide in this loft before someone found me or before idleness and the need to continue my search for Mama obliged me to go back to the woods. Could I make it until spring? Summer? Not even knowing if it was December or January made both seem so far away. What if Mama was standing next to that grandfather oak right now, looking down on this farm, looking for me? The thought made me anxious, but winter—the deadly, barren season of famine— caused almost as much fear as the thought of the SS or police.

The day exhausted itself, and night came all at once. With the people inside, I could pull away the straw and move about the loft to stretch my legs and use the horse stall as I waited for Paranka. Just when I thought she would not come, the house door opened, and then the barn was lit in golden lamplight.

In the pail was a boiled potato and onion and a tiny piece of chicken that smelled sour and had a gamy taste.

"I'm sorry if I worried you last night," she said as I ate.

"I'm sorry for your father." I bit into the potato then looked at Paranka. Her eyes were the shape of almonds and were a soft blue in the faint light. "Are the people here your family?"

"Yes, my mother's family."

I nodded. "Do they hate Jews?"

Her lips pressed together, flattening her cupid's bow. "They're afraid, Musia, afraid of everybody and everything. If they knew you were here, they would turn you over to the authorities, but maybe I could convince them to let you go back into the forest."

"They wouldn't let me stay?"

"Hiding a Jew would mean the death of us all."

The weight of their lives weighed like a stone on my chest. "Should I leave?"

Paranka looked up. "No. We'll just be sure they don't find you."

I nodded, but I heard the same uncertainty in her voice that ached in my heart. "What happened to your mother?"

She looked to the door, folded her hands in her lap, and shivered against the cold. Then in a whisper, "After the Germans liquidated the ghetto in Lwów, they came for the Poles, not all, but most. My mother wanted us to come here but thought it too much of a risk for the three of us—her, my sister, and me—to travel together, so she sent me first. That was almost two years ago, and I haven't seen or heard from them since."

"Paranka, I'm sorry."

A tear wavered down her cheek. "They killed my Polish father for being too Ukrainian and my Ukrainian mother for being too Polish. It doesn't make any sense."

"How do you know she's dead?"

"She and my sister would be here." She took a deep breath then said, "How did you lose your mother?"

"After the Germans took Papa, only the three of us were left, Mama, my sister, Tchiya, and me, and then after they stole everything we owned, they sent us to the ghetto—"

"In Lwów?"

"No, Horochów. We were there from the fall, through the winter, and into the summer when the rumors started that the Germans would liquidate the ghetto. You could tell it was going to happen. There were more guards and Germans, and there was just more activity, like they were preparing for something.

"People started to panic, and no one knew what to do. Mama worked outside the ghetto building roads for the Germans—"

"I remember the haunted eyes of the workers walking down the street in Lwów from the ghetto," Paranka said.

I sat up a bit. "Mama hoped she would run into a friend of ours from before, but she couldn't make a connection, and we could tell the end was coming closer. Then one night she came home smiling and said she'd found a place for us to hide—"

"How did she do it?"

"I don't know, but I think she paid them."

"Them?"

"It was two farmers; neither would take all three of us."

"And she had to decide which of you would go alone."

"Like you, Tchiya was to go on her own."

"She was older?"

"She *is* older, yes. The plan was that Tchiya would sneak away from her work and meet the farmer and go with him. If we didn't hear anything, we would assume she was safe, and then Mama and I would sneak out of the ghetto at night and go to our place to hide.

"The day came for Tchiya to go, and we hugged goodbye, and that was that. After two days it was our turn, but that was the night the liquidation began, and bullets hummed past our heads."

"Were they shooting at you?"

"No, they were shooting people in the streets or running to the river behind the ghetto to get away. We hid in bulrushes that spread out into the shallow water for two days and watched as they slaughtered every living thing in the ghetto. Then, at the end, I fell asleep."

Paranka held her hand up for me to be quiet and looked at the door, but there was only silence.

"When I woke up, Mama was gone."

"Gone?"

"She couldn't wake me, so she left. I've been looking for her since."

"Why would your mother leave you?"

"Because I don't remember one flaw in my mother, nothing, and I can't remember her doing anything that I don't admire. She is perfect, and I'm very, very, very lucky to have her as *my* mother."

Paranka placed her hand on my leg. "I'm sorry, Musia. I don't mean to doubt—"

She held up her hand again, and this time we both heard the house door grind open. "Paranka, where in the world are you?" a woman called out in Ukrainian. Behind her two dogs barked, and she told them to be quiet.

Paranka lifted the pail and pulled her coat tight around her. "I have to go." She climbed down the ladder and walked out into the cold night.

My head sank into the straw, and my heart ached. The pain of missing Mama was sharper than I'd ever felt, and for the first time, I doubted my own story.

The next morning the work continued, as did the frequent calls for Paranka to do this or that. Later that night she came with her pail, and we talked as I ate, but we didn't share stories of our families. I asked her where the food came from, with the Germans taking so much, and she said that people had learned to hide food in the woods, never in their homes. "The Germans or the police would shoot us if they knew we had anything."

On following nights, we talked about our friends, our schools, and homes. She asked questions about my time in the woods, and I asked about the farm. We also shared our dreams for the lives we would lead once this horrible war was over, but I couldn't imagine a time when the killing would stop or the Germans and police would no longer hunt me. Death, as always, hovered, waiting for me to emerge into the light.

After a few days I'd learned to tell time by the different sounds each chore made. Feeding chickens had its own song, as did the clinking and clanging of the man and boy working on this or that machine. The cows lowed, and the chickens clucked in their roosts. Paranka shoveled chicken and cow manure, then laid the new bedding. She made sure she was the one to gather fresh straw for bedding, though no one else seemed interested in the task. And then they went inside, and smoke poured from the chimney.

At night, after Paranka left and the loft was quiet and the night silent, I lay in the straw and smiled. Rather than worry about what was to be, I thought about what is. *I am safe tonight and will be safe tomorrow. That's enough for now.* And I let my worries spread their wings and fly away into the night.

The weather remained cold, and snow fell and collected on the barn's roof so that it creaked beneath the weight of it. When the sun shone, it warmed the roof and rafters and released heaps of snow that slid off and landed on the ground in a loud puff. The morning after one of these storms, with the sun shining and the sky a bright blue, the man and boy hitched the horses to a sled and left for the day. The women spent the morning inside and sent Paranka out to feed the animals and milk the cows. With everyone occupied, she climbed the ladder and gave me a cup of milk and said she would bring bread and butter that night.

After she left, my legs were restless, and my entire body felt wiggly, but I wasn't starving in the woods, and there was bread and butter to look forward to. The door to the house croaked open and then closed. I lay back in the hay, then heard a horse whinny. With the man and boy returning, I knew the farm would return to its regular rhythm. I burrowed deeper into the straw and lay still, so they wouldn't see me as they watered, fed, and brushed the horses.

I heard sleigh runners scrape and bounce through the snow, and a man whistled and called out to the horses in Ukrainian for them to slow. Their hooves crunched on the hard-packed snow between the barn and the house. I could hear the horses' lips flutter as the sled came to a stop, and I imagined their bodies, hot from exertion, steaming in the cold air.

A pair of boots landed hard on the snow and then another, and the two mumbled to each other. A fist pounded on the door, and the deep, husky voice of a man yelled, "Come out! Hello!"

The door creaked open, and a woman, Paranka's aunt I believe, asked what in the world they wanted. "We've given all we have to give and more. There's nothing left."

"Where's the man of this house?"

"He's gone for the day."

There was a pause. "Send Paranka out here, now!"

"What do you want with her?" The woman's voice was sharp but restrained.

"Send her out now."

"But what could she have—"

Then Paranka's voice, shaking, afraid, "It's all right, Auntie." I heard her step onto the snow.

"Where are your papers?"

"In the house."

"Fetch them."

Paranka's steps faded in the house.

"She's a good girl, loyal, why do you have to stir up

trouble? There are Jewish and Polish gangs in these woods, for God's sake."

The man did not answer her.

Paranka's boots scratched across the snow. "Here."

Silence.

And then a gunshot—my heart seized, and my breath left me—and a body landed hard on the snow followed by a scream. The horses nickered, and a second gunshot rang out.

"Paranka!" the woman cried, and I heard her fall to the ground. "My beautiful Paranka. You animals, she was not a Jew!"

"Shut up, bitch, or we'll kill you and burn the farm to the ground!"

The woman sobbed over Paranka's body as the two men climbed into the sleigh and the horses guided it down the frozen track. The scratch of the runners faded, and the old man and woman came out from the house as the other woman moaned over my friend.

They took Paranka inside, and a painful quiet settled over the farm. Tears streamed down my cheeks, and my body heaved from despair.

Is there no end to this, Mama?

Yes, neshomeleh, there is. Come to me in the forest, and you will see.

That night, I trudged up the beaten path through a sea of moonlit, phosphorescent snow beneath glittering stars. At the grandfather oak, I turned to look once more at the farm, then disappeared into the trees.

Treat Her Gently

Into the night I walked north and east along the edge of the forest.

Moonlight created a lacework of knotted and gnarled shadows that quivered at the slightest hint of a breeze. Dried leaves skittered across a frozen skin of snow, and in a distant yard or barn a dog barked, and somewhere in the woods a wolf howled a mournful response.

Maybe there is another Paranka, Mama?

It's too much to hope for, neshomeleh.

I paused to take a breath and looked out past the trees into an artist's dream of glittering fields tinted indigo-blue beneath a dome of black silk pricked by starlight. Here and there, bosks of crooked trees were girdled by wiry briars and windblown snowdrifts that all but swallowed fences and hedgerows. Scattered farmhouses with their off-kilter barn brides slept dark and quiet in the cold night.

On the farthest horizon was a charcoal-colored line, like an elongated brushstroke, cast by yet another vast forest. In that brushstroke, across from where I stood, a pinprick of light shimmered. There were no other lights, and I wondered who could be so bold.

Hunger twisted my stomach while my mind's eye ruminated on the sight of Paranka's blood, a bright red cloud in trampled snow. My fingers pressed into my temples to dislodge the image, but memory, like a grotesque zoetrope, replaced it with a projection of Zofia's deep blue, dead eyes followed by flashes of starved and murdered children.

Tears stung my chapped cheeks.

Are you alive, Mama?

I am here with you, neshomeleh.

But are you alive?

An inescapable chill inhabited my body, causing a shiver to run up my spine and coerce my legs into movement. The snow was deep with a thick, brittle crust that held me for a moment before giving way beneath my weight. Each step pained my muscles, scraped my shins raw, and sapped my will, but I continued, step by step, for hours until I stumbled on a fallen branch hidden beneath the snow and fell hard. Thin, spidery fractures rippled out around me as I rolled onto my back and tilted my head up. Trailing off along the fringe of the forest was a path that led from Paranka's frozen blood to the last living Jew of Wołyń.

If worries were birds that could fly away into the sky, so too was hope.

Go into the woods, Musia.

I'm too tired, Mama.

It will be safe.

No, Mama, it won't.

Yes, my love, please, into the forest.

The eastern horizon glowed dull copper, and beneath it, in that long brushstroke, were more glinting flecks of light. *More hunters, more killing,* I thought.

Sunlight caught the top of a chimney at the center of the open expanse of fields, and I wondered if someone kind might live there or if there was a cellar for me to find a bit of food and warmth, but it was a long way and the land too open. Unlike the forests and fields farther south, there weren't any farms or villages at the edge of these woods. There were only pairs and trios of low buildings nestled into the patchwork of fields like ladybugs clinging to an immense leaf.

Yes, Mama, into the woods.

Trees enfolded me as the snow resisted my full weight on the crust, then dropped me down into it again. Morning light burned on the horizon behind me, and the woods were silent except for the rasp of my steps, rattling of branches, and warning caws of crows. Hunger, inexhaustible and unyielding, wrapped around my belly like a tight fist, and cold ached outward from the marrow of my bones.

Why am I alive, Mama?

You are strong.

Others were stronger.

Not like you.

Others deserved to live more than me.

No one is more deserving than you, neshomeleh.

I have nothing to contribute to the world.

Your life is a gift.

I'm not worthy of this gift.

Copper dawn dissolved into blue sky, and on I pushed farther into the heart of the forest. Occasionally, I rested against a fat tree or beside a large rock and watched for anyone who might be following my trail, but the woods were free of any human sounds or sights. During one of these rests, I noticed acorn caps in the snow and kicked with my toe down to the dirt to pick through rotting leaves and pry the coffee-brown nuts from the ground. My teeth sank into their doughy flesh, and their flavor was of damp earth, but it was food. Later, as I leaned my back against a rock, I saw a tangled braid of fox or owl scat—it was black with gray fur that looked like mold and tiny white bones wound in it. I stuffed it in my mouth before the sight of it sickened me, though bile rose and burned the back of my throat as I chewed and swallowed the furry clump. When I came to birch trees, I stripped bark from them, which tasted like mint and camphor oil, and chewed on it as I bobbed up and down across the snow.

The sun traveled along a low arc in the southern horizon until midday transitioned to late afternoon and the forest was cast in a gray-hued light. The effort of walking exhausted my legs, body, and mind, and my belly, filled with the soft, earthen flesh of acorns and acidic animal feces, felt watery and ill. Behind me was a winding trail of footsteps, and I wished for snow or wind or rain to erode the evidence of my presence.

I crumpled to my knees and rested my shoulder and cheek against the rough bark of a fat, old oak. My eyes floated upward through spindly, gray branches where a blood-orange moon ascended in the eastern horizon. A wisp of cloud passed before it like a silken veil.

Mama?

Yes, my love.

I want to go home.

Home is with me, neshomeleh.

No, I want to go to our home. I want to run from the woods, past the pear and apple trees, and through the garden and hear the slap of the screen door behind me as I hurl myself into your arms and smell Papa's pipe and hear Tchiya practicing her scales on the piano and for you to kiss my forehead.

I know, my love. My arms miss you.

Tears bubbled from my eyes, and the salt of them burned on my cheeks.

Mama, I've walked so much I don't think I can walk any more.

Each step brings you closer to me.

But I don't even know if you are alive.

Musia, I'm with you—

No, Mama, I'm alone!

Remember Papa saying, "There is no God, only proof of his abundant compassion"?

Yes.

The proof of my love is abundant within you, and my love is why I am always with you.

Are you with God?

Can't I be both with God and with you?

Mama! Just please tell me because if you are, then that is where I want to be!

My face dropped into my hands, and I wept from frustration.

I'm sorry, I said, *but I'm alone, and all I want is to go home.*

My love can carry you, Musia, but you must take each step that brings us closer.

Aren't you looking for me?

Yes, Musia, I am, and I will never give up seeking you.

I lifted my face from my hands and looked into the pale face of an eventide moon.

Mama, I'm so very tired.

I know, neshomeleh.

Each breath wheezed from my chest, and the skin on my hands was wax-like and pockmarked by abscesses that flourished elsewhere on my body like lichen on a rock. With my fingers I lifted a pant leg to expose my shin to the air and saw that the inflamed skin bubbled with blisters coated by oily blood. Each beat of my heart pounded in my chest, then paused to gain enough momentum for the next pulse.

Paranka's kindness caused death to ebb from me like water seeping into sand, but not so much that my body and mind lost the unrelenting sensation of impending death.

I want to be home, and I want to be with you.

It may not be possible to have both, neshomeleh.

A gust of wind rattled frozen tree branches as it passed like a wave above me.

Death feels close, Mama.

Death has always been close.

Saliva made thick from crying choked in my throat.

I'm so tired.

Then let's sleep.

Wind rustled through the forest, and my eyes followed bursts of it through a canopy of birch and alder and oak and maple. Dispersed below these much taller trees were clutches of balsam, fir, and hemlock, and below these were looping strands of briars, juvenile trees, and bushes denuded by winter, except for those with small red or orange berries. Bowls and knobs the depth and size of large, round rocks pockmarked the forest floor, and not too far from me was a stand of mast-like pines. Pushing myself up against the papa oak, I stood and walked into the pines. Red-brown needles matted the snow, and wind or age had toppled an elder so that a section of its trunk lay across a bowl.

With the rusted shovel blade, I dug out the snow and piled it like a rampart on the lip of the hole beneath the pine. Then I used the penknife to cut and wrest small boughs from balsams and lay them on the ground in my den. Last, I gathered fallen branches from beneath the broadleaf trees and used them as a roof.

I ate the last four acorns, then pulled my coat tight around me and rested my head in the balsam; its pungent, pitchy scent colored the air and eased me to sleep.

• • •

Kaleidoscopes of color fanned and burst against the backs of my eyelids, and I blinked them open to bright sunlight peeking down into my hermitage. It was warm on my cheeks, though I shivered with a deep chill. I wanted to lie still, but an ache in my bones and knife-like pains in my belly forced me to sit up. With my knees pulled up to my chest, arms wrapped around them, and my head leaning forward, a throbbing soreness in my neck made itself known to me as did a severe pressure behind my eyes.

As much as I wanted to let go and be done and be with Mama, pain impelled me to seek something, anything, to put in my gaunt belly. By now, my body was so emaciated that I pressed a finger against my stomach to feel for the bones of my spine.

My back bumped against the roof of branches as I crawled out and stood in the sunlight. Without thinking, I pulled down a handful of pine needles and shoved them into my mouth. Their acidic flavor dried my mouth and tightened my throat so that they caught and I gagged on them. I spit what needles I could out then scooped snow into my mouth, held it there to melt, and swallowed the water in a gulp. I did this a couple more times until the melted snow cleared my throat and then looked out past the stand of pines into the forest.

Not too far away was a small clearing where a patch of spiky burdock pods dangled from their stems. With the shovel blade, I dug through the snow around each stem, pausing every so often to rub the back of my neck or my temples to relieve the pulsing pain, and teased out as much of the root as I could. For my effort, I had only a handful of the white flesh to eat, but it was mild and sweet and better than rotting acorns.

Look at the snow, Musia.

My footprints were strewn about.

They'll find you.

A sudden cramp cut through my stomach and my hands instinctively pressed against it to sooth the pain. In almost the same instant, the throbbing in my neck and pulsing behind my eyes became almost blinding. My vision blurred, and my legs shook from weakness.

If they come, they come, I replied.

My body felt as if it were on fire as I stumbled through the snow and then into my little grave. The smell of balsam, once reassuring and calming, only inflamed the cramp in my stomach and vice-like pain in my neck and head. The sun was warm, but its light splattered against my closed eyes and cast a fiery aura that blinkered like lightening in my eyes, through my brain and down through my spine. Turning from the light diminished the aura a bit, but a moment later, burning vomit surged up my throat and flowed from my mouth into the balsam.

Oh, my poor Musia.

I hate this, Mama, I hate it. Please hold me; make it go away.

I remember Papa's books.

An image of Papa reading in his library—the maple desk piled with books and papers, the cherry-wood card catalogue, and the globe with its blue-green ocean currents—came to me.

How could I forget, Mama?

Remember the poems he read to us in the evening before bed?

Of course.

I drew my knees up to curl my legs, and a small, acrid sip of vomit slid from my mouth.

Papa sat in his chair next to the fire while you and Tchiya curled around me on the sofa.

And the room was lit by candles and firelight.

Mama whispered the lines of a poem: *The tired day droops, slowly waning, the noisy waves are now tranquil. The sun has set, the moon is sailing, above the world, absorbed and still.*

Within these words echoed Papa's rich voice, but still, pain beat behind my eyes, and I squeezed my arms around my belly.

Remember this? "At the vegetable stall on market day, such conversations are the way: 'You may lean on me, Mr. Dill, you really have gone through the mill.' 'Now is that a surprise my dear chive, I've been withering here since five.'"

Her laughter vibrated in the air around me.

Or this, she said, *"I built on the sand, and it tumbled down, I built on a rock, and it tumbled down. Now when I build, I shall begin with the smoke from the chimney."*

Her fingers tickled the downy hairs on the back of my neck. A dribble of curdled saliva stuck in my throat, and I coughed to release it.

Is it the burdock root, neshomeleh?

No, Mama. We've seen this in others before.

A warm tear dropped onto the back of my neck and spilled down my collar.

Yes, neshomeleh. She took a breath. *"However keen may be your sting, however fatal, yellow bee, over my basket I have dropped, the merest dream of floating lace."*

A chill rattled through me, but with it came the lines of a poem. *"Mister Hilary runs and screams—"*

I love this one.

"—where on earth could my glasses be? A scandal, he yells, it's beyond belief! To have my glasses stolen by a thief! Though who would ever suppose, his glasses are on his very own nose."

That is so good you remembered that, Musia.

Thank you, Mama.

Her smile radiated. *One more, then please rest, my love.*

I pulled the coat over my head to block the light and tucked my hands beneath my cheek.

Okay, I'm ready.

"The tired day droops, slowly waning, the noisy waves are now tranquil. The sun has set, the moon is sailing above the world, absorbed and still."

My breath entered and left my body of its own accord—rasping like that of a sleeping baby—and the pain ebbed but did not leave me. My heart beat then gained strength for the next push, and with each, I wondered if it was the last. But then my heart summoned the will once more, and I wondered anew if it would beat again.

Wind blew through the trees above me, and from within my woolen chrysalis, I sensed clouds thickening against the sun. Before long, I heard the pit and pat of snow falling through the trees. My thoughts were at peace, but my body was in pain, and I prayed for sleep, or whatever may come. The response was calm and dreamless—not quite what I wanted nor what I feared.

...

Krak, krak, krak, krak-krak-krak.

The breathy echo of gunshots resounded through the forest, and my eyes opened to darkness and the delicate murmur of snow falling.

Krak, krak, krak-krak-krak.

Musia, get up. Those are rifles.

I know, Mama, but they are far away.

Not that far. Please, you need to get up.

Mama, I'm too tired, and the pain is too much.

My love, please.

Here is as good as anywhere else.

Musia, each step you take is one step closer to me.

Mama, I'm so tired.

A shiver snaked up my spine.

There is home, Musia. I swear to you there are violet lilacs, blooming pear and apple trees, beautiful roses, and love, so much love, but only if you get up.

The pressure behind my eyes and the burning in my belly and across my skin pulsed with each breath and slow beat of my heart.

How can you promise such things?

Because it will never exist if you don't come to me.

But Mama—

No buts, my love. I am through the forest; come to me.

No, I can't, Mama.

Musia, don't give up on me.

I'm not!

Tears fell down my cheeks, and I pressed my hands to my eyes and face.

Have I ever given up on you?

No, but—

I will never stop looking for you, and there is nothing I wouldn't give up for you, even my life, neshomeleh.

Sobs choked in my throat, and I buried my face in my

hands, knowing that I had no choice but to climb from my little grave and try once more to find Mama.

The gunshots seemed to come from the east and south, so bundled against the cold night, I started walking west and north. The snow crust had not changed, and I continued to bob up and then down with each step. Snow fell in large, eiderdown flakes and hung on hardwood tree branches in white tufted lines. The woods were silent, except for the static-like sound of falling snow, and the air smelled cold and metallic. Though I wore layers of woolen clothes, including the boots Paranka had given to me, and my muscles worked hard enough for me to sweat and my breath to come slow and heavy, the chill would not relent. Often, dizziness or the need to release my liquid bowels caused me to stop, and each of these times brought the temptation to curl up in the snow.

But guilt and shame are powerful and compelling emotions. They were set loose by Mama's words, which looped through me in her gentle, insistent, loving voice: *I will never stop looking for you.* Lying to Mama and sneaking beneath the fence, getting the beating across my back, losing my finger, and every other stumble I'd made over my twelve years caused visceral spasms of shame, but the memory that burned deepest was losing Mama at the river's edge.

Proof of love and my atonement to Mama was pulling my body up from the snow, making one more step, and believing it brought me that much closer to Mama and her love.

The snow eased, then stopped, and soon after a soft butternut dawn waxed on the eastern horizon. With it came more *krak, krak, krak* of gunshots. Their echo was sharp, and each lit through me like an electrical shock. The sound carried from some distance, but I couldn't be sure they were not close, not following my trail. Yet even as fear filled my heart, my legs could do no better than their same benumbed pace.

But I kept going until the forest gave way to a clearing filled with frail evergreens coated by fresh snow, none taller than an arms-length above my head. Hardwood forest surrounded the clearing on three sides, but at its farthest end it looked as if it opened out to yet another expanse of fields. I squinted and, in the distance rising above the white and reedy evergreens, saw the peaked roof of a barn.

I don't know, Musia.

It's all right, Mama.

The snow was billowy and free of human footprints. The only markings were where tufts of snow fell from a branch or where a squirrel had bounced by in its obsessive hunt for food. Though approaching the barn did not feel safe, the thought there could be food made it impossible to walk back into the forest. The immature grove of evergreens hid me as I walked toward the barn, and as I brushed past slouching boughs, snow fell onto me and dappled my brown, wool clothes so that I blended with the trees. Every couple of steps I paused with my ears pricked to listen for any human sound, and my eyes, blurred by malnutrition, searched for footprints or movement in the trees around me.

I heard only the cawing of crows, and the snow was smooth as a quilt. Sunlight breached the horizon in amber streaks that reflected off clouds and lent them a golden trim. Soon, the barn came into view as morning light sifted down upon it.

Lying on my belly beneath the trees, I watched and listened for people, but this was a lonely and silent place. Hardwood tree trunks formed the end of the slate-gray barn, their stump ends buried in the ground and each trunk lashed to the next. Whoever built the barn had cut the trunks to form a large and wide triangle upon which a roof of irregularly sized boards fitted together and descended from the roof's peak to the top of the snow. At the near end was an opening cut from the lashed trees where two large doors were open so that wind-blown snow piled against them, and a tongue of snow entered the barn.

Set to one side of the barn was a small house built in the same way as the barn. Its door was also open, as were the windows on the first story. A fieldstone chimney jutted up from the center of the roof. A picket fence ran along the front of the house, though many of its slats were missing and blown snow swallowed much of it. Beyond that was an immense patchwork of fields and farms across which cloud shadows passed.

There was no movement or sound until *krak, krak, krak, krak-krak-krak* reverberated through the air again. As before, the shots appeared to come from the south and east, but their echo made it difficult to be sure. I cupped my hands around my eyes like binoculars and squinted into them. Backlit by the rising sun and highlighted by a patchwork sea of white fields, four or five bleary columns of smoke curled into the sky, but I could not tell if they were the product of farmhouse chimneys or some other cause. My eyes were too weak and the smoke too distant and obscured by sunlight.

Hunched over and dragging my clothes and carrying my meager belongings, I made my way through the snow to the barn. Snow had blown in through the open doors, and as my eyes adjusted to the light I saw that the doors at the opposite end of the barn were open too, and wind had piled snow against them. No hay was in the loft or any on the ground. The stalls were empty and without any bedding or signs that animals recently lived in them. There were only rusted tools hanging from pegs on the walls or where someone put them down as if to take a break and left them. There weren't any hay tedders or ploughs or harnesses or wheat threshers or any large equipment a farm would need.

Light filtered in through the open doors as well as through cracks in the walls that were once filled by mud and clay mortar. I poked around the stalls and corners of the barn hoping to find an errant potato or anything I could put in my mouth, but there was nothing other than a pile of potato sacks in one corner. I grabbed them thinking I could bundle myself in them to keep warm and then walked to a small workbench. Any useful tools were gone but etched into the wall behind the bench were the words, "Without work, there will be no supper," written in Polish.

They're all dead, neshomeleh.

Or run away.

Krak, krak, krak, krak, krak-krak-krak-krak-krak echoed across the patchwork of fields. It was not close but sounded nearer than the earlier shots. With the potato sacks in hand, I walked outside and stood in the yard between the house and barn, looking across the farmland to the edge of the horizon. Something moved.

What is it, Musia?

I don't know.

I shaded my eyes with one hand and squinted into the vast white plain.

Do you see it, neshomeleh?

I think so.

My eyes could not focus.

I think it's cars.

Cars?

Or trucks.

Soldiers?

Cars and trucks, maybe?

Where are they going?

I don't know.

Are they getting closer?

Maybe, I can't tell.

Musia, you must leave.

I looked over the house, its windows were open, some cracked and broken, and I knew that someone would come, either to hide or look for someone who was hiding.

I know, Mama.

I pulled my clothes and coat tight around me and walked back into the forest of stunted pines with the same rise-and-fall stride through new snow and crust. As I grazed each pallid tree, snow dropped down my neck, and I swept at it with my fingers, which were white rather than red.

The mittens I'd taken from the partisans had weeks-ago disintegrated into uselessness, and now my bare fingers weren't even warm enough to melt the snow that stuck to them like hoar frost. I'd seen enough frozen corpses in the ghetto to know that I was becoming one.

A jagged spasm seized my stomach, and with it the aura of pain behind my eyes flashed. Like a hinge, I doubled over, and yellow bile spilled like raw egg from my mouth into the snow. My hand reached for a branch or anything to steady me, but grasping only air I fell to the ground. I raised myself up and braced my upper body with my hands against my knees and retched, but there was only bloody spittle for my stomach to retch.

Don't stop, Musia.

I know, Mama, I know.

My heart beat then paused and beat again. The aura of pain consumed my head, a fever burned within me, and my skin felt as if it were on fire, but even as heat consumed me, chills rattled out from the marrow of my bones through my chest.

I love you, Mama, but—

Don't give up on me, Musia. You are so close.

To what? Death?

To home, Musia.

My eyes flitted upward then closed. When they opened, there at the edge of the forest stood a man, tall and elegant in a black-wool suit and vest, his dark, wavy hair parted in the middle, and a wisp of black mustache crossed above his lips.

"Papa? Is that you? Papa!"

He removed his glasses and smiled. Then he held his hand to his heart, turned, and walked into the woods.

"Papaaaaaa! Please, help me, Papa!"

A thick bolus of phlegm caught in my throat, and my eyes lowered as I coughed it out. When I looked back up to the woods the man was gone.

Musia, please ...

A thick cough rasped from deep in my lungs up into my mouth, and my eyes opened. My face was lying against the ground so that all I saw was cold white.

Mama, what happened?

I lifted my head and fought to rise to my knees.

You fainted, my love.

Krak, krak, krak-krak-krak-krak.

My hands instinctively pressed against my belly to ease a barbed contraction.

Please, Musia, the forest is just there.

Slowly, painfully, I stood. Blistered skin rubbed against rough wool, and I held myself for a moment to adjust to the ever-shifting pain. Then I reached down to lift one of the potato sacks, and as it jerked upward in my hand, I felt a weight in one corner. My hand reached in expecting to feel the soft skin of a rotted and frozen potato, but instead what emerged in my fingers was the limp, bloated body of a rat. I tore it open and ate it.

Into the woods I stumbled, my stomach fighting to force the rat from it, but I would not let it go. Behind me the throaty echo of gunshots flowered then fell away, but I walked golem-like until surrounded by balsam and hemlock. With the last of my strength I dug my final little grave, lay down, and covered myself with branches, dead leaves, and a wide, green bough of balsam.

No one has loved more than you, my dear neshomeleh, no one.

I love you, Mama.

Sleep my darling girl. You are almost home.

Vomit spilled from my mouth, my body convulsed, and stool dripped from me. I brought one hand to my face. Hoar frost grew on the pale, translucent skin like tiny, feathery minerals. My eyes fluttered then closed as breathy echoes pulsated through the air and thunder broke over the horizon. Its clap rushed over me, and then, nothing.

...

"Doushenka, doushenka," said a moonfaced boy as he shook my arm. *"Doushenka, proshniece."* His eyes were bright with fear and darted from me to the woods and back again.

My chest quivered, and the boy and the woods dissolved into darkness.

"Proshniece, devotshka," urged a deep, tobacco-scarred voice. Silver haze resolved into an older man, face like a bulldog, kneeling beside the boy.

Krak-krak-krak-krak electrified the air. Their heads ducked, and their eyes searched the woods, then turned to me. Both wore brown, quilted cotton jackets and fur-lined hats with earflaps dangling down like floppy dog ears. The boy cradled my head with one hand, pulled a cloth from a jacket pocket with the other, licked it and wiped around my eyes and mouth.

His brows furrowed, and his lips pressed together, and sorrow haunted his eyes. Then he lifted me in his arms like a baby, and the trees and sky and odor of gunpowder and sweat diffused and faded into darkness.

...

I woke in darkness. A brown, wool blanket covered me up to my chin and scratched at my reddened skin. Beneath me was canvas, and as my senses came to me bit by bit, I realized I was lying in a cot inside a large canvas tent. In the gloom were people, some of whom moaned in pain or murmured to themselves.

Am I a prisoner?
I don't know, neshomeleh.
Should I try to escape?
No, I don't think you can.
But when the sun comes up, it will be too late.
Where would you go? Back to the woods?
No. I don't even know where I am.

You are warm, my love, and in a bed. Let that be enough for now.

With that, I closed my eyes and waited for sleep to outrace my pain.

When daybreak arrived, it became clear that the people around me were soldiers, and this tent was part of a sort of hospital. Female attendants moved between the beds, their muffled voices not loud enough for me to distinguish the language they spoke.

Moments later, a tall, thick woman burst in through the tent's canvas door. She wore the same quilted jacket as the soldiers as well as the dog-eared winter hat. When she turned toward us after sealing the door shut against the cold, her mouth was cast in a broad smile, and in loud, clear Russian she said, "Good morning, my friends."

With her smile and those words, *my friends,* the tightness within my chest, which began when the Germans took Papa and became tighter as we walked into the ghetto and throughout our ordeal, eased just a bit.

She stopped at the beds one by one and spoke with the nurse responsible for that soldier. Then she sat with them to check their dressings and speak to them. She gave each a light pat on their chest and reassured them with a kindness and care I'd not seen in a long time.

When she came to me, the woman stood at the end of my cot with her fists resting on her sturdy hips and exclaimed, "Well, it's the girl from the forest!" She walked toward me with her arms extended for a hug, and I sat up but fell back dizzy and lightheaded. "That's okay, my love, it's okay," and she bent down and stroked my cheek with her warm hand.

"You're a very lucky girl, you know that?"

I nodded, unable to voice the words that came to me.

Her lips crumpled in an empathetic smile. "You don't have to speak. I don't think you mean us any harm." Her smile broadened so that her teeth showed. "Have you seen this?" and she pulled the wool blanket down to expose my chest, which was covered by a clean, white undershirt. Pinned to it was a note. "The soldier that brought you in left this with you."

She held the note up. Written in pencil with an unsteady hand was, "This is a child of the forest. Care for her gently, with great care."

Tears bubbled from my eyes and fell across my cheeks onto the pillow beneath my head, yet the words born within me could not find my voice.

She patted my chest and said, "We will honor that boy's request. I promise."

Behind her, a nurse arrived with a tray that held a plate with a piece of dark bread with butter and marmalade and a cup. "Time for breakfast," the woman said, and she stood and walked to the next bed.

My hands and arms were unsteady and frail, so the nurse sat with me and broke bits of bread off and cradled the back of my head with her hand to hold me up to eat. Then she let me sip the dark, milky liquid in the cup that tasted like chicory. When I finished, she helped me with a bedpan and then tucked the blanket up under my chin.

"What's your name?" she asked.

My eyes widened.

"That's okay," she said. "For now, we'll call you *Child of the Forest,*" and she smiled.

She gave me another bit of toast then tilted her head to look beneath my cot. She reached down and dragged out my bundled belongs. "I think we'll need to burn these."

I shook my head and lifted one arm to wave my hand. She reached out and took my hand in hers. Her skin was warm and, compared to my emaciated limb, her hand was full and strong.

"I'm sorry, but these things can't ever be worn again. They shouldn't even be in a medical unit."

Panic wavered through my chest, and I shook my head, but she said, "I'm sorry."

With what strength I had, I tilted my shoulders over and pointed to the coat I wore the night Mama and I left the ghetto. The only sound I could make was an anxious, muted squeak, and with my eyes I pleaded, *Please.*

She looked at me then to the coat and pulled it from the pile. I nodded my head, and she opened the inside pocket and withdrew my knife and the key to my family's home in Horochów and placed them on the cot. She dropped the coat back onto the pile, but I shook my head again. She gave me a discerning side glance but picked the coat up once more and shook it. She felt the weight of the last two gold coins through her fingers and looked at me. Then, with the penknife, she cut them from the coat's lining.

She placed them with the penknife and the key and asked, "Is that it?"

I nodded. She reached into a pocket and pulled out a small, cotton bag, placed my belongings in it, folded it, and tucked it with me under the blanket. "I'll make sure they stay with you," she whispered.

After she left, the pulsing ache in my head returned, as did the jagged cramp in my belly. The wool blanket stung my skin as I moved my hands to place them on my belly, but doing that helped ease the cramp.

I'm safe, Mama, finally, safe.

Oh, my sweet, sweet love, I know! I am so proud of you, neshomeleh.

When I'm better, I'll come for you, Mama, I promise.

I know you will, Musia, and I'll be here waiting with Tchiya.

What about Papa?

And Papa too. Now sleep, my love.

■ ■ ■

I'm not sure how long I slept, but a young doctor woke me from a dream when he pulled the blanket down to examine me. His face was placid and eyes calm as he lifted the undershirt. "This won't hurt," he said and then began to press one hand against my belly and then my chest. I winced. "Sorry," he said.

I watched as his fingers, bright white and sunless, moved across the protruding lattice that were my ribs. He avoided the inflamed and bloody ulcers as well as the patches of skin made crimson by rashes and chafing, but still the pain was considerable.

Next, he lifted the blanket away from my legs. The skin was yellow with jaundice and ulcerated, as was the skin on the rest of my body. He peeled off one of the loose, wool socks they'd put on my feet, and I saw green-black blisters at the ends of my toes, which faded to white near my foot. The rest of my foot was red and puffy so that when he pressed a finger against the skin it left a mark like in a pillow.

He turned to the nurse standing at the end of the bed, "Severe malnutrition and peripheral frostbite at the feet and hands. Nothing new here." He turned back to me, "You're an incredibly lucky girl." After he left, the nurse rubbed a salve on the ulcers and wrapped towels soaked in warm water around my feet and hands and then left to tend a soldier. As my feet warmed and the circulation returned, a dull ache emerged and sharpened with time, but I lay in the cot silent and closed my eyes to think of home.

After about twenty minutes she removed the towels from my feet, then looked up at me. Her pink lips were straight and serious, but her brown eyes soft and caring. "I'm sorry, but this is going to hurt." I nodded and pressed my lips together in preparation for the pain. She lit a match and held a pin into the flame, then waved the match out and dropped it to the floor. She looked at me, "Ready?" I nodded. Quickly but gently she punctured each blister and squeezed the milky fluid out. Then with tweezers she pulled the dead skin away from my toes and feet. With each tug of the tweezers, I winced but kept still.

"Good girl," she said looking up to me.

She rubbed an ointment all over my feet, then wrapped them in gauze.

When she unwrapped my hands, she smiled. "These aren't so bad." She rubbed the ointment into them and wrapped them in gauze. Then she packed up her things and left to care for someone else, and I fell into a deep sleep until a nurse brought more toast and the chicory-flavored drink.

Within a day or two, soldiers and nurses broke the hospital down. They loaded some of the wounded into trucks and horse-drawn carts to take them back toward hospitals in Russia. Those who could still fight once they healed rode in horse-drawn carts with the doctors and nurses to the next location as the soldiers fought their way from Równe to Łuck, a distance of about eighty kilometers. Though I was safe and lying in a cart, sickness and malnutrition overwhelmed me. Consciousness came in bouts accentuated by pain that was unbearable, but death's touch waned.

The nurses and doctors were kind, though busy with a steady stream of wounded soldiers, many of whom died agonizing deaths. I watched the wounded come in from battles and the nurses do all they could. Often, I woke to find someone new in the bed beside mine and no idea what happened to the man who was there before him.

A doctor checked on me once a day, but it was the nurses who cared for me. And always, the big nurse whom I had met that first morning came to be sure she kept her promise to the young man who had carried me here from the woods. Never did I feel like a burden or unwelcome, but neither could I express my gratitude or even tell them my name. The words could not translate from thought to speech. So they called me *Child of the Forest* or, more often than not, *Child*.

Each day blended into the next. Then one morning the big nurse came to my bed as usual, but as she left she said, "We will be in Łuck soon." Within two days, the Russians forced the Nazis from Łuck, and a day later nurses and soldiers once again packed the medical tents, and we entered Łuck. I'd been there once before with Papa, and I remembered that Mama often came here by train for meetings for the summer camp she helped create, but Łuck was nothing like I remembered. Bullet holes pitted every wall, the snow was a dirty brown, and large potholes rutted the streets. Few trees remained standing, and the people moved about in a daze, unable to comprehend what had happened to them and, probably, what would happen to them.

We came to a large building with people milling about and bodies lying stiff in the snow. "I kept my promise."

My eyes widened.

"This is a hospital, and they can take much better care of you than we can. I made them promise they would care for you gently." She gave my chest a gentle pat, then walked away. Two men carried me into the building, asked an orderly where to put me, then took me up a flight of stairs, and left me in a damp, cold hallway.

My hands searched for the cotton bag carrying the penknife, key, and two gold coins. Reassured I'd tucked it safely in my blanket, I closed my eyes and waited for sleep to once again outrace my pain.

As I rose up through watery sleep to consciousness, I felt as if my skin were on fire and a pool of pain rose from my belly up to my eyes. My hands found their way to my stomach and pressed down, which helped. It was evening, and rather than still lying in the cot in a hallway, I was in a white room lying on a clean bed with clean sheets, a blanket, and a pillow. A blend of disinfectant and sour body odor rose to my nostrils. When my vision cleared, I saw the small, square room was full of beds, each occupied, mostly by children but two by women. At first, I thought they were all Jews and wondered why I'd never come across them as I wandered the forests, but within their muted voices I heard Polish and Ukrainian. No one spoke Yiddish.

Lifting the sheet and wool blanket covering me, I noticed a new, clean, white shirt that fell loosely around my wasted body. My skin was inflamed from a nurse or doctor wiping it clean and rubbing a new salve into the ulcers and rashes. Fresh gauze fell loosely around my feet, but not my hands.

A few moments more and a nurse rolled a cart to our door. On the cart were bowls with steam rising from a milky porridge as well as cups of water, and she delivered one to each of us. For the first time since the soldier found me, I could sit up, with some help, and feed myself.

A clean bed and warm food, Mama.

It's wonderful, neshomeleh.

When can I come home to you?

She paused. *Care for yourself, my love. Home will wait.*

But I want to see you. Can't you come to me?

Not now, neshomeleh, not now.

A nurse took the plates and the effort of eating so exhausted me that sleep easily outraced my pain.

A doctor came in the morning to check on us. He was gentle but quick and efficient as he passed from one bed to the next. He came to me and said hello in Ukrainian, but my words had no voice, so I shook my head. Then he tried Polish, but again I shook my head. Then he said, "Umhoo," and I nodded at him. He turned to the nurse and said in Ukrainian, "This one can't speak. Do what you can to get her to talk but don't push too hard." He looked at me. "She's been through a lot." Then he moved on.

Some of the children talked in hushed voices, as did the two women. A girl, younger than me, her brown hair, like us all, cut to her scalp, thin as a rail, and wearing a white dress with red polka dots, turned to me and in Ukrainian asked, "What's your name?"

My eyes watered, and I only looked at her for a moment before she turned and spoke to the girl in the bed on the other side of hers. I looked past the girl in the polka dot dress to the girl next to her. Gauze covered both of her arms as well as the stump where the lower half of her leg used to be. Next to her, a dazed baby boy stared at his fingers. Blood-stained gauze was wrapped around his bald head. A woman, thin, shaved head, sad eyes, and the lower half of both arms splinted and wrapped, was in the bed next to his and murmured to the boy, sometimes singing soft lullabies. All them, twelve or fourteen in all, wore an odd assemblage of clothes with various parts of their bodies wrapped in gauze. Some were missing limbs. Small round lesions mottled our bodies, the hallmark of lice, though the lesions on my skin grew one into the next.

For days I existed within this florid body, eating milky porridge and gaining a bit more strength. Sleep did not come so insistently or often, but still no voice was in my hollow throat. And then, one morning after the nurse came to feed us, a young attendant, her hair wrapped behind her in a red scarf, blue eyes, high cheekbones, and lips that formed a delicate cupid's bow, came into the room with a mop and bucket. As she worked she hummed a familiar melody and then in the slightest murmur sang in Polish:

> *Goodnight, goodnight,*
> *Goodnight, my small one,*
> *Goodnight grey eyes*
> *half closed,*
> *For all good children,*
> *Watched by a good angel.*

Tears watered my eyes, and without any thought I cried, "I want to go home! My name is Musia Perlmutter, and I want to go home!"

Everyone in the room was silent and stared at me. The young woman leaned her mop against a table and placed one hand on my arm. "Let me get the nurse," she said in Ukrainian.

Gazing into her cornflower blue eyes I asked in Polish, "Are you *Paranka?*"

A worried expression passed through her eyes, and she looked around the room at the faces staring at us. "No, I'm sorry," she whispered in Polish.

She left, and my shoulders heaved with sobs. Through the wetness of my crying, I murmured, "I just want to go home, I just want to go home ..."

A nurse came and wiped my face with a cloth, then held me in her arms as I cried. "Who are you?" she asked.

I sniffed and said, "My name is Musia Perlmutter."

"You're Jewish."

"Yes."

"Where are you from?"

"Horochów."

She patted my back.

Her face was round with wrinkles radiating from her lips and the corners of her eyes, and a white scarf with a red cross on her forehead held her graying hair from her face. "My Mama is Fruma Perlmutter. Have you seen her?"

Her eyes winced. "No, my dear, I haven't."

I buried my face into her chest. "She won't stop looking until she finds me."

The nurse held me closer. "If my daughter were alive, I'd never stop looking for her too."

■ ■ ■

I asked every nurse, every doctor, every person I met if they knew a Fruma Perlmutter, but it was as if she never existed, like she was a product of my imagination. No one had ever heard of her or my Papa or my sister or me. The most anyone would say is to be patient; when the war is over she would find me. When will that be, I asked. I don't know, but soon, was the common reply. Others, too, had their own wishes and hopes, and what they wanted was what I wanted—to go home and have it be like it was before.

As my health improved I became restless to go home, but

a doctor said the Germans still held Horochów and Lwów.

"When will the soldiers take Horochów?" I asked.

"I don't know," he said. "It's a very big war."

"Soon?"

"Probably not until after spring."

"Why?"

"The roads are nothing more than sucking mud that in some places is deep enough to drown the horses."

"What month is it?"

His eyes widened. "You don't know what month it is?"

My eyes glanced away from his. Papa would be disappointed I'd not kept track. "No."

He nodded. "It's March 20, 1944."

I wiped a tear from one eye with the back of my hand.

Tenderness creased his eyes. "How long were you alone in the woods? A couple weeks?"

"Since August 1942."

His head tilted forward.

"How did you ...," but his voice trailed off. "I'm sorry for what you've been through." Then he stood and moved on to the dazed baby and his mother.

● ● ●

By late April I'd recovered enough to leave the hospital, but the Russians still had not liberated Horochów and Lwów, nor was the army moving to attack. With nowhere else to go, the authorities sent me to a set of buildings in Łuck used to house the many—Ukrainian, Polish, and the scant Jews who survived—displaced people. Soldiers and military equipment filled the cobblestone streets of the small city so that as I traveled through Łuck with a group from the hospital, it was difficult to make our way through without some person, vehicle, or horse running us over.

My legs were weak and wobbly, but the sheer number of people occupied my attention. After being so lonely for so long and afraid of every human I encountered, the experience was overwhelming, and by the time we reached the barracks that would be our home, my hands were sweating, and fear bit into my belly.

We entered the first building, which was a long, narrow hall, and here they gave us a breakfast of bread and jam with bitter coffee. A desk sat at the end of the hall, and as we finished the food, a well-dressed woman with salt-and-pepper hair pulled into a tight bun sat at it and told us to line up.

When it was my turn, I sat in a wooden chair in front of the desk. Her mouth formed a faint smile, and sorrow wore at her large brown eyes. She studied me for a moment, and I sensed pity in her expression, which embarrassed me for looking so dirty and gaunt.

"What is your name?" she asked.

"Musia Perlmutter."

She wrote my name onto a paper form. "Where are you from?"

"Horochów"

She looked up. "It must be frustrating to be so close to home."

"Yes."

"Where were you born and when?"

"December 16, 1929, in Horochów."

She looked at my frail, thin body and its lack of any womanly attributes. "That makes you fourteen?"

It was hard to believe that when I entered the ghetto I was eleven. "Yes."

Sadness passed over her face like a shadow. "And you are an orphan?"

"No."

She looked up at me. "What do you mean, *no*?"

"My Mama is alive, as is my sister Tchiya."

"Are you sure?"

I shifted my bottom on the hard, wooden seat, and my eyes drifted from her stare. "Yes."

She looked at me, and heartbreak bathed her eyes. Then she stood and walked around the desk and gave me a quick, stiff hug. "You can go through that door there," she said pointing to a door on the side of the narrow hall.

The door led outside to a large courtyard with a garden set in its center. Someone had already tilled the soil into neat rows, and well-trimmed, aged trees grew in intervals around the courtyard's boundary.

"Strip," said a woman dressed in farmer's clothes, a white coat, and cloth surgical mask pulled down around her throat.

"What?"

"Strip, please." In her hands was a large tube with a lever. Connected to the tube was a hose that ran over a wall and to an engine that huffed on the opposite side of the wall.

"Why? No."

She pushed me into a corner and started to pull my clothes from me, which were a thin coat, dress, socks, and underwear given to me at the hospital. I grabbed the cloth sack from a pocket and held it in my hands. The woman tried to grab it, but I moved my hands away from her, and she relented.

Standing naked in a corner of the courtyard I watched the woman raise the surgical mask over her mouth and nose, and then a stream of white powder shot from the tube and hit my body. The spray was strong and felt like sharp needles pricking all over my skin. It smelled of rotten eggs, and within a few moments I vomited. The woman stopped the spray. Her lips were a straight line and her eyes menacing. She waited a minute for me, then opened the tube and resumed spraying me for what must have been twenty minutes or more.

She shut off the sprayer, and I opened my eyes to see that a thick coat of white powder covered every pore of my skin as well as my boyish hair. "Don't just stand there," she said pointing to a doorway across the garden. "Go to the showers."

Humiliated and naked, I walked with the bag in my hands and my head lowered through the garden to the door. Inside, the rush of water came from two or three of the twelve stalls, six on either side of the room, and I entered one and hung the bag on a hook. The water came out cold, but no matter, it was liberating, and I took my time to wash my body and hair with soap.

Towels sat on a table outside of the stalls, and I dried myself. For the first time in three years, I was clean, truly, truly clean.

With the towel wrapped around me and the cloth bag in my hand, I went to the end of the room. A gentle-looking woman with a white scarf wrapped around her hair and white coat motioned for me to come closer. On a table behind her were boxes of clothes that she rummaged through and dug out three pairs of underwear, three pairs of socks, and then several dresses, which she held up to me.

"Which one do you like best?" she asked.

I pointed to a blue dress, and she handed it to me with the socks and underwear. I dressed as she found shoes that fit as well as a cardigan, "So you don't catch cold when it starts getting chilly."

Next, she gave me a pillow, bedsheet, blanket, towel, cake of soap, toothbrush, and toothpaste. I'd not seen such things in three years.

"Your new home is barracks two, locker number twelve."

■ ■ ■

As April eased into May and the weather warmed and the roads and fields started to dry out, new rumors spread every day of when the Russians would liberate Horochów and Lwów. Most reflected the growing anxiety of the soldiers walking through the streets and the significant buildup of uniformed men, women, medical caravans, and the sounds of tanks and other heavy equipment gathering on the plains that surrounded Łuck.

With each passing day, as it appeared the fighting was imminent, my impatience to return home and look for Mama and Tchiya grew. In my imagination I saw myself walking up our quiet street, the sidewalk shaded by chestnut trees. I would run to our front door, where Mama would fly out toward me, her arms held wide, tears running down both our cheeks.

"My dear Musia," she would cry out as she wrapped herself around me.

"Mama, I love you so much; I'm so sorry," I would say.

"I love you, my neshomeleh." And she would cry out, "Tchiya, come quickly, it's your sister!" and we would hold each other and together wait for Papa's return.

My desire for this dream to play out was a passionate ache in my heart, and from my first day in the barracks I asked everyone if they'd heard of my mother or sister. "Do you have a picture?" many of them asked, but I had nothing. Every belonging, except for the knife, key, and two coins, that connected me to my family and our home was gone or, as I hoped, was waiting for me on the other side of a serpentine line of soldiers and guns.

When someone new arrived at the barracks, I raced to ask if they'd seen my family, but nothing came of it until one day a woman came to me and said a Jewish woman from Horochów just arrived and was looking for her family.

"Do you know her name?" I asked.

"No, but she's in barracks ten."

I ran down the alley between our buildings and all but exploded through the door. "Mama! It's me, Musia." Faces turned toward me, but none were Mama's or Tchiya's. Then from a bed in the corner, "Musia? Musia Perlmutter is that you?"

I ran toward her voice. "Mama!"

"No, Musia, I'm so sorry. It's me, Sonia Tesler." She raised her frail body from her cot and held out her arms. She was once a beautiful woman with shoulder-length brown hair, a small, full mouth, and gentle brown eyes that were incapable of any expression other than kindness. She was a former student of Papa's and a friend of Mama's and had a two-year-old child, brothers, sisters, parents, a home, and a lovely life before the war and the Germans came.

To believe my search was over, that Mama's arms were a few steps away, broke my heart in a way it hadn't broken before, and I fell into Mrs. Tesler's arms, now bony wisps of what they once were, and sobbed.

"I thought you were Mama."

She patted the back of my head and through her own tear-choked voice said, "I thought you might be my little Flora."

We sat, and I told her my story. Then she told me of her escape from the ghetto, also through the river, and that she'd made her way to the farm of a friend who hid her. When her safety and the safety of her friends became tenuous, they took her to another family who claimed she was a cousin from a village north of Równe. As the authorities seemed to be closing in, she moved again and then again until finally the Russians neared and there was no safe place for anyone. She and the people who took her in hid in the woods for almost two weeks as they waited for the Germans and the fighting to pass them by. Afterward, she came first to Równe to look for any of her family who may have survived and then to Łuck.

"I'm lucky to have found you," she said. "I haven't seen anyone from the ghetto, have you?"

"No, not a soul."

"I don't want to think we are the only two left," she said wiping tears from her eyes with her fingers.

"Neither do I."

She took a breath and sat up straight. "Well, the Russians will attack the Germans soon, and I hope they kill them all."

"Me too."

She patted my hand, "Then we'll go home and see what we find, okay?"

Never in my life had seeing and making a friend anew meant more to me. "Yes."

Rumors of the attack grew in intensity and then fell away as everything remained as it was. The weather warmed, our garden in the courtyard blossomed as did gardens in every inch of tillable land not occupied by a tank, truck, horse, or human. And throughout, the number of soldiers and equipment seemed to double and then triple until it felt as if there wasn't one square foot of space to put anything else.

Then, early in the morning of July 13, we heard the sound of sustained thunder, and the next day it was as if someone pulled a giant plug and the city drained of its soldiers and equipment. In the two weeks that followed, rumors of attacks and counter attacks, that the Germans were coming back, that Russians routed them, that the Russians collapsed, and then that the Russians destroyed the German army, floated through our barracks and throughout Łuck. Then, about two weeks after the attack began, word came through that the Russians had liberated Horochów and then Lwów.

Mrs. Tesler and I were ready to leave for Horochów the day we learned it was free of Germans, but the authorities said everyone had to stay off the roads. Only military vehicles and soldiers could use the roads or leave the city. It was too dangerous, and there were concerns of partisans sympathetic to the Nazis attacking civilians wandering the roads and forests.

For three weeks we waited with our hearts and bodies burning to move, to go home and find our people.

Then, at the end of August, almost exactly three years after the Germans herded us into the ghetto, Russian officials said it was safe and gave us the okay to go to Horochów. I offered to use my last two coins to pay for a train for us both, but only military trains could use the tracks. So we set out to hitch rides from anyone we could and to walk as much as needed. In all, what was a one-and-a-half-hour train ride took us two days as we made our way, mostly on foot, down roads clogged by the military—horses, some trucks, and long lines of marching soldiers—and displaced people trying to go west to their homes or east away from the fighting.

Scattered in the broad, brown fields were destroyed vehicles, bomb craters, and all sorts of battle debris. Fighting knocked over or plowed up much of the grain, but enough of it was left to create a surreal and vast sea of amber wheat tassels and stalks tilting in breezes as sparrows and swallows bobbed and weaved like kites and, in celebration of life, let loose staccato series of melodic trills.

As the setting sun reflected violet and peach against clouds that rose in tall thunderheads, with lightening flashing within them and down to the earth, Mrs. Tesler and I decided to find shelter and walk into Horochów in the morning. Lying beneath a copse of linden trees, their sweet, honey scent drifting down with a passing drizzle blown from a massive dark cloud hovering above the fields like a ghost ship, we burrowed into our blankets and slept like anxious children.

Morning came, and we woke with it and ate a small meal of bread and jam, then packed our belongings. I tucked the sack with my precious things in a pocket and walked down the road to the bridge that would bring us over the river and into Horochów.

The ghetto was gone, not a trace of it left, as if the Germans had plowed it into the ground to be rid of any memory of the Jews they'd murdered. The only remnant was a small pile of bricks. We looked across the open dirt littered with small bits of chipped concrete and brick, and lost to our own thoughts, we remembered. My mind replayed eating a meager breakfast of a potato and pinch of bread that wheezed sawdust and saying goodbye to Tchiya for the last time. Neither of us had cried, nor did Mama. We embraced and looked into each other's faces one last time.

"We'll meet again," Mama said, "and Papa will come home, and we'll have great celebrations."

She and my sister left for their work, and that evening Mama returned home alone.

"Everything is working according to plan," she said.

Mrs. Tesler and I walked toward the center of the city, and as we did, people, their eyes dark and bodies slouched, noticed us. After three years of Nazi occupation, looting, and neglect, there were still some untouched neighborhoods. Other neighborhoods bore the scars of the fight between the Germans and Russians. Everywhere was debris in the streets, and in some places bombs or artillery had caused the facades of buildings to fall into the street. What remained looked like a giant dollhouse of living rooms, kitchens, bedrooms, and stores left untouched. At one kitchen table, a man and woman ate their breakfast, blithely unaware of the people in the street below them.

The Orthodox Tserkva with its golden domes still stood, though fighting had damaged it, as did the big and beautiful Polish Catholic kościół. Across the street from the kościół was the statue of święto Matki Boskiej. Of course, three years ago Germans made us watch them burn our Shtiebels and synagogue to the ground.

We were almost to my home, and my heart beat as if it would burst from my chest. Mrs. Tesler said she would walk to where she lived, and we made plans to meet later, hoping this would include at least someone from our families.

She walked away, and I continued down the main street. As I walked, people looked at me, their eyes hard and angry. One woman called from her front stoop, "You're Professor Perlmutter's daughter."

"Yes, have you seen him or my mama or sister?"

She frowned and waved me away. Most people stared at me, but another older woman asked, "Are you Musia Perlmutter?"

"Yes, I am," I said.

"What are you doing here?"

"Going home."

She nodded.

"Have you seen my sister or mama?"

She pressed her hands to her hips and looked in the air past me. "No, of course not."

Farther down the street a handful of women stopped me and one of them asked, "Are you Professor Perlmutter's daughter?"

"I am."

"My dear, dear girl, you know if only we knew what was happening, what was going on, we would have helped."

The Nazis burned our synagogues and Torahs, they systematically stole our possessions in heaps from the main square, they rounded up my Papa and more than three-hundred men and took them away in a single day, and the stench of death emanated from the ghetto like a foul gas.

"How could you not know?" I asked.

An older man became indignant. "You know it was too dangerous for anybody to do anything."

A woman added, "They killed a lot of Poles and Ukrainians too."

Soon after, I came to my street and stood at the end of it. The chestnuts were full, and fighting and occupation had not damaged the pavement and sidewalk. The same houses were at the corners and along each side of the street, and though it looked as I remembered, something was off, something not quite like home. A man stood in his yard at the house on the corner, but it wasn't the same person I knew who lived there before. Each house was dingier and on some were broken windows or shutters hanging loose from a hinge.

I walked down the middle of the street looking at each house and remembering who had lived there and what it used to look like. And then I came to our house, and I stood before it. When I left I was eleven and pencil straight. Now, at age fourteen, my body was still pencil straight as the result of starvation, emaciation, and cold. I remembered how the hedges, yard, and gardens looked, still tended and bristling with late summer bloom and life. Now, dirt patches marred the yard; the hedges had grown so that shoots shot out like unruly, wiry hair; and the gardens were overrun by weeds. The paint was peeling, two cracked windows stared out at the street, and the front door looked beaten and weathered.

I pulled the brass key out of the cloth bag and felt its weight in my hand. Shafts of sunlight poked down through the leaves, and one warmed my legs.

"Musia? Musia Perlmutter?"

I turned, and standing on the sidewalk in front of his house was Mr. Kijek.

"Yes, hello, Mr. Kijek."

He walked out into the street and gave me a light hug and then stood next to me with his hands in his pockets looking at my home. "They're not there," he said.

My soul withered, and tears welled then fell from my eyes and down my cheeks. "Have you seen them?" I asked.

He put one hand on my shoulder. "I remember seeing you hide in the cemetery behind the chapel one day when the Germans came through."

"You didn't turn me in?"

"No, I couldn't, I wouldn't. I was friends with your father and mother and loved them both. I also remember how beautifully your sister played piano and would open the windows in the summer to hear her play." He looked down to me. "And I remember you running like a demon around that yard of yours and through the garden and the woods. For three years I've missed that as well as your mother calling for you to come in each summer evening. It was like a song she sang to lure you from the woods or the garden, and it was always followed by the slap of your screen door."

Tears flowed down my cheeks, and I wiped at them with the backs of my hands. "I remember."

"Let's sit on my steps and have something to drink, okay?"

I nodded, and we walked to his house, and I sat while he went inside. Through a window in my family's house, a woman was watching me, and then she disappeared. Mr. Kijek brought out two glasses of cool water and sat with me.

We sipped at the water for a minute or two. "I'm glad you survived, Musia, but of anyone, I'm not surprised it was you."

"Why?"

He looked up through the trees to the sky. "You're a strong girl."

"Thank you."

He handed me a handkerchief. "How did you do it? Did someone hide you?"

I wiped my eyes and told him about the river and losing Mama and then Mr. Voitenko and the haystack and the woods, all of it. He listened with grief and sadness in his eyes and face. When I finished, I asked if he knew anything about Papa, Mama, or Tchiya.

He looked at the empty glass in his hands. "I'm not sure you want to hear what I have to say."

My heart wilted, and my chest tightened. "I've seen so much and looked for them for so long, please."

He turned the glass in his fingers. "I suppose it isn't a surprise that your father is dead. When they took those men that day, they drove out into the forest and made them dig a pit and shot them. I'm sorry, Musia."

I put the glass down in the step and folded my hands across my knees.

He winced before he spoke. "Someone, I don't know who, gave Tchiya up. The Germans ordered us to go out and stand near the Catholic Church where they marched her and a handful of women down the street. The Germans had stripped them naked and beaten them badly." Tears welled in his eyes, and he wiped them away. "After that, I don't know when or where, the Nazis killed them all."

The air around me became thick, and through my tears I asked, "And Mama?"

He wiped his eyes with his shirt sleeve. "I don't know, Musia. I hoped she was with you and that the two of you were together. She loved you and Tchiya so much; I just can't believe she would have left you at the river unless she had to."

"But when I woke up she was gone."

"She did that to save you, Musia. There's nothing else that I could believe. It was the last thing she did, and it was out of love for you. And look," he held his arms out, "here you are, alive. By living you did something incredible, and if your mother were here, she would be very proud of you, very proud."

I opened my right hand, and the brass key was still in it, its outline pressed into my skin. My eyes wandered to the house across the street. The woman's face was back in the window, and the sun was easing down toward the horizon behind it. I knew then that as much as I wanted it to not be true, it was no longer my home. I put the key back in the cloth bag and tucked it into my pocket.

I wiped my eyes with the handkerchief, handed it back to Mr. Kijek, and stood.

"I have to go meet a friend," I said and reached my hand out to shake his.

He grasped it with both of his. "I'm sorry, Musia, and I wish you well."

"Thank you. I wish you well too."

I walked down his front walk to the street and turned to wave goodbye. He waved back and then walked into his home. A breeze blew in the chestnut trees and the leaves whispered a late afternoon song.

Are you there, Mama?

Yes, neshomeleh, I always will be.

I'll never stop looking for you.

Each step brings you closer to me.

I love you.

I love you too.

Afterword

Though Musia never again confronted anything as difficult as the ghetto and then her search for her mother in the woods, her life was a mix of joys and sorrows.

After their visit to Horochów, Musia and Sonia made their way back to Łuck where they waited for another eight months for the war in Europe to end. As they waited, they searched for their families and any other survivors of the Horochów ghetto, but there were none.

With the end of the war, word spread that Jewish survivors were gathering in displaced persons camps in the American sector of Germany, considered by many to be safer than the Soviet-occupied territories. Without any papers, food, transportation, or money, Sonia and Musia joined a group of survivors and began the long trek from Łuck to the Föhrenwald displaced persons camp located about forty miles south of Munich.

With much of eastern Poland still lawless or brutally managed by the Soviets, Musia and her small group of survivors made their way to Kraków, then Bratislava , then Vienna. It was in Austria that they came to the first United Nations Relief and Rehabilitation Administration displaced persons (DP) camp. Here they went through another delousing process and received food and clothing. Musia would go through this routine a few more times before reaching Föhrenwald.

After the DP camp near Vienna, Musia and Sonia split up and would not see each other again until well after both had made it to the United States.

Throughout her journey to Föhrenwald, Musia continued to search for her mother and ask everyone she met if they'd heard of her, but to no avail.

At Föhrenwald, which was the largest of the camps and in 1957 the last to close, Musia began the process of applying to immigrate to the United States. She'd remembered her grandmother's (Hanna Perlmutter's) address in the Bronx and wrote her a letter to inform her and the rest of her family that she had survived. The first reply she received was from one of her five aunts in the United States who told her that her grandmother had died of what she said was a broken heart knowing her son and his family were likely all dead.

Overjoyed that Musia had survived, her family worked to gather the necessary documents and affidavits, all in English, which Musia did not speak, and send them to her. Delivering these papers was no small task as it required traveling to a town quite a distance away. Once there, she had to wait a long while for her turn only to have an official tell her she needed even more papers.

In the end, the process took three long years. As she noted in an interview with the United States Holocaust Memorial Museum (USHMM), "After the war, you would think that Jewish survivors would have a priority to get out of Germany but no. There were quotas. There were always quotas."

Not wanting to waste her time as she waited to immigrate and remembering her father's constant emphasis on education, Musia left Föhrenwald and went to a DP camp near Heidelberg, Germany. Once there, she walked to Heidelberg University where she met with a representative of the school and requested admittance. He looked her up and down and asked if she had any school papers. In good German, she said she had none and that the Germans interrupted her education in about the fifth grade. That was enough for the interviewer who accepted her, and the university provided her with tutors to help her catch up on her studies.

Eventually, Musia received permission to come to the United States, and on June 25, 1948, she disembarked from the troop ship Marine Flasher in New York where her aunts, uncles, and cousins embraced her and welcomed her into their lives. From the docks, they took her to the apartment of one aunt, where they agreed she would live, and almost immediately they began to help her transform into an American teenager. They got rid of the DP camp clothes, gave her a whole new set of American clothes, and cut her hair to fit with the style of the times. As one cousin said, "You're a young girl in America now, so let's help you look like one." Musia later said, "I felt like a plucked chicken."

As soon as possible, her aunt threw her into public school in the Bronx, which added to Musia's sense of culture shock. However, this immersion helped Musia quickly learn to speak, read, and write in English, the fifth language she became fluent in. Along the way, Musia's name, which was a pet name given to her by her parents—her real name was Shulamit— was Americanized to Charlene.

Throughout, she was still in considerable emotional and physical pain. As she noted in an interview with the USHMM, she kept her story and her pain to herself, only letting it out in tears when alone.

Upon graduation from high school, Charlene attended Ohio State University where at a party she met Erwin "Ed" Schiff. He was immediately taken by her, and for three months Charlene played hard to get, but eventually he won her over. In an interview she said, "And he has been blind ever since because he doesn't see any of my faults, and I am forever grateful. If I wanted to line up a million men, I couldn't have picked a better husband."

Not long after they became a couple, Charlene told Ed her story. "We sat up the whole night, and I told him. Then I asked, 'Do you still want me?' I was so lucky because he had such a big heart, and he said, 'You are the most beautiful creature in the whole wide world.'"

The two married and started their lives together. Unfortunately, war interrupted their dreams of calm, domestic bliss. Ed was in the military at the end of World War II, and though discharged, he remained in the Army Reserve. When the Korean War started, the United States Army called

Ed back into service. Unbelievably, the Army stationed him in Munich, Germany. Charlene was beside herself and refused to go back to Germany. However, the thought of being without Ed was far more difficult, so after receiving her American citizenship she packed up and left for Germany.

She hated being in Germany and would rarely even let on that she spoke German. In one instance though, she and her sister-in-law, who was visiting from the States, went to a store, and a female sales clerk asked another woman in German what to charge the *Ammies,* a derogatory term for Americans. "In my purest *holk Deutsch* I answered that if the price is different for the *Ammies,* we are not buying here. That gave me great satisfaction."

In Germany, Ed was an officer, which meant Charlene had the responsibilities of being an officer's wife. This included hosting dinner parties, volunteering on the base, and learning the social role for such a woman. At first, this was a challenge, but as with all other things, Charlene worked hard at it and soon began to change, to let go of a little bit of the pain and anger. "I was becoming a different person, and that was good for me," she later said.

After about two years, Ed and Charlene returned to the States, but Ed believed he'd found something in the military he couldn't find in civilian life, so he signed up for another three years. This was the beginning of his life's career.

On September 22, 1956, Charlene and Ed had their only child, Stephen Schiff.

Soon after the birth of Stephen, the Army sent Ed to Japan. After Stephen received a medical exam by future Surgeon General of the United States Dr. C. Everett Koop that cleared Stephen for the trip, he and Charlene joined Ed.

Charlene was busy with her young son but happy in Japan. Then one evening, as a typhoon swept across the islands, Charlene received a call from the military telling her that Ed drowned when a boat he was on capsized. For the next two days Charlene could not get any more information from the military until she received a second call to say the first was a mistake. Ed was alive.

The family moved back to the States and like any other military family was subject to frequent moves. Stephen attended seventeen different schools before high school, but for the most part, these were happy times. Then came Vietnam. From the start, Ed did not believe Vietnam was a war the United States should fight. The United States military, he argued, was not designed or capable of winning a guerrilla war. However, he was a man of duty and in 1965 willingly went to Saigon.

A few months later, Charlene heard news reports of a large bombing by Viet Cong guerillas at a hotel in Saigon. Worried for Ed, she called the Red Cross who told her that Ed was in the building when the bomb exploded and died because of his injuries. Again, Charlene found herself mourning her beloved husband until she received word that he was in fact still alive. He had been in a meeting in that hotel but left five minutes before the bomb exploded. In an interview with the USHMM, Charlene said, "I will never give another penny to the Red Cross."

After a year of service in Vietnam, Ed returned home. He smoked two-packs of cigarettes per day, was skin and bones, his hands shook, and he believed more than ever that the war was a mistake. In 1969, they sent him back. Again, he came home believing the war was a mistake and argued this with his superiors. According to Charlene, a superior of Ed's told him that if he stopped arguing against the war the higher ups would make him a general—he was a brigadier general by then—but Ed said no and retired instead.

Though life for the most part was happy, Charlene continued to suffer from her experiences during the Holocaust. "I have ulcers and other serious health problems and am always sick, which is one reason why my son wanted to be a doctor from an early age," she said in a 2003 interview. "When my husband went to Vietnam for the first time, my son said, 'I'm going to be the man of the family. I'll take care of mommy.' And he did. He was a wonderful boy from the very beginning."

Along with the physical ailments and wounds were many emotional wounds that had not healed. "My son's father was a wonderful father, very even tempered, but I was the explosive one. I was the one who demanded more than perfection because, in retrospect, I think I tried to live my youth through my son."

She also felt incredible guilt for having survived and felt she was undeserving of surviving when so many died. In an interview with the USHMM in 1993, she said, "I have an enormous amount of guilt for surviving. Why? Why did I survive when there were so many worthy people who really deserved to survive who were killed? I mean, these were people who could contribute to culture, to history, to education. Why did I survive? I have nothing to contribute, nothing. And here I am a self-elected, self-appointed spokesperson for all these millions, and I'm not eloquent enough to speak in their name, and yet I have to."

In fact, her healing began when she first came to this country with the love and support of her family in the Bronx. It continued with meeting and falling in love with Ed and then through the love and courage of her son Stephen.

But still, she was angry and deeply pained by the loss of her family and the suffering she had endured, and she wanted to leave it all behind.

Then with the urging and support of her rabbi, she began to reach out to other survivors and attended a Holocaust survivors' meeting in Washington, DC. She began testifying to her experience. Though she'd told her story to Ed and bits and pieces of it to Stephen, this marked her first step onto a public stage to share what she had endured during the Holocaust.

This led to more meetings with survivors and sharing her story with even more groups of people. In 1985, she traveled to Israel where she met with her father's students who, at his urging and with his help, escaped Poland just before the war. This culminated in a party to celebrate her father, mother, and sister, a moment that held immense significance for Charlene and her emotional healing.

In 1993, the United States Holocaust Memorial Museum opened, and within a short amount of time, Charlene became one of their autobiographical storytellers. In this capacity, she routinely spoke at the USHMM and was asked to speak on their behalf at schools, synagogues, churches, clubs, military and veterans' organizations, and anywhere else across the country where there were people whom she could touch with her story.

Bit by bit, she healed herself as she raised awareness of the horror of the Holocaust and genocides in places such as Rwanda and Bosnia. As her son noted in an interview with the authors of this book, "My mother was an incredibly smart woman who was able to display a quality that was not quite forgiveness, but looking beyond the immediate emotion, to not be driven by anger and animosity and hatred for what people did to her. I marveled at this quality in my mother because she had every reason to be angry and depressed and hateful for what happened to her and her family, but she rose above it.

"She was very strong willed, driven, and incredibly smart. She was also an incredibly demonstrative person who had a hug for everyone, which I believe is a lasting legacy of her parents and sister and the experience of losing them."

Charlene was inexhaustible in her desire to share her story with as many people as possible. To them, she gave a gift of awareness and of personal experience that none will ever forget. In their rapt attention and desire to learn and become aware, they gave her a sense of purpose, a reason for which she survived.

"Every day it hurts the same and even more," she said in an interview, "because I remember details that I haven't spoken about before. I'm trying to learn to forgive, but I can never forget, and I don't want the world to ever forget, and that is one of my missions, to, as Elie Wiesel says, bear witness. He was one of my early inspirations, and I feel that if he can talk about it, I have to make myself talk about it. I'm not as eloquent as he, and I'm not as smart as he is, but in my own small way I try to do the best I know how, and maybe that's my mission in life and the reason why I survived. I don't know."

In a later interview, Charlene described how she'd found a greater sense of peace. "I felt enormous guilt for surviving. Why me? A nobody like me when people who had so much to contribute to humankind were just blown away like flies. Why me? So that's why I feel very strongly that I must do what I can in in my own small way. I have to contribute what I can, and this is my contribution.

"I often say I'm very proud to be who I am. I wouldn't change it for the world. And I'm proud of being a Jew. And I'm proud of having survived, but until recently I had enormous guilt. Now, I am still imprisoned by my memories, but I don't feel guilty anymore."

On August 15, 2008, Charlene's beloved husband Ed passed away. His body was laid to rest in Arlington National Cemetery.

On January 19, 2013, Charlene passed away. She is interred next to Ed in Arlington National Cemetery.

Acknowledgements

As with any piece of writing—especially narrative nonfiction—it would be impossible to recreate a decades-old experience with the same emotional intensity as when it occurred without the support of many people. *Child of the Forest* is no exception and has deeply benefited by the help, words, and kindness of the following people.

First, of course, is Charlene (Shulamit "Musia" Perlmutter) Schiff. Up until the mid-1980s, Charlene rarely talked about her experiences during the Holocaust. But then, at the urging of her rabbi, she began to tell her story and did so with a calm grace that affected anyone fortunate enough to see her speak. The United States Holocaust Memorial Museum gave her the ability to speak with new audiences either at the museum or while traveling to schools, synagogues, and other receptive audiences. It was at one of these talks that I first heard Charlene tell her story and was immediately touched. I introduced myself, and ultimately we became dear friends. My last promise to her shortly before she died was that I would continue to testify to her experience and share her story with the world. She often asked me, "Why did I live through this experience and so many died?" I would respond, "So you can tell your story to the world." Thank you for changing my life.

Thank you Mateus Bacci Gayoso for your keen interest in *Child of the Forest*. I would also like to thank Tim and Ryan Goff for their role in seeking out James Buchanan, a prolific writer, to assist me with this project. James proved to be perfect for this project. In addition to his exceptional writing skills, he did a tremendous amount of research, including many interviews. His conversations with Diane Saltzman and the United States Holocaust Memorial Museum proved invaluable. Diane and the museum deserve praise for their extraordinary efforts to maintain an enduring legacy and tribute to those who survived and those who perished in the Holocaust. Though Charlene passed before writing *Child of the Forest* commenced, the record she left behind with the museum and the generosity of Ms. Saltzman ensured the details of Charlene's story were not lost. This book would not be possible without Ms. Saltzman and the Unites States Holocaust Memorial Museum, and I owe a deep debt of gratitude to them both. Thank you.

I also owe a deep debt of gratitude to the Holocaust survivors and friends of Charlene who provided their stories, remembrances of Charlene, and details that could not have been found anywhere else. James Buchanan did an excellent job of identifying these amazing individuals and communicating with them. They are Estelle Laughlin, Marcel and Ania Drimer, Halina (Litman) Yasharoff Peabody, Henryk Grynberg, and Rabbi Jack Moline. Thank you.

Charlene's son, Stephen Schiff, has also played an instrumental role supporting this project. He provided details of his mother that could not have been learned from anyone else and has been an enthusiastic advocate for his mother and seeing her story brought to as large an audience as possible. Thank you, Stephen, for your support, even through the many challenges. Your encouragement was always appreciated.

And to those whose names are not listed here but in some way played a role in helping create *Child of the Forest,* thank you.

Bibliography

Since this is a work of creative nonfiction, the sources for *Child of the Forest* were used to create an understanding of the place, time, history, and emotional and mental effects of the trauma Musia suffered. Other than interviews of Charlene Schiff (née Shulamit "Musia" Perlmutter) and selected lines from traditional songs, hymns, and poems, sources are not quoted or directly referenced in the text. Rather, they helped inform the story and therefore deserve to be noted to provide proper credit and help the reader understand the depth of research used to recreate Musia's story.

American Psychiatric Association. *Diagnostic and Statistical Manual (fifth edition).* Washington, D.C., 2013. (In particular: Trauma in children, acute stress, depersonalization/derealization, and dissociation/dissociative state).

Ania and Marcel Drimer (Holocaust survivors and friends of Charlene), interview by James Buchanan.

Charlene Schiff, *A Lesson in Geography,* 2011, United States Holocaust Memorial Museum. Retrieved from https://www.ushmm.org/remember/office-of-survivor-affairs/memory-project/featured-writers/schiff-geography.

Charlene Schiff, *A Special Diet,* 2008, United States Holocaust Memorial Museum. Retrieved from https://www.ushmm.org/remember/office-of-survivor-affairs/memory-project/featured-writers/the-girl-from-the-forest.

Charlene Schiff, *Don't Ask for Soap,* 2011, United States Holocaust Memorial Museum. Retrieved from https://www.ushmm.org/remember/office-of-survivor-affairs/memory-project/featured-writers/schiff-soap.

Charlene Schiff, *For a Rainy Day (Men Zol Nit Bedarfin)*, 2005, United States Holocaust Memorial Museum. Retrieved from https://www.ushmm.org/remember/office-of-survivor-affairs/memory-project/featured-writers/for-a-rainy-day.

Charlene Schiff, *I Remember*, 2011, United States Holocaust Memorial Museum. Retrieved from https://www.ushmm.org/remember/office-of-survivor-affairs/memory-project/featured-writers/schiff-remember.

Charlene Schiff, *If Rivers Could Speak*, 2011, United States Holocaust Memorial Museum. Retrieved from https://www.ushmm.org/remember/office-of-survivor-affairs/memory-project/featured-writers/schiff-rivers.

Charlene Schiff, *Kasia*, 2011, United States Holocaust Memorial Museum. Retrieved from https://www.ushmm.org/remember/office-of-survivor-affairs/memory-project/featured-writers/schiff-kasia.

Charlene Schiff, *Naughty, Naughty*, 2011, United States Holocaust Memorial Museum. Retrieved from https://www.ushmm.org/remember/office-of-survivor-affairs/memory-project/featured-writers/schiff-naughty.

Charlene Schiff, *Papa's Magnificent Obsession*, 2006, United States Holocaust Memorial Museum. Retrieved from https://www.ushmm.org/remember/office-of-survivor-affairs/memory-project/featured-writers/papas-magnificent-obsession.

Charlene Schiff, *Paranka*, 2006, United States Holocaust Memorial Museum. Retrieved from https://www.ushmm.org/remember/office-of-survivor-affairs/memory-project/featured-writers/schiff-paranka.

Charlene Schiff, *That First Day,* 2005, United States Holocaust Memorial Museum. Retrieved from https://www.ushmm.org/remember/office-of-survivor-affairs/memory-project/featured-writers/that-first-day.

Charlene Schiff, *The Girl from the Forest,* 2008, United States Holocaust Memorial Museum. Retrieved from https://www.ushmm.org/remember/office-of-survivor-affairs/memory-project/featured-writers/the-girl-from-the-forest.

Charlene Schiff, *The Haystack-1942,* 2002, United States Holocaust Memorial Museum. Retrieved from https://www.ushmm.org/remember/office-of-survivor-affairs/memory-project/featured-writers/schiff-haystack.

Charlene Schiff, *The Promise,* 2011, United States Holocaust Memorial Museum. Retrieved from https://www.ushmm.org/remember/office-of-survivor-affairs/memory-project/featured-writers/schiff-promise.

Charlene Schiff, *What Mattered Most,* 2005, United States Holocaust Memorial Museum. Retrieved from https://www.ushmm.org/remember/office-of-survivor-affairs/memory-project/featured-writers/what-mattered-most.

Diane Saltzman (director of institutional stewardship at the United States Holocaust Memorial Museum and friend of Charlene) interview by James Buchanan.

Estelle Glaser Laughlin, *Transcending Darkness: A Girl's Journey Out of the Holocaust.* Lubbock: Texas Tech University Press, November 15, 2012.

Estelle Laughlin (Holocaust survivor and friend of Charlene), interview by James Buchanan.

Esther Finder, interviewer for United States Holocaust Memorial Museum, *Oral History Interview with Marcel Drimer,* 1996. United Sates Holocaust Memorial Museum. Retrieved from https://collections.ushmm.org/search/catalog/irn507554.

Geni, *Lutsk (Luck) Ghetto.* Retrieved from https://www.geni.com/projects/Lutsk-Luck-Ghetto/11424.

Halina (Litman) Yasharoff Peabody (Holocaust survivor and friend of Charlene), interview by James Buchanan.

Henryk Grynberg (Holocaust survivor and friend of Charlene), interview by James Buchanan.

Jack Grossman (Charlene's friend and principal author of this book), interview by James Buchanan.

Jan Brzechwa (1898-1966) translated by Dr. Aniela Korzeniowska, *At the Vegetable Stall.* Retrieved from http://konicki.com/blog2/2009/07/09/july-9-at-the-vegtable-stall-by-jan-brzechwa.

Jewish Virtual Library, *Virtual Jewish World: Lvov, Ukraine.* Retrieved from http://www.jewishvirtuallibrary.org/lvov-ukraine-jewish-history-tour.

Joan Ringelheim (interviewer for United States Holocaust Memorial Museum), *Interview with Charlene Perlmutter Schiff, March 23, 1993, RG-50.030*0203,* United States Holocaust Memorial Museum. Retrieved from https://collections.ushmm.org/oh_findingaids/RG-50.030.0203_trs_en.pdf.

Leopold Staff (1878-1957), *Foundations,* All Poetry. Retrieved from https://allpoetry.com/Leopold-Staff.

Linda N. Edelstein, PH.D. *Writer's Guide to Character Traits: Includes Profiles of Human Behaviors and Personality Traits (second edition).* Cincinnati: Writer's Digest Books, 2006.

Marcel Drimer, *The First Few Days* (shared by author). Washington D.C.: United States Holocaust Memorial Museum, 2015.

Nina Ellis (interviewer for United States Holocaust Memorial Museum), Interview with Charlene Schiff, January 29, 2003, RG-50.549.02*0068, United States Holocaust Memorial Museum. Retrieved from https://collections.ushmm.org/oh_findingaids/RG-50.549.02.0068_trs_en.pdf.

Paul Valéry (1871-1945) translated by Nathaniel Rudavsky-Brody, *The Bee.* Retrieved from http://intranslation.brooklynrail.org/french/six-poems-from-charms-by-paul-valery.

Rabbi Jack Moline (Charlene's rabbi and friend), interview by James Buchanan.

Ray Brandon and Wendy Lower (editors). *The Shoah in Ukraine: History, Testimony, Memorialization.* Bloomington: Indiana University Press in association with the United States Holocaust Museum, 2008.

Sergey Yesenin (1895-1925), *The Night.* Retrieved from https://www.poetryverse.com/foreign-poets/sergei-yesenin-poems/the-night.

Shimon Redlich, *Metropolitan Andrii Sheptyts'kyi and the Complexities of Ukrainian-Jewish Relations* found in *Bitter Legacy: Confronting the Holocaust in the USSR,* Edited by Zvi Gitelman. Bloomington: Indiana University Press, 1997.

Shmuel Spector (Editor in Chief) and Geoffrey Wigoder (Coonsulting Editor), *The Encyclopedia of Jewish Life.* New York: New York University Press, 2001.

Stephen Schiff (Charlene's son), interview by James Buchanan.

Traditional hymn translation by Rabbi Shai Gluskin, *Anim Zemirot,* Zemirot Database. Retrieved from http://www.zemirotdatabase.org/view_song.php?id=59.

United States Holocaust Memorial Museum, *Charlene Schiff (Shulamit Perlmutter).* Retrieved from https://www.ushmm.org/remember/office-of-survivor-affairs/memory-project/featured-writers/the-girl-from-the-forest.

United States Holocaust Memorial Museum, *Charlene Schiff: A Daughter's Separation from Her Mother,* May 19, 2009. Retrieved from https://www.ushmm.org/information/visit-the-museum/programs-activities/first-person-program/first-person-podcast/charlene-schiff-a-daughters-separation-from-her-mother.

United States Holocaust Memorial Museum, *Interview with Charlene Schiff, March 2, 1993, Alexandria, Virginia*. Retrieved at https://collections.ushmm.org/oh_findingaids/RG-50.233.0120_trs_en.pdf.

United States Holocaust Memorial Museum, *Oral History, Charlene Schiff, Describes the Soviet occupation of Horochow after the outbreak of World War II,* 1993. Retrieved from https://www.ushmm.org/wlc/en/media_oi.php?ModuleId=0&MediaId=4353.

United States Holocaust Memorial Museum, *Oral History, Charlene Schiff, Describes anti-Jewish decrees and anti-Jewish measures after the German invasion of Horochow,* 1993. Retrieved from https://www.ushmm.org/wlc/en/media_oi.php?ModuleId=0&MediaId=2856.

United States Holocaust Memorial Museum, *Oral History, Charlene Schiff, Describes conditions in the Horochow ghetto,* 1993. Retrieved from https://www.ushmm.org/wlc/en/media_oi.php?ModuleId=0&MediaId=2854.

United States Holocaust Memorial Museum, *Oral History, Charlene Schiff, Describes children smuggling food into the Horochow ghetto,* 1993. Retrieved from https://www.ushmm.org/wlc/en/media_oi.php?ModuleId=0&MediaId=1111.

United States Holocaust Memorial Museum, *Oral History, Charlene Schiff, Describes being caught while trying to smuggle food into the Horochow ghetto,* 1993. Retrieved from https://www.ushmm.org/wlc/en/media_oi.php?ModuleId=0&MediaId=2857.

United States Holocaust Memorial Museum, *Oral History, Charlene Schiff, Describes foraging for food in order to survive in forests after escaping from the Horochow ghetto,* 1993. Retrieved from https://www.ushmm.org/wlc/en/media_oi.php?ModuleId=0&MediaId=2853.

United States Holocaust Memorial Museum, *Oral History, Charlene Schiff, Describes her liberation by Soviet troops,* 1993. Retrieved from https://www.ushmm.org/wlc/en/media_oi.php?ModuleId=0&MediaId=2855.

University of Southern California Shoah Foundation Visual History Archive Online, *Schiff Charlene Interview #7437,* tapes 1 through 4. Retrieved from http://vhaonline.usc.edu/viewingPage?testimonyID=6284&returnIndex=0.

Wikipedia, *Lvov-Sandomierz Offensive.*
Retrieved from https://en.wikipedia.org/wiki/
Lvov%E2%80%93Sandomierz_Offensive.

Wikipedia, *Lwów Ghetto.* Retrieved from https://
en.wikipedia.org/wiki/Lw%C3%B3w_Ghetto.

Wikipedia, *Tzadikim Nistarim.* Retrieved from https://
en.wikipedia.org/wiki/Tzadikim_Nistarim.

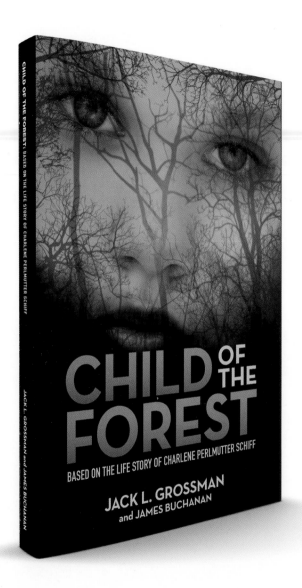

Visit **jackgrossman.com** to connect with the author and to sign up for updates and announcements about the book.